Aris and Phillips Classical Texts

# Greek Orators IX

## *Isaeus Orations 5 and 11*

*Edited with an Introduction, Translation, and Commentary by*

**_Brenda Griffith-Williams_**

LIVERPOOL UNIVERSITY PRESS

First published 2025
Liverpool University Press
4 Cambridge Street
Liverpool, L69 7ZU



British Library Cataloguing-in-Publication Data
A British Library CIP Record is available.

ISBN 978-1-83624-340-3
eISBN 978-1-83624-358-8

Cover image: Courtroom equipment (a *klērōtērion* and *psēphoi*) in the Museum of the Ancient Agora, Athens. Photograph: Brenda Griffith-Williams.

Typeset by Carnegie Book Production, Lancaster
Printed and bound by CPI Group (UK) Ltd, Croydon CR0 4YY

# CONTENTS

# ACKNOWLEDGEMENTS

I owe an enormous debt of thanks to all the various colleagues and friends who have helped and encouraged me in the preparation of this book. I am especially grateful to Dr Jakub Filonik (University of Silesia in Katowice) for sharing with me the results of his recent research on aspects of Athenian legal procedure, to Dr Janek Kucharski (University of Silesia in Katowice) for his prompt and helpful responses to my queries about Athenian rhetoric and legal procedure, and to Professor Mike Edwards (RHUL) for a thought-provoking discussion of Isaeus 11.

I am also grateful to Professor Ifigeneia Giannadaki (University of Florida) for inviting me to deliver a paper ('Theopompus (speaker of Isaeus 11): fraudulent guardian or victim of a malicious prosecution?') at the Cassas Seminar in Greek Law and Society on 27 October 2023, and to the participants in the seminar for their helpful and constructive feedback.

It has been a pleasure to work with Clare Litt, commissioning editor at Liverpool University Press, and with Professor Alan Sommerstein, the series editor for Aris & Phillips Classical Texts. I thank them both for their support.

Finally, I dedicate this book to Professor Chris Carey (UCL), the most inspirational of mentors.

# ABBREVIATIONS

## Ancient authors and works

| | |
|---|---|
| Aesch. | Aeschines |
| Andoc. | Andocides |
| Ant. | Antiphon |
| Ar. | Aristophanes |
| *Ach.* | *Acharnians* |
| *Thesm.* | *Thesmophoriazousai* |
| Arist. | Aristotle |
| *Rhet.* | *Rhetoric* |
| *Ath. Pol.* | *Athēnaiōn Politeia* (pseudo-Arist. 'Constitution of the Athenians') |
| Dem. | Demosthenes |
| D. H. | Dionysius of Halicarnassus |
| Din. | Dinarchus |
| Eur. | Euripides |
| *Hell. Oxy.* | *Hellenica Oxyrhynchia* |
| Hyp. | Hyperides |
| *Athenog.* | Prosecution of Athenogenes |
| *Eux.* | Defence of Euxenippus |
| *Lyc.* | Defence of Lycophron |
| *Phil.* | Prosecution of Philippides |
| Isae. | Isaeus |
| Isoc. | Isocrates |
| Lyc. | Lycurgus |
| Lys. | Lysias |
| Paus. | Pausanias |
| *P.Oxy.* | *Oxyrhynchus Papyri* |
| Thuc. | Thucydides |

**Modern works**

| | |
|---|---|
| *LGPN* | *Lexicon of Greek Personal Names* |
| *OCD* | *Oxford Classical Dictionary* |
| *OCT* | *Oxford Classical Texts* |
| *PAA* | *Persons of Ancient Athens*: https://attica.artsci.utoronto.ca/paa.search.php |

**General**

| | |
|---|---|
| acc. | accusative |
| ca. | *circa* |
| dat. | dative |
| dau. | daughter |
| ed./eds | editor(s)/edited (by) |
| esp. | especially |
| fr(r). | fragment(s) |
| Gk. | Greek |
| Lat. | Latin |
| lit. | literally |
| m. | married |
| ms./mss | manuscript(s) |
| n. | note |
| plur. | plural |
| trans. | translated by/translator |

# GENERAL INTRODUCTION

Isaeus, who wrote the two speeches in this book, was one of the ten 'Attic orators' recognized for their classic status since late antiquity. He was not, in the strict sense, an orator, since (so far as we know) he never participated in Athenian politics or spoke in court himself, but rather a logographer (professional speechwriter) who earned a living by writing speeches for litigants to deliver in court. Although most of the speeches attributed to him in antiquity are now lost, 11 of the 12 that survive are concerned with disputes about inheritance, an area of the law in which he was apparently a specialist.

Virtually nothing is known about Isaeus's life, and few of his speeches can be dated with complete certainty, but his career appears to have spanned four or five decades from the late 390s to the 350s or 340s BC. Isaeus 5 *On the estate of Dicaeogenes*, if it is correctly dated to the late 390s,[1] is his earliest extant speech, while Isaeus 11 *On the estate of Hagnias* (ca. 359) dates from the height of his career.

These speeches expose bitter rivalries over property in two of the richest and most distinguished families of classical Athens; each of them is concerned with the inheritance of a man who has died some years previously and whose surviving relatives continue to fight for a share of his property. Both speeches include accounts of earlier litigation over the disputed estates, in the course of which they provide a wealth of information for modern scholars about various aspects of Athenian law and legal procedure. These include wills and intestate succession, the enforcement of agreements, the use of oral and written witness testimony, voting procedures in the Athenian courts, the choice between 'public' and 'private' legal actions, prosecutions for false testimony, and character evidence. Both speeches provide some insights into the duties of guardians appointed to manage the property of orphans,[2] and both

---

1 See the introduction to Isaeus 5, pp. 18–19.

2 An orphan (Gk. *orphanos*) in classical Athens was a child whose father had died, regardless of whether the mother was still alive.

of them also reflect, from different angles, the role of women and the importance of inheritance through a female line in the Athenian system.

Forensic speeches such as these are our principal source of information on Athenian law and legal procedure, but, since they are not legal textbooks or official law reports, they are open to interpretation and sometimes misunderstanding or controversy. Isaeus 11, in particular, has long been the subject of debate, and often misunderstanding, among modern scholars. So, while the main purpose of my translations and commentaries is to explain the legal framework and the logographer's rhetorical strategy in each case, I also identify and discuss some of the key points of scholarly controversy. This General Introduction provides a brief outline of Athenian inheritance law and other aspects of the legal system relevant to these two speeches.[3]

## ATHENIAN INHERITANCE LAW

The central feature of the Athenian inheritance system was the transmission of property from father to son. An Athenian could not disinherit his legitimate offspring, and every male citizen had an absolute right to take over the paternal estate after his father's death, without recourse to the courts. If a man left more than one legitimate son, his property was divided equally among them. If his oldest son was still a minor at the time of his death, the estate would be managed by a guardian or guardians (Gk. *epitropos*, plur. *epitropoi*) until the son became an adult.[4]

Laws attributed to the great sixth-century legislator, Solon, determined what happened to the property of an Athenian with no legitimate sons. First, according to Solon's 'law on wills':

> Those citizens who had not been adopted and thereby may neither renounce [the inheritance] nor claim their rights in an *epidikasia*,[5]

3 For a more detailed account of Isaeus's work and the Athenian inheritance system, see Griffith-Williams (2013, 1–2).

4 On the appointment of guardians for Athenian orphans, see commentary on 'guardian', 5.10.

5 See commentary on 'awarded by the court', 5.6.

> when Solon entered on his archonship shall be allowed to bequeath (*diathesthai*) their own property as they wish, as long as they do not have male legitimate children, and their intellect was not disturbed by insanity, senility, drugs, sickness or by the manipulation of a woman, or forced by necessity or imprisonment.[6]

As this law was interpreted in the fourth century, it enabled a childless Athenian to adopt anyone he chose as his son and heir, either *inter vivos* – that is, during the lifetime of the adoptive father – or by will (testamentary adoption). A typical Athenian nominated a son as heir to the testator's entire estate, but we learn from Isaeus 5 and 11 that there were other possibilities. The will of Dicaeogenes II was unusual in that he gave only one third of his estate to his adopted son, while Hagnias was one of only two Athenians known to have adopted a daughter rather than a son.[7]

Secondly, if an Athenian left no legitimate sons, natural or adopted, his estate would go to his daughter(s), if any. A daughter in this position was known as an *epiklēros* (loosely translated as 'heiress'), and she could be claimed in marriage by her father's next of kin. The estate of a man who left no offspring (natural or adopted) went to his next of kin, that is, his closest collateral relative(s) in the order prescribed by another Solonian law (modified in the late fifth century):

> If a man dies without having made a will, if he leaves daughters, the property shall be to them; if not, the following relatives shall be entitled to the property: if there are brothers of the same father or legitimate children of brothers, they shall take the part of the father; if there are no brothers or children of brothers, then ‹the cousins on the father's side and the children› of them shall inherit in the same way. The male relatives and their male descendants shall take precedence, if they are from the same ancestors, even if they are of remoter affinity. If there is nobody on the father's side to the degree of children of cousins, the relatives of the deceased on the maternal side shall inherit in the same way. And if there is nobody on both sides covered by these degrees, then the next of kin on the father's

6 Cited at [Dem.] 46.14: Leão and Rhodes (2016), fr. 49a.

7 See commentary on 'adopted his niece as his daughter', 11.8.

> side shall inherit. Neither an illegitimate son nor an illegitimate daughter shall have rights of kinship, either in sacred or in secular affairs. (Effective from the archonship of Eucleides.)[8]

Finally, it was possible in some circumstances for one of the surviving family members to become the son and heir of their deceased relative through what modern scholars call 'posthumous adoption', but this practice appears to have evolved as a matter of custom rather than law. Unlike adoption *inter vivos* or by will, posthumous adoption did not necessarily involve the express wishes of the adoptive father, but it did require the agreement of the family.[9]

Unless an adoptive father and son were already closely related by blood, there was obviously scope for conflict of interest between the adopted son and his new father's collateral relatives, so it is not surprising that in the majority of attested inheritance disputes in the Athenian courts, a will or adoption *inter vivos* is contested by the deceased's next of kin. There was also potential for conflict of interest between an orphan and his guardian, especially when the child's father was the guardian's next of kin (a situation exemplified, at least as the speaker's opponent presents it, in Isaeus 11). Hence, while it is relatively rare for litigants in the Athenian courts to praise or thank their guardians, there is sufficient evidence of mistreatment or financial mismanagement (whether through neglect or deliberate fraud) to suggest that such cases were not uncommon.[10] Menexenus, the speaker of Isaeus 5, accuses Dicaeogenes III of neglecting the orphans who were left in his care as their guardian, painting a vivid picture of the destitution and misery to which the children and their widowed mother were reduced by his callousness.[11] But Menexenus brings no

---

8 Cited at [Dem.] 43.51; Leão and Rhodes (2016), fr. 50b. For further discussion, see pp. 113–14, 124.

9 Cf. commentary on 'persuaded by her', 11.49, and see Rubinstein (1993, 25–28) for a full discussion of posthumous adoption.

10 Cases in which a guardian was prosecuted by or on behalf of his ward: Dem. 27–31, Hyp. *Timandrus*, Isae. 11, fr. X Teubner, Lys. 32, fr. 174 *OCT*, *P.Oxy.* XXVII 2464. Cf. Dem. 38.8, Isae. 7.6–7.

11 See the commentary on 5.9–11.

evidence in support of his accusations, and makes no suggestion that Dicaeogenes was ever prosecuted for the alleged offences.

The law provided two means of redress for wronged orphans. First, the orphan himself could, within five years of coming of age, prosecute the guardian(s) in a private action (*dikē epitropēs*) for the restitution of any property which the guardian(s) had illegally withheld. But a private action, available only when the orphan became an adult, might not provide adequate redress. The Athenians' concern for orphans as a vulnerable group in need of protection from society is reflected in the existence of the *eisangelia kakōseōs orphanou* ('denunciation for mistreatment of an orphan'), a public action which could be brought by any citizen on the victim's behalf without waiting for him to reach adulthood.[12] That is the procedure under which Theopompus, the speaker of Isaeus 11, was prosecuted by his fellow guardian.

## ATHENIAN WOMEN: PROPERTY AND INHERITANCE

In Athens, as compared with other ancient Greek city-states, female citizens had relatively limited rights of property ownership and inheritance; Athenian inheritance law did not completely exclude women, but they were severely disadvantaged by the principle of male precedence. Unless she was an *epiklēros*, an Athenian woman would get no share in her father's estate apart from her dowry.[13] She could inherit property from her brother(s) or another male family member, but only if she was more closely related to him than any of his surviving male relatives.[14]

Any property an Athenian woman inherited would be administered by her *kyrios*, the male citizen who had legal responsibility for her. (This would normally be her husband, or, if she was a widow, an adult son or other male relative.) She could not make a legally enforceable will,[15] and, while it is possible that she could make an informal

12 On the differences between 'public' and 'private' actions, see pp. 6–7.

13 See commentary on 'a dowry of 40 minas', 5.26.

14 Cf. Griffith-Williams (2016, 111).

15 Isae. 10.10, with Griffith-Williams (2013).

agreement with her *kyrios*, relying on him to carry out her wishes after her death, we have no positive evidence that this happened. Nor do we know whether a woman's property would routinely pass to her children after her death, or whether it was treated as part of her husband's estate and remained in his control until his own death.

The two speeches in this volume illustrate both the limited legal capacity of Athenian women and the importance – for men – of inheritance through a female line. Theopompus, the speaker of Isaeus 11, took advantage of male precedence when he successfully claimed the estate of Hagnias from its previous holder, Phylomache.[16] The situation in Isaeus 5, where the sisters of Dicaeogenes II are fighting to recover their share of his estate from his adopted son, illustrates the vulnerability of women and raises questions about the transmission of the property they inherited from their brother. Menexenus, the speaker, represents his mother in the litigation, and implies that her share of the estate will eventually belong to him (and his brothers), but scholars have sometimes speculated that a daughter could also inherit a share of her mother's property, even if she had brothers.[17] In the absence of evidence to the contrary, such a hypothesis is legitimate, but in the light of what we know about the Athenian system it is safer to assume that the ultimate recipient of property inherited by a woman would always be her son(s).

## ATHENIAN LEGAL PROCEDURE: PUBLIC AND PRIVATE CASES

The distinction between 'public' and 'private' actions was fundamental to the Athenian legal system, but there was no public prosecuting authority in classical Athens, and all prosecutions, including those of serious offences against the state, were dependent on the initiative of private citizens. The defining feature of a 'public action', even if it involved an individual victim, was that it was perceived to entail

16 See commentary on 'excluded by the law, which prescribes that males have precedence', 11.17.

17 E.g. Hunter (1994, 200, n.39); see p. 33.

some harm to the state. It was open not only to the victim to bring a prosecution (as in a private action), but also to any male citizen acting as 'volunteer prosecutor' (Gk. *ho boulomenos*, lit. 'he who is willing'). The penalty in a private action would normally be the payment of damages to the victim. In a public action any financial penalty would be payable to the state, and more serious punishments such as death or disfranchisement (*atimia*) might also be available.

In many circumstances a potential prosecutor could choose to proceed by way of either a private or a public action. The chosen procedure sometimes led to complaints by the defendant, as in Isaeus 11 where a key part of Theopompus's defence is his counter-attack on his opponent's inappropriate choice of a public action.[18]

Most Athenian trials, in both public and private cases, were adversarial: there were two opposing litigants, the prosecutor and defendant, and a penalty would be imposed on the defendant if he lost the case. The special, non-adversarial procedure used to determine contested inheritance claims, the *diadikasia*, was different: there was no prosecutor or defendant, and no penalty for the loser apart from the loss of a deposit.[19] In principle, there could be any number of claimants in a *diadikasia*, although in practice there were rarely more than two, and all were treated on an equal footing. (A previous trial in the dispute over the estate of Hagnias, described at Isae. 11.15–19, provides one of our rare examples of a *diadikasia* involving three or more rival claimants.)[20]

There was no means of appeal against the decision of an Athenian court, but a defeated litigant could prosecute one or more of his opponent's witnesses in an action for false testimony (*dikē pseudomartyriōn*). As discussed in the introduction to Isaeus 5,[21] that could have the effect of re-opening the substantive issues in the dispute, but there is no conclusive evidence that a conviction for false

18 See the introduction to Isae. 11, pp. 126–30.

19 See commentary on 'pay a deposit', 11.13.

20 For the alternative account of this trial by the speaker of [Dem.] 43, see the introduction to Isae. 11, pp. 115–20.

21 See pp. 30–31.

testimony would actually annul the court's decision at the original trial.[22]

A natural son, or one adopted *inter vivos*, could take over his deceased father's estate without submitting a claim to the court. If his right to the estate was challenged by a collateral relative of his father's, he could block the rival claim with a *diamartyria*: a formal declaration, made either by the son himself or a witness on his behalf, that the estate was not adjudicable by the court because the deceased had left a legitimate son. It appears from Isaeus 5 that this procedure was also available to a son adopted by will, once the adoption had been approved by the court.[23] If the collateral relative(s) still wanted to proceed with their claim, they could only do so by prosecuting the man who had testified in the *diamartyria* for false testimony – as Menexenus and his associates did against Dicaeogenes's witness (5.17–18).

It is important to note that an Athenian court's decision at a *diadikasia* was not final: the judges' task was simply to decide which of the rival litigants had the best claim to the estate, and it was open to other claimants to come forward (or to a defeated claimant to put forward a different case) within five years of the latest decision. This could result, as in the case of Hagnias's estate, in a succession of *diadikasiai*, sometimes spread over many years. It could also lead to adversarial litigation over ancillary issues relating to the disputed inheritance, as in the cases of both Dicaeogenes and Hagnias. Menexenus, the speaker of Isaeus 5, is the prosecutor in an action to enforce an agreement under which Dicaeogenes III, the adopted son of Dicaeogenes II and current holder of the estate, had promised to relinquish part of the estate to Menexenus's mother (a sister of Dicaeogenes II). The speaker of Isaeus 11, Theopompus, is the current holder of Hagnias's estate after winning a recent *diadikasia*. Now, as one of the guardians of his nephew, he is the defendant in a public action for mistreatment of an orphan, facing a claim from his fellow guardian that the nephew is entitled to half of the estate.

22 Cf. Volonaki and Edwards (2023, xxxv); Volonaki (2024, 33).

23 See commentary on 'a *diamartyria* …', 5.16.

## DEME MEMBERSHIP, KINSHIP TIES, AND PROPERTY

After the reforms introduced in the sixth century by the politician Cleisthenes, the 139 local territorial districts of Attica known as demes became the main unit of local administration. Every deme had its own political institutions, and was also represented on the Athenian Council (the Boule), whose total membership was 500. The number of members representing each deme varied in proportion to its size; in the fourth century, the largest deme (Acharnae) had 22 representatives. More information about the size and location of the demes mentioned in the two speeches (seven in Isaeus 5 and two in Isaeus 11) is provided in the commentaries.

Membership of a deme, which was compulsory for Athenian citizens, was transmitted from father to son, and Athenians retained their affiliation to the family's deme and often still held property there, even if they no longer lived within its territory. Property holdings and kinship ties could be consolidated or reinforced by marriage and adoption within or outside the deme.

The ancestral deme of Dicaeogenes was Cydathenaeum, while that of Hagnias's family, the Buselids, was Oeum Ceramicum, both in the city of Athens. Isaeus 5 provides five examples of inter-deme marriage, which was apparently more common in classical Athens than marriage within a deme.[24] The marriage of Proxenus of Aphidna to a daughter of Dicaeogenes I created a link between the rural deme Aphidna and Cydathenaeum in the city, a link that was reinforced when Dicaeogenes III, as the adopted son of Dicaeogenes II, transferred from Aphidna to Cydathenaeum.[25] And at least three of Menexenus I's four daughters were married out of Cydathenaeum: one of them to Polyaratus of Cholargus (father of Menexenus, the speaker), another to Cephisophon of Paeania, and the third to Democles of Phrearrhii (§5). One of the daughters later married

24 Osborne (1985, 135).
25 Cox (1998, 13).

Protarchides of Potamus (§26).[26] Most of the Buselids, on the other hand, married within their ancestral deme, but Theopompus was able to acquire property in Prospalta through his marriage to a daughter of Apolexis of that deme.[27]

## THE MANUSCRIPT TRADITION AND THE TEXT OF THE SPEECHES

The principal source for the text of Isaeus's speeches is the Codex Crippsianus (A), a thirteenth-century manuscript now in the British Library, which also contains the speeches of Andocides, Antiphon, Dinarchus, and Lycurgus. All other existing manuscripts of Isaeus are considered to be derived from A, apart from Ambrosianus, D 42 sup. (Q), which contains only Isaeus 1 and 2. Wyse (1904, i–lii) gives an exhaustive overview of the manuscript tradition, including a detailed description of A. Forster (1927, xiv–xvi) provides a brief summary.

My text is based on that of Forster's 1927 Loeb edition (also available online at Perseus Digital Library), which should be consulted for a full critical apparatus. As explained in the commentary, I have departed from the Loeb text in the following places:

5.9 γυναῖκα Edwards (2002): θυγατέρα

5.9 ἀδελφήν Edwards (2002): ἀδελφιδῆν

5.26 τὴν ἀδελφὴν τὴν <τοῦ> ἑαυτοῦ <πατρὸς>: τὴν ἀδελφὴν τὴν ἑαυτοῦ

11.2 ἐὰν δὲ καὶ τοῦτ᾽ ἐκλείπῃ, εἰς τὸ γένος πάλιν ἐπανέρχεται (mss): ἐὰν δὲ καὶ τοῦτ᾽ ἐκλείπῃ [εἰς] τὸ γένος, πάλιν ἐπανέρχεται

11.27 αὐτοῖς Thompson (1976, 39): αὐτούς

---

26 For a more detailed study of the kinship group of Dicaeogenes I, see Cox (1998, 10–15).

27 See commentary on 'Prospalta', 11.44.

# ISAEUS 5

# ON THE ESTATE OF DICAEOGENES

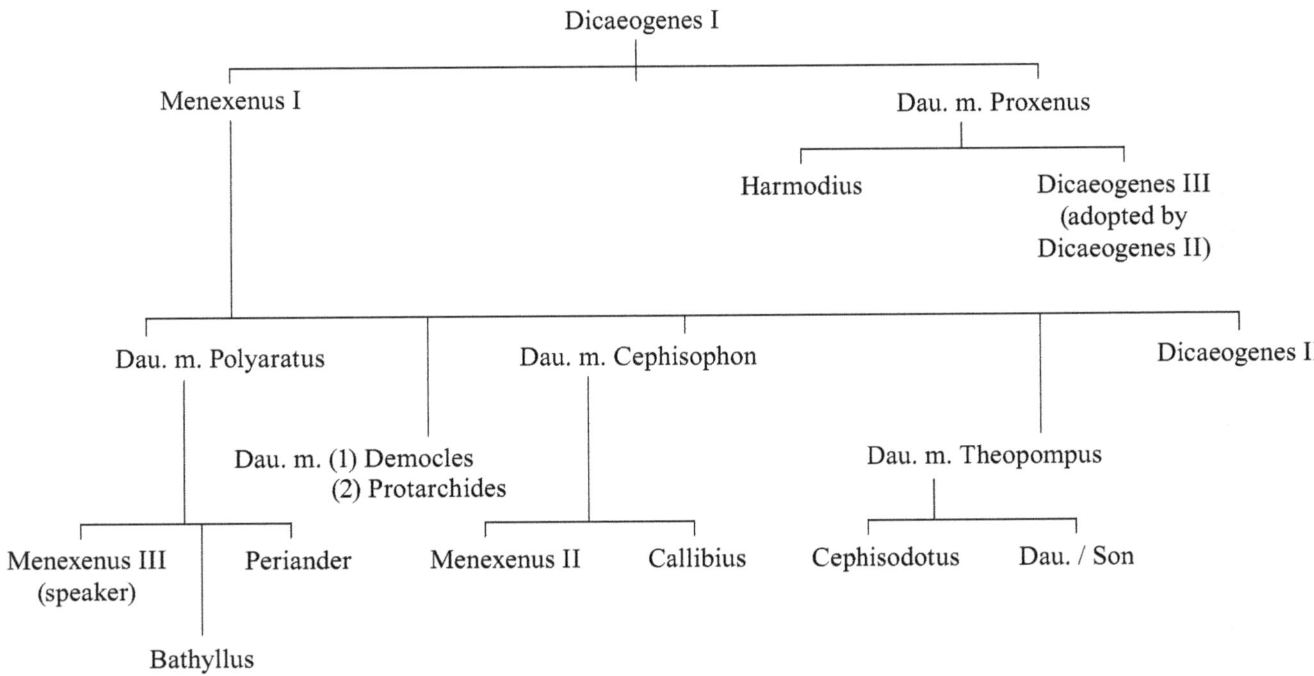


The Family of Dicaeogenes: Partial stemma

# INTRODUCTION

## THE DISPUTE AND THE PROTAGONISTS

Isaeus 5 is the prosecution speech from a private action for the enforcement of a surety, delivered in court in around 391 BC.[1] The procedure was probably a *dikē engyēs*, although some scholars have argued that the case might have been brought as a more general action for damages (*dikē blabēs*).[2] This trial was the latest stage in a long-running dispute about the estate of Dicaeogenes II,[3] who had died about 22 years previously, between his four sisters (his next of kin) and his adopted son (Dicaeogenes III) who was currently in possession of most of the estate. The prosecutors were sons of two of the sisters, and the defendant was Leochares, a surety for Dicaeogenes III for the fulfilment of an agreement under which Dicaeogenes had promised to relinquish two thirds of the estate to the sisters of Dicaeogenes II. Much of the speech is devoted to an account of the previous litigation over the estate, which, for students of legal history or the Athenian legal system, provides valuable information on several aspects of law and procedure.

---

1 On the dating of the speech, see pp. 18–19.

2 It has also been suggested that the procedure could have been a *dikē synthēkōn parabaseōs* (action for breach of contract), but such an action is attested only by the grammarian Pollux (second century AD) and most modern scholars doubt its existence. See, e.g., Harrison (1971, 79, n.3), Todd (1993, 105), and, for full discussion, Cobetto Ghiggia (2002, 40–44).

3 In the introduction and commentary, I follow the conventional use of Roman numerals to distinguish Dicaeogenes I (the speaker's great-grandfather) from Dicaeogenes II (the speaker's uncle), and Dicaeogenes III (the son of Proxenus and adopted son of Dicaeogenes II). Similarly, to distinguish the three men named Menexenus: Menexenus I is the speaker's grandfather, Menexenus II the speaker's cousin (son of Cephisophon), and Menexenus III the speaker himself. In the translation, I do not use this system but rely on Isaeus's own method of disambiguation (see commentary on 'our dispute with Dicaeogenes', §1).

This, more than any other of Isaeus's extant speeches, is rich in allusions to Athenian history and to individuals who can be identified from contemporary classical sources.[4] The protagonists in the dispute came from an elite Athenian family, distinguished not only by their great wealth but also by their record of civic and military service. Menexenus III, the speaker, traces his maternal ancestry back to the first half of the sixth century: his great-grandfather, Dicaeogenes I, of the deme Cydathenaeum, was a general who died in battle at Eleusis, probably around 460 BC (§42). The line of succession passed through his son, Menexenus I, a cavalry commander killed at Spartolus in 429 (§42) and then to Menexenus I's only son, Dicaeogenes II, who died while in command of one of the state triremes, the Paralus, in a battle near Cnidus probably around 414/3 (§5).

In addition to his only son, Dicaeogenes II, Menexenus I had four daughters, who (following the conventions of Athenian forensic oratory) are not named in the speech but identified only in relation to their male 'guardians' (*kyrioi*), the husbands or sons who represented them in litigation. (Like all other Athenian women, they had limited civic and legal rights, and could not speak for themselves in court.) One of these women, the speaker's mother, was the wife of Polyaratus of Cholargus, an assessor to the public treasurers (Hellenotamiae) in 410/09 BC and member of the Athenian Boule (Council) in 405/4 (§5). The second was married to Cephisophon of Paeania, who was Secretary of the Boule in 403/2 BC and one of the Treasurers of Athena and the other gods in 398/7. The third was the wife of Theopompus, whose identity is otherwise unknown, and the fourth was married to Democles of Phrearrhii. Since Dicaeogenes II was childless, the whole of his paternal estate would have passed to his sisters on his death if he had not left an adopted son.

Dicaeogenes III, who claimed to have been adopted by Dicaeogenes II, was also descended through his mother from Dicaeogenes I, and he came of very distinguished lineage on his

4 The individuals named in Isaeus 5 are listed on p. 37. The simplified stemma on p. 12 does not include individuals whose existence is doubtful, or who were not directly involved in the litigation over the estate of Dicaeogenes II.

father's side: he was the second son of Proxenus of Aphidna, a public treasurer (Hellenotamias) in 410/09 BC and a descendant of Harmodius, one of the so-called 'tyrant-slayers' reputed to have brought an end to the Athenian tyranny in the late sixth century.[5] If, as most scholars believe, his mother was a daughter of Dicaeogenes I and sister of Menexenus I, Dicaeogenes III was by birth a first cousin of his adoptive father, Dicaeogenes II.[6] In that case, it is possible that Dicaeogenes III was named after his maternal grandfather, Dicaeogenes I, or he may have taken the name Dicaeogenes only after the adoption.

Isaeus's client, who delivered the speech in court,[7] does not identify himself by name, but he says that his father was Polyaratus. We know that Polyaratus of Cholargus had three sons: Menexenus, Bathyllos, and Periander, of whom the youngest, Periander, was probably still a minor at the time of the present trial.[8] Menexenus was apparently the oldest, and I follow the scholarly convention in naming him as the speaker of Isaeus 5. There is, however, no firm evidence that this was the case, and we cannot rule out the possibility that the speech was delivered by Bathyllus.[9] One of Menexenus's cousins, Cephisodotus (son of Theopompus) seems to have been a joint prosecutor in the action against Leochares (§2). Another cousin, also called Menexenus (the son of Cephisophon) had been associated with them in previous litigation over the estate of Dicaeogenes II, but it is not clear whether he was directly involved in the present case. There is no indication that Democles or his sons (if any) ever participated on behalf of the fourth sister.

5 See commentary on §46.

6 An alternative conjecture is that the daughter of Dicaeogenes I was the mother, not the wife, of Proxenus, in which case Dicaeogenes II and Dicaeogenes III would have been first cousins once removed. See commentary on 'Proxenus ... produced a will', §6.

7 Todd (1993, 95, n.19) includes Isae. 5 in a list of speeches delivered by a supporting speaker (*synēgoros*), but this seems mistaken; there is nothing to suggest that Menexenus was not himself the prosecutor.

8 See commentary on §5.

9 Cf. Cobetto Ghiggia (2002, 74).

## THE SPEECH IN THE CONTEXT OF ISAEUS'S CAREER

This is the earliest of Isaeus's extant speeches, dating from the late 390s or very early 380s, when he was a young man, but it is unlikely to have been his first: although some of the characteristic features of his style are not yet fully developed, the speech displays considerable rhetorical skill and is clearly not the work of a complete novice. Moreover, the fact that he was hired by such a wealthy litigant as Menexenus, in a dispute about such a substantial estate, suggests that he already had a reputation. According to pseudo-Plutarch's *Vitae decem oratorum*, Isaeus was mentioned (presumably as an object of satire) in the comedy *Theseus* of Theopompus, which has been dated to 390–380 BC.[10] That, if true, and if the dating is correct, would also suggest that Isaeus had become well known at an early stage in his career as a professional speechwriter.

## SUMMARY OF EVENTS NARRATED IN THE SPEECH

After Dicaeogenes II died, Proxenus of Aphidna produced a will in which his son, Dicaeogenes III, had been adopted as the son of Dicaeogenes II and given one third of the estate. No-one contested the will, and the remaining two thirds of the estate were shared by the four sisters of Dicaeogenes II. Twelve years later, Dicaeogenes III himself produced a document purporting to be a second will of Dicaeogenes II, in which he had been adopted with the whole of the estate. The speaker's father, Polyaratus, disputed the will on behalf of his wife, and the case went to court as a *diadikasia*,[11] which Dicaeogenes won. At the end of the trial, Polyaratus lodged an objection to the testimony of Dicaeogenes's witnesses (or some of them) but he died before he could proceed with a prosecution for false testimony and his sons were too young to do so. Dicaeogenes III was thus able to take over the whole estate; he seized all the property occupied by the sisters of

10 Cf. Griffith-Williams (2013, 25–26).

11 See General Introduction, pp. 7–8.

Dicaeogenes II, leaving one of them, the widow of Theopompus, and her children destitute.

Ten more years elapsed before the current trial, the prosecution of Leochares as surety for Dicaeogenes III. During this time, the speaker's cousin Menexenus (son of Cephisophon) had prosecuted Lycon, one of Dicaeogenes's witnesses at the *diadikasia*, for false testimony. Menexenus won the case, but before he could prosecute the remaining witnesses he was (according to Menexenus the speaker) persuaded by Dicaeogenes III to take his own share of the estate but abandon the cousins on whose behalf he had been acting and give up the prosecution of the remaining witnesses. But Dicaeogenes cheated Menexenus, who joined forces again with his cousins.

At this stage the cousins changed tactics and submitted a claim to the whole estate on behalf of their mothers as next of kin to Dicaeogenes II, on the basis that there was no longer a valid will because the first had been annulled by the decision of the court and the second was discredited by the conviction of Lycon for false testimony. Their claim did not go to court because Dicaeogenes III made use of the *diamartyria*, a procedural device that enabled a legitimate son to block a claim to his father's estate from collateral relatives.[12] Leochares, as Dicaeogenes's witness, asserted in the *diamartyria* that the estate was not available for adjudication to the next of kin. The cousins then prosecuted Leochares for false testimony in the *diamartyria*. At the end of the trial, when the judges had voted but before the votes had been counted, it became obvious that Leochares would be convicted. So, with the agreement of the archon, a last-minute compromise was reached: the votes were not counted but mixed together, and Dicaeogenes agreed to return two thirds of the estate to the sisters of Dicaeogenes II, free of any further claims or liabilities. Leochares and Mnesiptolemus of Plotheia stood surety that Dicaeogenes would carry out what he had agreed.

Menexenus and his cousins found it impossible to recover more than a small part of what was due to them under the agreement, because much of the property was occupied by tenants or mortgagees,

12 See commentary on 'a *diamartyria* ...', §15.

and Dicaeogenes obstructed the cousins' attempts to evict them. The cousins then decided to prosecute Leochares as surety, but when the case was about to come to court, Dicaeogenes and Leochares persuaded them to submit the dispute to arbitration. Arbitrators were appointed, but after questioning the disputants they declined to announce a decision. The prosecution, accordingly, went ahead – about 22 years after the death of Dicaeogenes II.

## DATING AND HISTORICAL BACKGROUND

The private conflict narrated in Isaeus 5 played out during an eventful period in Athenian history, encompassing the last years of the Peloponnesian War, the brutal and turbulent regime of the Thirty Tyrants in 404–403 BC and its aftermath, and the Corinthian War of 395–386, which was still in progress when the speech was delivered. Determining the date of the speech is, nevertheless, not an entirely straightforward exercise.

The narrative starts with the death of Dicaeogenes II in a sea battle near Cnidus, which recent scholars have generally taken as a reference to an incident near Syme in 411 BC.[13] Accordingly, since the original division of the estate lasted 12 years (§7), the *diadikasia* at which Dicaeogenes III gained possession of the whole estate would have taken place in 399. He held the estate for 10 years before the prosecution of Leochares, so the date of Isaeus 5 would be 389.

There are some difficulties with this chronology, not least the allusion to the civil unrest at the time of the oligarchy: after the initial division of the estate, 'each possessed the share he had received for 12 years, and in that time, although cases were being heard, none of them thought of saying that what had been done was unjust until

13 There was a more famous battle at Cnidus in 394 BC, which led some nineteenth-century scholars to think that the date of the speech was 372. R. C. Jebb, who initially took this view, later changed his mind; see commentary on §37. Wyse (1904, 413) had reservations about the identification of a sea battle 'at Cnidus' with one near Syme, and suggests that Dicaeogenes II was killed in 412. (See commentary on 'at Cnidus', §6.)

there was disorder and civil war in the city' (§7). In the light of this, it would be surprising if the *diadikasia* between Dicaeogenes III and Polyaratus did not come to court until 399 BC – four years after the restoration of the democracy in September 403. Moreover, it is clearly implied that Menexenus the speaker was still under 20, and therefore too young to prosecute Dicaeogenes's witnesses for false testimony, when his father Polyaratus died shortly after the *diadikasia* (§9). Menexenus is thought to have been born around 420 BC,[14] so, even if this is an approximate date, he is likely to have been at least 20 in 399.

A critical factor in the dating of the speech is the reference to the capture of Lechaeum by the Spartans, which took place in 392 and is mentioned by Menexenus in terms which suggest it was a recent event at the time of the trial (§36). On that basis, the speech could have been delivered as early as 391 or even in late 392. So the *diadikasia* could have taken place in 402 or 401, which would make the allusion to the oligarchy of the Thirty more intelligible. Given the interval of 12 years between the death of Dicaeogenes II and the *diadikasia*, he would have died in 414 or 413. There is, admittedly, no record of a naval battle in the vicinity of Cnidus in either of those years, but this would not be the only reference in the Attic orators to a military encounter that does not appear on the historical record.[15] On balance, then, although any conclusion must inevitably be speculative, I think it most likely that Isaeus 5 was delivered very shortly after the capture of Lechaeum, in late 392 or in 391.[16]

---

14 ca. 420–365 (*LGPN* V-2. 44815).

15 On 'insignificant battles' and family memory, see commentary on 'the battle at Eleusis', §42.

16 Wevers (1969, 14–16) treats Isae. 5 as one of four speeches by Isaeus that can be 'firmly dated' from the internal evidence, and his statistical analysis of 'good' and 'bad' rhythms confirms the accepted date of 389, but he stresses that the dates suggested by that method are 'only an approximation'. An adjustment of two or three years would not invalidate his method.

## THE ESTATE OF DICAEOGENES II

The first piece of documentary evidence produced at the trial was an inventory of the property left by Dicaeogenes II. Dicaeogenes III derived an annual rent of 80 minas (a talent and a third) from this property over the ten years during which he held the entire estate (§§11, 35), so its capital value was clearly very substantial. But (as with nearly all the documentary evidence cited in the Attic orators) the text of the inventory has not survived, and only a few items of property are mentioned in the speech: two small houses outside the city walls (§22), 60 plethra of land 'in the Plain' (§22), a bathhouse (§22), and a house in the city that was sold for 5,000 drachmas (§28). Exact locations are not mentioned, but the bathhouse and the house 'in the city' may have been in Cydathenaeum (the ancestral deme of Dicaeogenes II), while land 'in the plain' could have been in Polyaratus's deme, Cholargus.

## THE ADOPTION

We know nothing about Dicaeogenes II except that he died in battle at Cnidus while in command of the Paralus, and that he was childless (§6). Since he had no natural legitimate son, he was legally entitled to adopt anyone he chose as his son and heir, either during his lifetime (adoption *inter vivos*) or by will (testamentary adoption).[17] The latter was the natural choice for someone who, like Dicaeogenes II, was about to undertake military service or some other risky activity, if he still had hopes of fathering a natural son after surviving the imminent danger.[18] Dicaeogenes's reasons for the adoption are not discussed in the speech, but we may surmise that, as a typical Athenian, he

17 For details of the relevant law, see the General Introduction, pp. 2–3. A son adopted *inter vivos*, like a natural legitimate son, could simply take possession of the estate after his father's death, without legal formalities, but someone claiming to have been adopted by will had to secure the approval of the court before taking possession.

18 Of the ten attested Athenian cases of testamentary adoption, six were carried out by men who died in war or while travelling (Rubinstein, 1993, 23).

wanted a successor who would continue his line of descent (*oikos*) and perform the annual commemorative rituals for him, as well as inherit his material property (or part of it, according to the terms of the first will).[19] He also followed what seems to have been a common Athenian practice in adopting someone to whom he was already related by blood,[20] but his reasons for choosing a cousin rather than one of his sisters' sons are unknown. In any event, the adoption was accepted by the family, and when, 12 years later, Dicaeogenes III claimed the whole estate under the second will, it was the disposition of the property that was challenged by Polyaratus, not the adoption in itself.

## THE TWO WILLS

Apart from a case known only from fragments,[21] this is the only attested Athenian case involving two wills, the first of which was accepted as valid until it was challenged by a claimant producing a later one. As far as we can judge from the available sources, a typical Athenian will nominated an adopted son as heir to the father's entire estate. So the first will, in which Dicaeogenes III was adopted with only a third of the estate, was evidently unusual, though it was not illegal.[22] As to how Dicaeogenes persuaded a court to annul the first will and award him the whole estate, we can only speculate, since we know nothing about the circumstances in which Dicaeogenes II made the two wills or the competing arguments put forward by Dicaeogenes III and Polyaratus at the *diadikasia*.[23] Dicaeogenes is unlikely to have argued that the first will was a forgery, or invalid under Solon's law

19 Such a motive is regularly cited in speeches in which an adoption is defended; see, e.g., Isae. 2.15, 6.5, 7.30; [Dem.] 43.11; and, for discussion, Griffith-Williams (2012, 146–48).

20 Rubinstein (1993, 22–23); cf. Griffith-Williams (2022, 71).

21 Isae. fr. III Teubner.

22 See commentary on 'with a third of the estate', §6.

23 Cf. Todd (1993, 222, n.23): 'What makes this episode particularly odd is that Dikaiogenes subsequently produces a further will giving him the entire estate, and persuades a court to accept it'.

for some other reason, since it was produced by his own father and he had benefited from it for 12 years.[24]

Perhaps Dicaeogenes III explained the unusual terms of the first will by claiming that it had only ever been intended as an interim measure, and that Dicaeogenes II had always wanted him to succeed to the whole estate when he came of age.[25] Another possibility is that the original division of the estate did not follow the terms of the will but was a compromise between Proxenus and Dicaeogenes's sisters; Dicaeogenes III was a minor when Dicaeogenes II died, and (in accordance with the compromise) claimed the whole estate when he came of age.[26] Or perhaps it was argued that Dicaeogenes II had simply changed his mind, although in that case it would have been difficult to explain why he had not destroyed the first will,[27] and why the second had not come to light for 12 years.

According to Wesley Thompson's reconstruction of the case, Dicaeogenes

> originally made the will to assure that his sisters would receive an adequate dowry, but once they were all married he changed his will and gave his heir the entire estate (5.7). The second will was not discovered until after the first had been probated. If the man who had custody of the will was abroad for several years during the Ionian War, that would explain why it took so long for it to come to light.[28]

To support the suggestion that the delay in producing the second will could have been caused by the custodian's absence from Athens, Thompson cites the case where a claimant to the estate of Archippus produced a second will that had allegedly been made on Lemnos (Isae. fr. III Teubner). Ingenious as it is, however, his explanation[29]

---

24 Cf. commentary on 'not the true one', §15.

25 Cf. Harrison (1968, 86).

26 Wyse (1904, 414).

27 On physical destruction as the only means of revoking an Athenian will, see Isae. 1.25 and 6.32, with Griffith-Williams (2022).

28 Thompson (1981, 18, n.22).

29 Described by Todd (1993, 222, n.23) as 'ingenious but unconvincing'.

still does not account for Dicaeogenes's failure to destroy the original will, or why he did not tell Proxenus and other family members of his changed intentions.

## THE AGREEMENT

The essence of the agreement between Dicaeogenes III and his opponents, made at the end of the trial of Leochares for false testimony, was that Dicaeogenes would relinquish two thirds of the estate to the sisters of Dicaeogenes II. Some of the terms of the agreement, according to the speaker, were committed to writing, but others, in view of the urgency of the situation, were simply agreed orally in the presence of witnesses. He does not produce the written document in court, and provides no details of the terms of the agreement except that the property was to be handed over 'free of any further claims or liabilities' (*anamphisbētēta*, §§1, 18, 20, 21). The intended effect of the agreement was thus to restore the position under the original will, giving only a third of the estate to Dicaeogenes III while the rest would be shared among the sisters of Dicaeogenes II. This is presented as a concession on the part of Menexenus and his cousins, who had been hoping to win the whole estate, but in practice they may have been happy enough with the compromise.

The fact that only part of the agreement was in written form was a serious difficulty for Menexenus – not, as some commentators have suggested,[30] because the terms agreed orally were not legally enforceable, but because their existence was more difficult for the prosecutor to prove, and much easier for the defendant to dispute. Dicaeogenes and Leochares clearly could not deny that an agreement had been made, or that Leochares had agreed to act as one of the sureties for Dicaeogenes III, since this had taken place in a public setting in the presence of many witnesses. But they evidently did deny that the agreement required Dicaeogenes to restore the property in its original condition, free from further claims or liabilities. They probably said that he could not afford to repay the full original value

30 See the introductory note on §§25–30.

of his opponents' share in the estate, and had returned as much of the property as he could.

It is, in fact, more than likely that the original value of the property had depreciated in the 22 years since the death of Dicaeogenes II; a reference to 'the repairs to the bathhouse and the cost of building' (§28) gives some indication of what was probably a much larger problem. Then there was the additional difficulty that Dicaeogenes III had mortgaged some of the property, and would need to pay off his mortgagees in order to recover it. So, even if the sisters of Dicaeogenes II were legally entitled to reclaim the full value of the estate that they had previously enjoyed, restoring it to them would have been an expensive matter for Dicaeogenes III. If he did, under pressure, make an agreement on the terms claimed by Menexenus, he might well have denied it in the knowledge that Menexenus would find it impossible to prove.

That, then, is the weak point in Menexenus's case, and Isaeus does not attempt to address it directly by spelling out the terms of the agreement in full. Instead, he strives to convey the impression that Dicaeogenes III was a slippery character who was highly likely to dishonour an agreement and who, despite pleading poverty, had more than enough resources to repay his opponents in full.

## THE CHARACTER OF DICAEOGENES III

The final 12 sections of this speech – about a quarter of its entire length – are devoted to an attack on the character of Dicaeogenes III. Character assassination of an opponent is not unusual in the speeches of the Attic orators, but what is striking about Isaeus 5 is the length and ferocity of the attack. The fact that the target is not the defendant, Leochares, but Dicaeogenes III, is not really surprising: if Dicaeogenes had honoured the agreement with Menexenus and his associates, Leochares would have had no case to answer, so in order to convict Leochares, Menexenus has to prove that Dicaeogenes had reneged on the agreement. Indeed, Dicaeogenes III is treated throughout the speech as the speaker's real opponent, and the narrative, far from being a straightforward factual account, is carefully designed to present him in the worst possible light.

Modern scholars have sometimes dismissed the character evidence[31] in Athenian forensic speeches as 'extra-legal' or 'irrelevant'. In the context of inheritance in particular, it has sometimes been assumed that, when the legal issues are too complex or difficult to determine, speakers use character evidence to show that one claimant is more deserving than his opponent on moral grounds, offering the judges an alternative basis for their decision. That is the view taken by David Cohen, who comments, on Isaeus 5 specifically:

> In the present case, the speaker devotes a substantial part of the oration … to arguing, in great detail, that the adoptee is a worthless citizen who has squandered his wealth rather than using it to benefit the city. [The speaker's] part of the family, on the other hand, has distinguished itself through benefactions to the state. Perhaps such extensive appeals on this point were felt to be necessary since the adoptee had previously been victorious in two previous suits against this branch of the family and the speaker felt it opportune to offer the judges another criterion for deciding the case in their favor.[32]

But this misunderstands the issue in the case, and the use of character evidence by the Attic orators may be more subtle than Cohen suggests. As Andrew Alwine points out:

> When a speaker attempts to paint himself or his opponent in a certain light, he does not necessarily ask the jurors to vote for whomever they find more acceptable as a person. He uses character portraits to create implicit arguments from probability about the key claims of the case.[33]

The 'relevance' of character evidence (as of any other evidence) needs to be assessed on a case by case basis: a particular piece of evidence is 'relevant' if it has some connection with the issue(s) in

31 A useful definition of 'character evidence' is 'proof or attestations about an individual's moral standing, his general nature, behavioural traits, and reputation in the general community' (Adamidis, 2017, 101–02).

32 Cohen (1995, 172–73).

33 Alwine (2015, 93).

dispute.[34] In some of his other cases, Isaeus does argue that if an estate is awarded to his client it will be put to good use for the benefit of the city, whereas his client's opponent would squander it,[35] but he never invites the judges simply to ignore the law and award an estate to the claimant who is more morally deserving. Typically, as part of an argument from probability, the good character of a claimant shows why the testator chose to adopt him, while the bad character of an opponent shows why the testator wanted to avoid leaving him his property.[36]

That argument is not deployed in Isaeus 5, because the issue in this case is not the validity of the adoption but Dicaeogenes III's alleged breach of the agreement with his opponents. The negative characterization of Dicaeogenes III – throughout the speech, not just in §§35–47 – does, nevertheless, support Menexenus's case by establishing a pattern of behaviour: Dicaeogenes III has (according to the speaker) repeatedly swindled his relatives, reneging on promises, cheating them out of property that lawfully belongs to them, and treating them with callous contempt. In the public sphere he has failed to carry out all but the most trivial of the military and civic duties that would be expected from a citizen of his wealth. All of this, it is clearly implied, makes it more than likely that he did dishonour the agreement, so the character evidence in this speech is relevant to the legal issue, although it does not amount to conclusive proof.

Leaving aside the question of relevance, we may wonder how accurate, or fair, Isaeus's characterization of Dicaeogenes III was. Most of it is unsupported by evidence, the only exception being the testimony from witnesses that Dicaeogenes defaulted on his promise to contribute 300 drachmas to the Athenian war fund (§38). Much of it, even if it had some foundation in fact, is likely to have been

---

34 For the modern legal theory of evidence on which this is based, and its application to the Athenian system, see Griffith-Williams (2012, 154–55).

35 Isae. 4.27, 6.61, with Griffith-Williams (2022, 127–28).

36 See, e.g., Isae. 4.27–31, with Griffith-Williams (2022), Isae. 7.33–42, with Griffith-Williams (2013).

exaggerated, and amounts to little more than rumour or gossip, portraying Dicaeogenes as not only the stereotypical 'bad citizen'[37] but also a transgressive family member.[38] It would, nevertheless, have had a powerful impact on the judges, if they believed it, making them more inclined to accept Menexenus's version of the agreement.

## WITNESS TESTIMONY: RELEVANCE TO THE DISPUTE

Eight items of witness testimony are produced in the course of the speech, but, as is almost invariably the case in the corpus of the Attic orators, we do not have the text of these depositions. Some indication of their content is given in the speech itself, but the wording is often vague, typically with formulations such as 'I will produce witnesses on these matters' or 'I will produce witnesses of these facts', from which it is not clear precisely which aspects of the preceding narrative are covered in the testimony.

Only two of the eight witness statements relate to the agreement between Dicaeogenes III and his opponents. First, the speaker states clearly in §1 that he is about to produce witnesses who will testify 'first, that Dicaeogenes ceded two thirds of the estate to us, and secondly, that Leochares became his surety'. This wording, which notably does not include the words 'without further dispute', is substantially repeated, with reference to the same testimony, in §4.

Secondly, at the end of the section of narrative dealing with the trial of Leochares for false testimony, the speaker says (§18):

> When we agreed with the archon that the ballots should not be counted but mixed together, Dicaeogenes surrendered two thirds of the estate to the sisters of Dicaeogenes, agreeing to hand over these shares to us without further dispute. And Leochares here became his surety,

37 Hunter (1994, 110).

38 Hunter (1994, 118) identifies 'treatment of kin' as one of the most common topics of gossip in the Attic orators. The examples she cites, in addition to Isae. 5.9–11 and 5.39, are Aesch. 1.102–04; Dem. 21.130, 24.127, 202–03, 25.55, 45.70; Isae. 7.31, 42, 44–45, 8.37, 40–43, 9.16–18, 11.37–38.

> pledging that he would carry out his promise, with Mnesiptolemus of Plotheia as his fellow surety. And I will now produce witnesses of these facts.

It is not clear from this whether the witnesses who were present at the earlier trial actually testified that the agreement included the words 'without further dispute'.

Most of the remaining witness statements relate to the speaker's story about the history of his dispute with Dicaeogenes III (although it is notable that there are no witnesses to his allegations about Dicaeogenes's callous treatment of his relatives) and the final one supports part of his character evidence, but none is directly relevant to the terms of the agreement. They relate to the terms of the first will (§5); the conviction of Lycon for false testimony and the subsequent change of sides by the speaker's cousin Menexenus (§12); the failed attempt to evict Micion from the bathhouse (§24); Leochares's duplicity in his dealings with Protarchides (§24); the inconclusive arbitration (§33); and Dicaeogenes's failure to pay his promised contribution to the war effort (§38).

## WITNESS TESTIMONY: ORAL OR WRITTEN?

A striking feature of this speech is that, while most of the witnesses' depositions are introduced with variations on the formula 'I will produce witnesses' (§§6, 13, 18, 24, 27, 33, 38), the first is introduced with an instruction to the court clerk to read out the testimony. This, if the text is correct,[39] is the earliest unequivocal evidence of written testimony in the Attic orators. In the forensic speeches of the earlier orators (Antiphon, Andocides, Isocrates, and Lysias) there are no direct references to written witness statements, and testimony is introduced with formulae such as 'I will produce witnesses', 'Let the witnesses come forward', or 'Please call the witnesses for me'. These formulae reflect the position that, until some time in the early fourth

39 Some earlier scholars argued for an emendation of the text; see, e.g., Bonner and Smith (1930, 359–61).

century, witnesses in the Athenian courts gave their testimony orally and could be questioned by the litigants.

Following a change in the law, witness statements had to be submitted in writing at the *anakrisis* (preliminary hearing before the archon) or arbitration hearing.[40] Then, along with other documentary evidence, they were kept in sealed boxes (*echinoi*) until the trial, in the course of which they were read out by the court clerk. The exact date of the change from oral to written testimony is uncertain, and has been the subject of much scholarly debate. According to Bonner, 'the law requiring evidence to be reduced to writing was … later than 380 BC, when the public career of Lysias was ended, and earlier than the bulk of the speeches of Isaeus'.[41] Calhoun thought that written testimony became mandatory at the same time as a change from oral to written pleading, in 379/8 BC, at least ten years later than the date of Isaeus 5. He explained the isolated occurrence of a reference to written testimony in this speech with the suggestion that 'there is not the slightest reason why evidence should not occasionally have been produced in writing prior to the enactment of a legal requirement that it be so presented'.[42]

A 'problem' identified by modern scholars is that several speeches later than Isaeus 5 include a mixture of formulae, some referring to the testimony as documentary evidence and others to the witnesses in person. Taken at face value, that might indicate that some witnesses gave their evidence orally while at the same trial there were others whose testimony was produced in written form and read by the clerk, implying a longer transition between oral and written testimony with no mandatory cut-off point prescribed in legislation.[43] It seems unlikely, however, that both oral and written testimony would have been permitted at the litigant's discretion, given the concern to maintain fairness between opposing litigants and to ensure that witnesses could not alter their testimony between the preliminary

---

40 Dem. 45.44.

41 Bonner (1905, 47).

42 Calhoun (1919, 191).

43 Thus Edwards (2024).

hearing and the trial.[44] While it remains impossible to be certain about the date of the change, the continuing use of formulae referring to the witnesses rather than the document is best explained by the requirement for witnesses to be present in court and come forward to affirm the testimony that was read out on their behalf.[45]

## FALSE TESTIMONY: *EPISKĒPSIS* AND *DIKĒ PSEUDOMARTYRIŌN*

There was no appeal against the decision of an Athenian *dikastērion* ('people's court'), but at least in some circumstances a case could be reopened if the losing party successfully prosecuted one or more of his opponent's witnesses for false testimony. (The Greek word *pseudomartyria* is sometimes translated as 'perjury', but that is inaccurate because Athenian witnesses did not routinely testify on oath.) An essential preliminary to such a prosecution was the *episkēpsis* ('objection'), which had to be made orally at the original trial, before the judges had voted.[46] The witness who testified in a *diamartyria* could also be denounced and prosecuted for false testimony. There are two instances of *episkēpsis* in Isaeus 5: Polyaratus made an objection to Dicaeogenes's witnesses at the *diadikasia* (§9); then Menexenus and his cousins objected to Leochares's testimony in the *diamartyria* (§17).

It was up to the litigant who had made the objection whether or not to proceed with a prosecution. It is reasonable to assume, despite the lack of evidence on this point, that if he chose to proceed he had to do so within a specified time after the *episkēpsis*.

According to the speaker of Isaeus 11, the conviction of a witness for false testimony in a *diadikasia* required the claim for the estate to start afresh.[47] Scholars have interpreted this in various ways; a conviction for false testimony clearly put the loser at a significant

44 Cf. Dem. 45.44.

45 Cf. commentary on 'Please read the witness testimony', §2.

46 See commentary on 'objected', §9.

47 See commentary on 'the law prescribes …', 11.46.

disadvantage, whether or not it formally annulled the decision of the court at the *diadikasia*.[48]

## THE STRUCTURE AND STYLE OF THE SPEECH

The structure of the speech seems designed to play down the weakness in the speaker's case, his difficulty in proving the terms of the agreement, while making the most of the points in his favour. After a confident start, producing evidence of the agreement and of Leochares's obligation as surety, Isaeus does not mention the terms of the agreement until more than halfway through the speech (§§25–30). The intervening narrative, ostensibly a factual account of the background to the current dispute, paints a negative portrait of Dicaeogenes III calculated to prejudice the judges against him even before the issues are discussed. The speech concludes with a lengthy and vicious character assassination.

Two characteristic features of Isaeus's style, repetition and rhetorical questions, are exemplified in this speech. The crucial term *anamphisbētēta* ('without further dispute' or 'free of further claims and liabilities') is first used in §1 and repeated at §§18, 20, and 21, to ensure that the judges grasp its significance and retain it in their memory. Of the 11 rhetorical questions in the speech, six are directed at the judges (§§12, 21(x2), 34(x2), 38) and five at Dicaeogenes III (§§43, 45(x3), 46). They create the sense of a dialogue between the speaker and his audience, or his opponent, and are often couched in an ironic tone that ridicules the opponent's character or behaviour.

Apostrophe (direct address to an opponent of the speaker) is a stylistic device that Isaeus uses much more rarely. In all his extant speeches, the most striking example is found at the end of Isaeus 5,[49] where the concluding five paragraphs (§§43–47) are addressed directly to Dicaeogenes III, and the name Dicaeogenes occurs four times in the vocative case.

48 See commentary on 'the witnesses who had not yet been convicted', §13.

49 See commentary on §43 for examples from other speeches.

## TEXTUAL PROBLEMS IN ISAEUS 5

There are, notoriously, two textual cruces in the speech, each involving the identity of one of the women in the family of Dicaeogenes II. First, one of those deprived of her inheritance, after Dicaeogenes III gained control of the whole estate, is identified in the manuscripts as 'the daughter of Cephisophon and niece of Dicaeogenes II' (§9). But Cephisophon's daughter could not have been in possession of a share of the estate unless her parents were already dead and she had no surviving brother. That does not appear to have been the case: §16 implies that Cephisophon's wife (to whom the share had originally devolved) was still alive at the time of the present trial in the late 390s, and her son Menexenus (first mentioned at §12 as the prosecutor of Dicaeogenes's witnesses for false testimony) had been actively involved in the earlier litigation.

Common sense, therefore, suggests that the woman in question was in fact the wife of Cephisophon and sister of Dicaeogenes II, and the nineteenth-century scholar Buermann[50] proposed that the text should be emended accordingly. But most editors (Thalheim 1903, Wyse 1904, Roussel 1926, Forster 1927, Cobetto Ghiggia 2002 and 2012), while recognizing the difficulty, have, nevertheless, retained the manuscript reading. Wyse justifies this on the ground that the corruption of γυναῖκα to θυγατέρα is unlikely. He concludes, with his characteristic bias: 'Is it not possible that Isaeus deliberately distorted the truth to get a rhetorical effect, wishing to represent Dicaeogenes III as the cruel oppressor of a defenceless girl?'[51]

A more objective commentator might have recognized that Isaeus had no need of rhetorical exaggeration at this point in his narrative: the plight of Cephisophon's wife is the first element of 'a neat tricolon *crescens* of the increasingly parlous situations of the three sisters',[52] culminating in the exceptionally callous treatment by Dicaeogenes of Cephisodotus and his mother (the widow and

50 Cited by Wyse (1904, 416).

51 Wyse (1904, 416–17).

52 Edwards (2002, 595).

son of Theopompus). I follow Edwards in emending the text, on the basis that the scribal error was 'one of mental association rather than palaeographical'.[53]

It is worth recording a dissident view, propounded by Virginia Hunter: that Cephisophon's daughter might have inherited at least part of her mother's property even if she had a brother still living.[54] That suggestion is, rightly, discredited by Edwards on the basis of the speaker's statements, at §§12 and 13, that his cousin Menexenus (the son of Cephisophon) was 'entitled to the same share of the estate as I was', and was persuaded by Dicaeogenes 'to take his own share of the estate'.[55] In fact, if we accept that the text of §9 is corrupt, there is no evidence in the speech that Cephisophon and his wife actually had a daughter at all, but Hunter is right in her more general point that we are not well informed about the *post mortem* disposition of property inherited by Athenian women.[56]

The second textual problem arises at §26, where, according to the manuscripts, Dicaeogenes gave his sister (ἀδελφὴν) in marriage to Protarchides with a dowry of 40 minas. In the next sentence, the speaker says that the woman in question 'is entitled to the same share of the estate as my mother', so she cannot have been a sister of Dicaeogenes III. If the manuscript text is correct, therefore, it must have been Dicaeogenes II who betrothed one of his sisters to Protarchides as her second husband. But that is problematic, and modern editors and commentators have taken different approaches to the text, based on their answers to two questions: which of the two men named Dicaeogenes betrothed the wife of Protarchides, and who was the woman in question? It is not necessary here to rehearse the debate in full detail, but it is worth summarizing the different conclusions of three scholars who have discussed the issues at some length, before considering the main arguments for and against each hypothesis.

---

53 Edwards (2002, 595).

54 Hunter (1994, 200, n.39).

55 Edwards (2002, 594, n.8).

56 Cf. General Introduction, pp. 5–6.

1. Wyse (1904) rejects all the textual emendations suggested by earlier editors, opting simply to obelize the words τὴν ἀδελφὴν τὴν ἑαυτοῦ ('his sister'). But he concludes that 'The giver of the dowry must be Dicaeogenes III' and 'The wife of Protarchides must be either a sister of Dicaeogenes II or the sole heir of a sister of Dicaeogenes II; she is either the sister who married Democles or her only child'.[57]
2. Cobetto Ghiggia (2002) concludes that it was indeed Dicaeogenes II who betrothed his sister (the former wife of Democles) to Protarchides, so no emendation of the text is needed.[58]
3. Edwards (2002) agrees with Wyse that the betrother was Dicaeogenes III, but concludes that the woman in question was not the former wife of Democles but her daughter. So the relationship of Protarchides's wife to Dicaeogenes III was that of 'cousin's daughter' or 'first cousin once removed' (ἀνεψιαδῆν) and Edwards emends the text accordingly.[59]

As to the first question, the identity of the Dicaeogenes who dowered the wife of Protarchides, Cobetto Ghiggia finds nothing to contradict the assumption that this happened during the lifetime of Dicaeogenes II. Yet it appears from the earlier narrative that none of the sisters was married to Protarchides when Dicaeogenes II died; if such a marriage had indeed taken place during his lifetime, one would have expected Protarchides to be mentioned at §5 or §9. Secondly, from its position in the narrative, the betrothal to Protarchides seems to have taken place after the death of Dicaeogenes II, closer to the time when Menexenus and his cousins were trying to recover the mortgaged property. The speaker says (§27) that after Dicaeogenes III agreed to hand over two thirds of the estate to the sisters of Dicaeogenes II, Leochares persuaded Protarchides to return the dowry in return for his wife's share of the estate, then swindled him by failing to return the share. This incident, obscure in itself, makes better sense if the dowry was

57 Wyse (1904, 445).
58 Cobetto Ghiggia (2002, 200).
59 Edwards (2002, 595–97).

given by Dicaeogenes III.[60] Finally, as Edwards notes, the betrother is identified simply as 'Dicaeogenes' with no qualification, which – although it is not conclusive proof – strongly suggests that he was Dicaeogenes III.[61] (This point is overlooked by Cobetto Ghiggia, who accuses Isaeus of lack of clarity in his identification of the betrother.)[62]

Turning to the second question, if Protarchides's wife was one of the sisters of Dicaeogenes II, she could have been either the former wife of Democles, who was either widowed or divorced, or the widow of Theopompus. The possibility that she was a *daughter* of Democles and his wife presupposes not only that her mother had died (of which there is no evidence in the speech) but also that she died leaving no sons, so that her claim to a share in the estate passed to her surviving daughter. That, of course, is not impossible, but there is a more serious objection (not mentioned by Wyse or Edwards): an Athenian woman left with no brothers after her father's death was an *epiklēros* ('heiress'), and should have been married by *epidikasia* (i.e. adjudicated by the court) to her father's next of kin, not betrothed with a dowry to a man who was not even a member of her father's deme. (And if Dicaeogenes III had defrauded an *epiklēros* by marrying her out of the family, in addition to all his other alleged offences against his relatives, Isaeus would undoubtedly have said so.)[63]

On balance, I conclude that it was certainly Dicaeogenes III who betrothed the wife of Protarchides, and that she must have been a sister (not a niece) of Dicaeogenes II. She was probably the former wife of Democles, but she could have been the widow of Theopompus,[64] whose *kyrios* we know to have been Dicaeogenes III.

60 According to Wyse (1904, 443): 'if Dicaeogenes here [§26] means Dicaeogenes II, the bargain between Leochares and Protarchides is inexplicable'. Cf. Edwards (2002, 596).

61 Edwards (2002, 596); cf. commentary on 'our dispute with Dicaeogenes', §1.

62 'Scarsa chiarezza' (Cobetto Ghiggia, 2002, 200).

63 Cases of (allegedly) defrauded heiresses were not unknown in classical Athens; see, e.g., Isae. 3 and, esp., Isae. 10.

64 Edwards (2002, 595, n.14) argues plausibly that if Dicaeogenes III had subjected the widow of Theopompus to the 'further humiliation' of insisting on the return of her dowry but failing to hand over her share of the estate (§27), 'we would

As to the text, Dicaeogenes III was, *de jure*, the nephew of his adoptive father's sisters, but it is hardly conceivable that a scribe would have written ἀδελφὴν ('sister') in error for τηθίδα ('aunt'). My preferred solution is to retain the ms. ἀδελφὴν and add the words τοῦ πατρὸς ('of his father').

## CONCLUSION

This is a highly complex case, and many of the factual details are obscure. The outcome of the trial is unknown, and it is impossible for us – more than 2,000 years after the event, and without seeing the defence speech – to judge which of the opposing parties had the stronger case. We may reasonably infer that the speaker was vulnerable when it came to the details of his agreement with Dicaeogenes III, but we should not conclude, simply because it was difficult for him to prove his case, that he was in the wrong.

Isaeus, like any advocate (ancient or modern) whose client lacks conclusive proof, relied heavily on argumentation from probability to persuade the judges that his client's story was, if not certainly true, at least more credible than his opponent's. In an adversarial Athenian trial, where each of the opposing parties put his case in a single main speech, it was the prosecutor who spoke first; and that (at least from the point of view of a worried or disgruntled defendant) gave him the opportunity to impress the judges with his client's version of events and prejudice them against the defence.[65] In his speech for the prosecution of Leochares (and, by extension, Dicaeogenes III), Isaeus exploited that advantage to the full.

---

expect Isaeus to have made the most of this rhetorical opportunity'. It is, however, Leochares rather than Dicaeogenes who is blamed for this episode, and I do not consider the objection to be fatal.

65 For the 'prosecuting is better than defending' topos in Attic oratory, see Hyp. *Lyc.* 8–10 with Whitehead (2000, 123–24) who cites as parallels Andoc. 1.6, Dem. 18.3–7, Isoc. 15.21–22, Lys. 19.3.

# PEOPLE IN ISAEUS 5

Aristogeiton of Aphidna, tyrant-slayer (§47); *PAA* 168195.

Cephisodotus, son of Theopompus (§§2, 5, 11, 12); *PAA* 567595.

Cephisophon of Paeania, husband of one of Dicaeogenes II's sisters and father of Menexenus II (§§5, 9, 12); *PAA* 569290.

Cleonymus the Cretan (§37); *PAA* 579500.

Demaratus of Plotheia, brother of Mnesiptolemus, arbitrator nominated by Leochares (§33); *PAA* 306345.

Democles of Phrearrhii, husband of one of Dicaeogenes II's sisters (§§5, 9); *PAA* 315975.

Dicaeogenes I of Cydathenaeum, speaker's maternal great-grandfather (§42); *PAA* 324265.

Dicaeogenes II, son of Menexenus I of Cydathenaeum, testator; *PAA* 324270.

Dicaeogenes III, natural son of Proxenus of Aphidna and adopted son of Dicaeogenes II of Cydathenaeum; *PAA* 324245.

Diopeithes, brother-in-law of Leochares, arbitrator nominated by Leochares (§§33, 34); *PAA* 363135.

Diotimus, arbitrator nominated by the speaker (§32); *PAA* 365440.

Harmodius of Aphidna, tyrant-slayer, ancestor of Dicaeogenes III (§47); *PAA* 203425.

Harmodius, son of Proxenus of Aphidna and brother of Dicaeogenes III (§11; cf. Lys. 1.41, fr. 18, Dem. 23.130, Din. 1.63, D.H. *Lys.* 12); *PAA* 203435.

Leochares, surety for Dicaeogenes III (defendant); *PAA* 607125.

Lycon, witness for Dicaeogenes III, prosecuted for false testimony by Menexenus II (§12); *PAA* 611750.

Melanopus, arbitrator nominated by the speaker (§32); *PAA* 638690.

Melas the Egyptian, friend of Dicaeogenes III (§§7, 8, 40); *PAA* 638910.

Menexenus I of Cydathenaeum, speaker's maternal grandfather (§5); *PAA* 644875.

Menexenus II, son of Cephisophon of Paeania, speaker's cousin; *PAA* 644910.

Menexenus III, son of Polyaratus of Cholargus, ca. 420–365 BC (speaker); *PAA* 644925.

Micion, mortgagee of bathhouse owned by Dicaeogenes III (§§22–24); *PAA* 652960.

Mnesiptolemus of Plotheia, surety for Dicaeogenes III (§18); *PAA* 657410.

Philonicus, purchaser of townhouse from Dicaeogenes III (§29); *PAA* 940120.

Polyaratus of Cholargus, husband of one of Dicaeogenes II's sisters and father of the speaker; *PAA* 777540.

Protarchides of Potamus, second husband of one of Dicaeogenes II's sisters (§26), named as a witness (§27); *PAA* 790905.

Proxenus of Aphidna, natural father of Dicaeogenes III before his adoption by Dicaeogenes II; *PAA* 789825.

Theopompus, husband of one of Dicaeogenes II's sisters and father of Cephisodotus; *PAA* 509500.

# ISAEUS 5: ON THE ESTATE OF DICAEOGENES

# ΠΕΡΙ ΤΟΥ ΔΙΚΑΙΟΓΕΝΟΥΣ ΚΛΗΡΟΥ

Ὠιόμεθα μέν, ὦ ἄνδρες, περὶ ὧν διεφερόμεθα πρὸς Δικαιογένην, τὰ ὡμολογημένα ἐπὶ τοῦ δικαστηρίου κύρια ἡμῖν ἔσεσθαι· ἀποστάντος γὰρ Δικαιογένους τοῖν δυοῖν μεροῖν τοῦ κλήρου, καὶ ἐγγυητὰς καταστήσαντος ἦ μὴν παραδώσειν ἡμῖν ταῦτα τὰ μέρη ἀναμφισβήτητα, ἀφήκαμεν ἀλλήλους τῶν ἐγκλημάτων· ἐπειδὴ δέ, ὦ ἄνδρες, οὐ ποιεῖ Δικαιογένης ἃ ὡμολόγησε, δικαζόμεθα Λεωχάρει ἐγγυητῇ γενομένῳ Δικαιογένους, ὥσπερ ἀντωμόσαμεν. [2] καί μοι ἀνάγνωθι τὴν ἀντωμοσίαν.

ΑΝΤΩΜΟΣΙΑ

Ὡς τοίνυν ἀληθῆ ἀντωμόσαμεν, Κηφισόδοτος οὑτοσὶ οἶδε, καὶ μάρτυρας ὑμῖν παρεξόμεθα πρῶτον μὲν ὡς ἀπέστη Δικαιογένης ἡμῖν τοῖν δυοῖν μεροῖν τοῦ κλήρου, εἶτα ὡς ἠγγυήσατο Λεωχάρης. καί μοι ἀνάγνωθι τὴν μαρτυρίαν.

ΜΑΡΤΥΡΊΑ

[3] Τῶν μὲν μαρτύρων ἀκηκόατε, καὶ ὡς οὐ τἀληθῆ μεμαρτυρήκασιν, οὐδ' ἂν αὐτὸν οἶμαι Λεωχάρην εἰπεῖν· ἴσως δὲ ἐπ' ἐκεῖνον τρέψεται τὸν λόγον, ὡς Δικαιογένης τε ἃ ἡμῖν ὡμολόγησεν ἅπαντα πεποίηκε, καὶ αὐτὸς τὴν ἐξεγγύην ὅτι ἀπέδωκεν. εἰ οὖν ταῦτ' ἐρεῖ, ψεύσεται καὶ ῥᾳδίως ἐλεγχθήσεται. ἀναγνώσεται γὰρ ὑμῖν ὅσα κατέλιπε Δικαιογένης ὁ Μενεξένου ἐν τῷ κλήρῳ καὶ τὰ χρήματα ἃ ἔλαβεν.

<ΑΠΟΓΡΑΦΗ>

[4] Ταῦτα εἰ μὲν μή φασι Δικαιογένην τὸν ἡμέτερον θεῖον ζῶντα κεκτῆσθαι καὶ ἀποθνήσκοντα ἡμῖν δοῦναι, ἀποδειξάτωσαν· εἰ δὲ καὶ ἐκεῖνον καταλιπεῖν καὶ ἡμᾶς κεκομίσθαι, μαρτυρησάτω τις αὐτοῖς. ὅτι μὲν γὰρ Δικαιογένης ὡμολόγει παραδώσειν ἡμῖν ὧν κατέλιπεν ὁ Μενεξένου τὰ δύο μέρη, ἡμεῖς μάρτυρας παρεχόμεθα, καὶ ὅτι Λεωχάρης ἠγγυήσατο αὐτὸν ταῦτα ποιήσειν· καὶ γὰρ δικαζόμεθα διὰ τοῦτο, καὶ ταῦτα ἀντωμόσαμεν. καί μοι ἀνάγνωθι τὴν ἀντωμοσίαν.

ΑΝΤΩΜΟΣΙΑ

[5] Εἰ μὲν τοίνυν, ὦ ἄνδρες, περὶ τούτων ἔμελλον ἀπολογήσεσθαι μόνον Λεωχάρης ἢ Δικαιογένης, ἤρκει ἄν μοι τὰ εἰρημένα· ἐπειδὴ δὲ παρεσκευασμένοι εἰσὶν ἐξ ἀρχῆς περὶ <τοῦ> κλήρου λέγειν, βούλομαι ὑμᾶς καὶ παρ' ἐμοῦ τὰ πραχθέντα πυθέσθαι, ἵνα εἰδότες τἀληθῆ, ὅ τι ἂν δοκῇ ὑμῖν, ψηφίσησθε, ἀλλὰ μὴ ἐξηπατημένοι.

(1) We thought, gentlemen, that in the matter of our dispute with Dicaeogenes, what was agreed in court would prevail. For when Dicaeogenes gave up two thirds of the estate, and provided sureties that he would hand over that share to us without further dispute, both sides abandoned our claims. But, gentlemen, since Dicaeogenes is not doing what he agreed to do, we are suing Leochares, his surety, in accordance with our sworn statement. (2) Please read the statement.

SWORN STATEMENT

Cephisodotus here knows that what we said in the sworn statement is the truth, and I will produce witnesses for you who testify, first, that Dicaeogenes ceded two thirds of the estate to us, and secondly, that Leochares became his surety. Please read the witness testimony.

TESTIMONY

(3) You have heard the witnesses, and I don't think even Leochares himself would deny that their testimony is true. But perhaps he will argue that Dicaeogenes has done everything he agreed to do, and that he himself has carried out his duty as surety. If he says this, he will be lying, and he will easily be convicted. For the inventory will be read to you of all the property that Dicaeogenes (the son of Menexenus) left in his estate, and the property that Dicaeogenes received.

INVENTORY

(4) If they say that our uncle Dicaeogenes did not acquire this property in his lifetime, and give it to us after his death, let them prove it. Or if they say that he did leave it to us, and we received it, let someone testify to that on their behalf. We produce witnesses to testify that Dicaeogenes agreed to hand over to us two thirds of the property left by the son of Menexenus, and that Leochares pledged that he would do so. As we have said in our sworn statement, that is why we are bringing this action. Please read the statement.

SWORN STATEMENT

(5) So, gentlemen, if these were the only points to be made by Leochares or Dicaeogenes in their defence, what I have already said would be sufficient. But since they are prepared to discuss the inheritance from the beginning, I want you also to learn the facts from my side, so that you are not deceived but know the truth when you cast your votes.

Μενεξένῳ γὰρ τῷ ἡμετέρῳ πάππῳ ἐγένετο ὑὸς μὲν εἷς, Δικαιογένης, θυγατέρες δὲ τέτταρες, ὧν ἔλαβε μίαν μὲν Πολυάρατος ὁ πατὴρ ὁ ἐμός, ἄλλην δὲ Δημοκλῆς ὁ Φρεάρριος, τὴν δὲ Κηφισοφῶν ὁ Παιανιεύς· ἡ δὲ <τετάρτη> Θεοπόμπῳ ἐγήματο τῷ Κηφισοδότου πατρί. [6] καὶ ὁ μὲν Δικαιογένης, τριήραρχος ἐκπλεύσας τῆς Παράλου, ἐτελεύτησε μαχόμενος ἐν Κνίδῳ· ἀποθανόντος δ' αὐτοῦ ἄπαιδος διαθήκην ἀπέφηνε Πρόξενος ὁ Δικαιογένους <τουδὶ> πατήρ, ᾗ πιστεύσαντες οἱ ἡμέτεροι πατέρες ἐνείμαντο τὸν κλῆρον. καὶ ἐπὶ μὲν τῷ τρίτῳ μέρει τοῦ κλήρου Δικαιογένης ὅδε τῷ Μενεξένου Δικαιογένει, ἡμετέρῳ δὲ θείῳ, ὑὸς ἐγίγνετο ποιητός· τῶν δὲ λοιπῶν ἑκάστη τὸ μέρος ἐπεδικάσατο τῶν Μενεξένου θυγατέρων. ὧν ἐγὼ τοὺς τότε παρόντας ὑμῖν μάρτυρας παρέξομαι.

<ΜΑΡΤΥΡΕΣ>

[7] Ἐπειδὴ δὲ ἐνείμαντο τὸν κλῆρον, ὀμόσαντες μὴ παραβήσεσθαι τὰ ὡμολογημένα, ἐκέκτητο ἕκαστος δώδεκα ἔτη ἃ ἔλαχε· καὶ ἐν τοσούτῳ χρόνῳ οὐσῶν δικῶν οὐδεὶς αὐτῶν ἠξίωσε τὰ πεπραγμένα εἰπεῖν ἀδίκως πεπρᾶχθαι, πρὶν δυστυχησάσης τῆς πόλεως καὶ στάσεως γενομένης Δικαιογένης οὑτοσὶ πεισθεὶς ὑπὸ Μέλανος τοῦ Αἰγυπτίου, ᾧ περ καὶ τἆλλα ἐπείθετο, ἠμφισβήτει ἡμῖν ἅπαντος τοῦ κλήρου, φάσκων ἐφ' ὅλῃ ποιηθῆναι ὑὸς ὑπὸ τοῦ θείου τοῦ ἡμετέρου. [8] ἡμεῖς μὲν οὖν μαίνεσθαι αὐτὸν ἡγούμεθα τῇ λήξει, οὐκ ἄν ποτε οἰόμενοι τὸν αὐτὸν ἄνδρα τοτὲ μὲν φάσκοντα ἐπὶ τῷ τρίτῳ μέρει ποιηθῆναι τοτὲ δ' ἐφ' ἅπαντι τῷ κλήρῳ δόξαι τἀληθὲς λέγειν ὑμῖν· εἰς δὲ τὸ δικαστήριον εἰσελθόντες καὶ πολλῷ πλείω καὶ δικαιότερα λέγοντες ἠδικήθημεν, οὐχ ὑπὸ τῶν δικαστῶν ἀλλ' ὑπὸ Μέλανος τοῦ Αἰγυπτίου καὶ τῶν ἐκείνου φίλων, οἳ διὰ τὰς τῆς πόλεως συμφορὰς ἐξουσίαν σφίσιν αὐτοῖς ἡγοῦντο εἶναι κεκτῆσθαί τε τἀλλότρια καὶ τὰ ψευδῆ ἀλλήλοις μαρτυρεῖν· ὑπὸ δὲ τῶν τὰ τοιαῦτα ποιούντων ἐξηπατήθησαν οἱ δικασταί. [9] καὶ ἡμεῖς μὲν καταψευδομαρτυρηθέντες ἀπωλέσαμεν τὰ ὄντα· καὶ γὰρ ὁ πατὴρ οὐ πολλῷ χρόνῳ ὕστερον μετὰ τὴν δίκην ἐτελεύτησε, πρὶν ἐπεξελθεῖν οἷς ἐπεσκήψατο τῶν μαρτύρων· Δικαιογένης δὲ πρὸς ἡμᾶς ὡς ἐβούλετο ἀγωνισάμενος τῇ αὐτῇ ἡμέρᾳ ἐξήλασε μὲν τὴν Κηφισοφῶντος τοῦ Παιανιέως γυναῖκα ἐκ τοῦ μέρους, ἀδελφήν οὖσαν Δικαιογένους τοῦ καταλιπόντος τὰ χρήματα, ἀφείλετο δὲ τὴν Δημοκλέους γενομένην γυναῖκα, ἃ Δικαιογένης ἀδελφὸς ὢν ἔδωκεν, ἀφείλετο <δὲ> καὶ τὴν Κηφισοδότου μητέρα καὶ αὐτὸν τοῦτον ἅπαντα. [10] καὶ γὰρ τούτων [τε] ἅμα καὶ ἐπίτροπος καὶ κύριος καὶ ἀντίδικος ἦν, καὶ οὐδὲ κατὰ τὸ ἐλάχιστον μέρος τῆς οἰκειότητος ἐλέου παρ' αὐτοῦ ἔτυχον, ἀλλ' ὀρφανοὶ καὶ ἔρημοι καὶ πένητες γενόμενοι πάντων καὶ τῶν καθ' ἡμέραν ἐπιτηδείων ἦσαν ἐνδεεῖς. οὕτως αὐτοὺς Δικαιογένης οὑτοσὶ ἐγγυτάτω ὢν γένους ἐπετρόπευεν· ὅς γε, ἃ μὲν ὁ πατὴρ αὐτοῖς Θεόπομπος κατέλιπε,

Our grandfather, Menexenus, had one son, Dicaeogenes, and four daughters. My father, Polyaratus, married one of them, Democles of Phrearrhii another, and Cephisophon of Paeania the third. The fourth was married to Theopompus, the father of Cephisodotus. (6) And Dicaeogenes sailed out as trierarch of the Paralus, and died in action at Cnidus. He died childless, and Proxenus, the father of Dicaeogenes here, produced a will on which our fathers relied when they divided the estate. Under the will, Dicaeogenes was to become the adopted son of our uncle Dicaeogenes, son of Menexenus, with a third of the estate. The rest was awarded by the court to the daughters of Menexenus in equal shares. I will produce witnesses who were present at the time.

WITNESSES

(7) When they had divided the estate, after swearing to observe the agreed terms, each possessed the share he had received for 12 years, and in that time, although cases were being heard, none of them thought of saying that what had been done was unjust until there was disorder and civil war in the city. Then Dicaeogenes here was persuaded by Melas the Egyptian (whose advice he always accepted) to contest the entire estate with us, asserting that he had been adopted as our uncle's son with the whole of the property. (8) We thought he was mad to bring the claim, never believing that you would think the same man who had once claimed to have been adopted with a third of the estate, but then with the entirety, was telling the truth. But when we came to court, although we had a much better case, we were deprived of justice, not by the judges but by Melas the Egyptian and his friends, who thought that because of the city's misfortune they were entitled to take possession of other people's property and support one another with false testimony. And the judges were deceived by them when they acted in this way. (9) And we, victims of false testimony, lost our property, for our father died not long after the trial, before he could proceed against the witnesses to whose evidence he had objected. And Dicaeogenes, after winning the result he wanted against us, on the same day ejected the wife of Cephisophon of Paeania (sister of Dicaeogenes who left the property) from her share, robbed the former wife of Democles of what her brother Dicaeogenes had given her, and also robbed both Cephisodotos and his mother of everything. (10) For he was, at the same time, their guardian, legal representative and legal opponent; he did not have the slightest pity for them on account of their relationship, but they were orphans, alone and destitute, lacking all the everyday necessities. That was how Dicaeogenes here, their next of kin, treated them as their guardian. What their father Theopompus had left them, he handed over to their enemies; and what

τοῖς τούτων ἐχθροῖς παρέδωκεν, ἃ δὲ ὁ πρὸς μητρὸς θεῖος καὶ ὁ πάππος αὐτοῖς ἔδωκεν, αὐτὸς ἀφείλετο πρὸ δίκης. [11] καὶ ὃ πάντων δεινότατον, τὴν οἰκίαν αὐτῶν τὴν πατρῴαν, παίδων ὄντων τούτων, πριάμενος καὶ κατασκάψας [τὸν] κῆπον ἐποιήσατο πρὸς τῇ αὑτοῦ οἰκίᾳ τῇ ἐν ἄστει. καὶ λαμβάνων μίσθωσιν ὀγδοήκοντα μνᾶς ἐκ τῶν Δικαιογένους τοῦ ἡμετέρου θείου χρημάτων, τὸν ἐκείνου ἀδελφιδοῦν Κηφισόδοτον τῷ ἑαυτοῦ ἀδελφῷ Ἁρμοδίῳ συνέπεμψεν εἰς Κόρινθον ἀντ᾽ ἀκολούθου· εἰς τοῦτο ὕβρεως καὶ μιαρίας ἀφίκετο. καὶ πρὸς τοῖς ἄλλοις κακοῖς ὀνειδίζει καὶ ἐγκαλεῖ αὐτῷ ὅτι ἐμβάδας καὶ τρίβωνα φορεῖ, ὥσπερ ἀδικούμενός τι εἰ ἐμβάδας Κηφισόδοτος φορεῖ, ἀλλ᾽ οὐκ ἀδικῶν ὅτι ἀφελόμενος αὐτὸν τὰ ὄντα πένητα πεποίηκεν. [12] ἀλλὰ περὶ μὲν τούτων τοσαῦτά μοι εἰρήσθω· πάλιν δ᾽ ἐπάνειμι ὅθεν ἀπέλιπον. Μενέξενος γὰρ ὁ Κηφισοφῶντος ὑός, ἀνεψιὸς ὢν Κηφισοδότῳ τουτῳὶ καὶ ἐμοί, καὶ προσῆκον αὐτῷ τοῦ κλήρου μέρος ὅσον περ ἐμοί, ἐπεξῄει τοῖς καταμαρτυρήσασιν ἡμῶν καὶ ἐκείνου τὰ ψευδῆ, καὶ Λύκωνα, ὅν περ εἰσήγαγε πρῶτον εἰς τὸ δικαστήριον, τοῦτον εἷλεν· ὃς ἐμαρτύρησε Δικαιογένην ποιηθῆναι τὸν νῦν ὄντα ὑπὸ τοῦ θείου τοῦ ἡμετέρου ὑὸν ἐπὶ παντὶ τῷ κλήρῳ. [13] μαρτυρήσας δὲ ταῦτα ἑάλω ψευδομαρτυρίων. ἐπειδὴ δὲ Δικαιογένης, ὦ ἄνδρες, οὐκέτι ὑμᾶς δύναται ἐξαπατᾶν, πείθει Μενέξενον τὸν ὑπὲρ ἡμῶν τε καὶ ὑπὲρ αὑτοῦ πράττοντα, ἃ ἐγὼ αἰσχυνόμενος ἀναγκάζομαι διὰ τὴν ἐκείνου πονηρίαν λέγειν, - τί ποιῆσαι; κομισάμενον αὐτὸν μέρος ἐκ τοῦ κλήρου ὅ τι ἐγίγνετο, ἡμᾶς μὲν ὑπὲρ ὧν ἔπραττε προδοῦναι, τοὺς δὲ μήπω ἑαλωκότας τῶν μαρτύρων ἀφεῖναι. καὶ ἡμεῖς μὲν ταῦτα ὑπὸ τῶν φίλων καὶ τῶν ἐχθρῶν παθόντες εἴχομεν ἡσυχίαν. τούτων δ᾽ ὑμῖν μάρτυρας παρέξομαι.

ΜΑΡΤΥΡΕΣ

[14] Ὁ μὲν τοίνυν Μενέξενος παθὼν ἄξια τῶν ἑαυτοῦ τρόπων ἠπατήθη ὑπὸ τοῦ Δικαιογένους· ἀφεὶς γὰρ τοὺς μάρτυρας καὶ ἡμᾶς προδούς, ὧν ἕνεκα ταῦτ᾽ ἔπραξεν οὐκ ἐκομίσατο. ἀδικηθεὶς δὲ ὑπὸ Δικαιογένους μεθ᾽ ἡμῶν πάλιν ἔπραττεν. ἡμεῖς δὲ καθηγούμενοι οὐκέτι προσήκειν Δικαιογένει ἔχειν τῶν ἐκ τοῦ κλήρου μέρος οὐδέν, ἐπειδὴ οἱ μάρτυρες ἑάλωσαν, ἀμφισβητοῦμεν αὐτῷ ἅπαντος τοῦ οἴκου κατ᾽ ἀγχιστείαν. καὶ ὅτι ἡμεῖς τε ὀρθῶς ἐγνώκαμεν καὶ οὐδὲν ἔτι προσήκει Δικαιογένει τοῦ κλήρου, ῥᾳδίως διδάξω. [15] δύο γὰρ διαθῆκαι <ἀπ> εφάνησαν, ἡ μὲν πάλαι, ἡ δὲ πολλῷ ὕστερον· καὶ κατὰ μὲν τὴν παλαιάν, ἣν ἀπέφηνε Πρόξενος ὁ Δικαιογένους τουτουὶ πατήρ, ἐπὶ τῷ τρίτῳ μέρει τοῦ κλήρου ἐγίγνετο τῷ θείῳ τῷ ἡμετέρῳ ὑὸς ποιητός, καθ᾽ ἣν δ᾽ αὐτὸς ἀπέφηνε Δικαιογένης, ἐπὶ παντὶ τῷ οἴκῳ. τούτοιν δὲ τοῖν διαθήκαιν ἣν μὲν Πρόξενος ἀπέφηνε, Δικαιογένης ἔπεισε τοὺς δικαστὰς ὡς οὐκ ἀληθὴς εἴη· ἣν δὲ Δικαιογένης ἀπέφηνεν, οἱ μαρτυρήσαντες αὐτὴν τὸν θεῖον τὸν ἡμέτερον

their maternal uncle and their grandfather had given them, he took for himself without waiting for a judgment. (11) And worst of all, while they were children, he bought the house they had inherited from their father, demolished it, and turned the site into a garden next to his own house in the city. What's more, so great were his insolence and brutality that, although he was receiving 80 minas in rent from the estate of our uncle Dicaeogenes, he sent Dicaeogenes's nephew Cephisodotus to Corinth as an attendant for his brother Harmodius. And on top of everything else he blamed and criticized Cephisodotus for wearing cheap shoes and a threadbare cloak, as if it were Cephisodotus who was somehow wronging him by wearing cheap shoes, not he who was wronging Cephisodotus by robbing him of his property and making him destitute.

(12) But I've said enough about that; now I'll get back to the point. For Menexenus the son of Cephisophon, my cousin and the cousin of Cephisodotus, being entitled to the same share of the estate as I was, proceeded against those who had testified falsely against him and us, and won his case against the first man he took to court, Lycon, who had testified that Dicaeogenes had been adopted by our uncle with the whole estate. (13) And he was convicted of false testimony on account of that evidence. And when, gentlemen, Dicaeogenes was no longer able to deceive you (I'm ashamed that his wickedness forces me to tell you this) he persuaded Menexenus, who was acting on our behalf as well as for himself – to do what? To take his own share of the estate but abandon us, for whom he had been acting, and to give up his prosecution of the witnesses who had not yet been convicted. And we, treated in this way by friends and enemies alike, kept quiet. And I will produce witnesses on these matters for you.

WITNESSES

(14) Well now, Menexenus was deceived by Dicaeogenes and suffered what he deserved, for he did give up his prosecution of the witnesses and abandon us, but got nothing in return. After being wronged by Dicaeogenes, he joined forces with us again. And we, thinking that Dicaeogenes no longer had a claim to any part of the estate, since the witnesses had been convicted, contested the whole estate with him on grounds of kinship. And I shall easily explain to you that we made the right decision, and that Dicaeogenes is not entitled to the estate. (15) For two wills have been produced, one long ago and the other much later. And according to the old will, produced by Proxenus the father of Dicaeogenes here, Dicaeogenes was to become our uncle's adopted son with one third of the estate, but according to the will which Dicaeogenes himself produced, with the whole of the estate. And of these two wills, Dicaeogenes persuaded the judges that the one produced by Proxenus was not the true one, while the witnesses who

διαθέσθαι ἑάλωσαν ψευδομαρτυρίων. [16] ἀμφοῖν δὲ τοῖν διαθήκαιν ἀκύροιν γιγνομέναιν, καὶ ἑτέρας μηδεμιᾶς ὁμολογουμένης εἶναι, κατὰ δόσιν μὲν οὐδενὶ προσῆκε τοῦ κλήρου, κατ᾽ ἀγχιστείαν δὲ ταῖς Δικαιογένους τοῦ ἀποθανόντος ἀδελφαῖς, ὧν εἰσιν αἱ ἡμέτεραι μητέρες. διὰ δὲ ταῦτα ἔδοξέ τε ἡμῖν λαχεῖν τοῦ κλήρου κατ᾽ ἀγχιστείαν, καὶ ἐλάχομεν τοῦ μέρους ἕκαστος. μελλόντων δ᾽ ἡμῶν ἀντόμνυσθαι διεμαρτύρησε Λεωχάρης οὑτοσὶ μὴ ἐπίδικον εἶναι τὸν κλῆρον ἡμῖν. [17] ἐπισκηψαμένων δ᾽ ἡμῶν ἡ μὲν λῆξις τοῦ κλήρου διεγράφη, ἡ δὲ τῶν ψευδομαρτυρίων δίκη εἰσῄει. ἐν δὲ τῷ δικαστηρίῳ πάντα μὲν ἡμῶν εἰπόντων ἅ περ νυνί, πολλὰ δὲ Λεωχάρους ἀνταπολογησαμένου, ἔγνωσαν τὰ ψευδῆ μαρτυρῆσαι Λεωχάρην οἱ δικασταί. ἐπειδὴ δὲ τοῦτο φανερὸν ἐγένετο ἐξαιρεθεισῶν τῶν ψήφων, ἃ μὲν τῶν δικαστῶν καὶ ἡμῶν ἐδεήθη Λεωχάρης ἢ ὅσα ἡμῖν ἐξεγένετο διαπράξασθαι τότε, οὐκ οἶδ᾽ ὅ τι δεῖ λέγειν, ἃ δὲ ὡμολογήθη ἡμῖν, ταῦτα ἀκούσατε. [18] συγχωρούντων γὰρ ἡμῶν τῷ ἄρχοντι μὴ συναριθμεῖν ἀλλὰ συγχέαι τὰς ψήφους, ἀφίστατο μὲν Δικαιογένης τοῖν δυοῖν μεροῖν τοῦ κλήρου ταῖς Δικαιογένους ἀδελφαῖς, καὶ ὡμολόγει ἀναμφισβήτητα παραδώσειν ἡμῖν ταῦτα τὰ μέρη· καὶ ταῦτα ἠγγυᾶτο αὐτὸν Λεωχάρης οὑτοσὶ ἃ ὡμολόγει ποιήσειν, οὐ μόνος ἀλλὰ καὶ Μνησιπτόλεμος ὁ Πλωθειεύς. καὶ τούτων ὑμῖν τοὺς μάρτυρας παρέξομαι.

ΜΑΡΤΥΡΕΣ

[19] Ἡμεῖς τοίνυν ταῦτα παθόντες ὑπὸ Λεωχάρους, καὶ ἐγγενόμενον ἡμῖν αὐτὸν ἐπειδὴ εἵλομεν τῶν ψευδομαρτυρίων ἀτιμῶσαι, οὐκ ἐβουλήθημεν, ἀλλ᾽ ἐξήρκεσε τὰ ἡμέτερα ἡμῖν κομισαμένοις ἀπηλλάχθαι. τοιοῦτοι δὲ γενόμενοι περὶ Λεωχάρην καὶ Δικαιογένην ἐξηπατήθημεν ὑπ᾽ αὐτῶν, ὦ ἄνδρες· οὔτε γὰρ Δικαιογένης τὰ δύο μέρη ἡμῖν τοῦ κλήρου παρέδωκεν, ὁμολογήσας ἐπὶ τοῦ δικαστηρίου, οὔτε Λεωχάρης ὁμολογεῖ ἐγγυήσασθαι αὐτὸν τότε. [20] καίτοι εἰ μὴ ἐναντίον μὲν τῶν δικαστῶν, πεντακοσίων ὄντων, ἐναντίον δὲ τῶν περιεστηκότων ἠγγυᾶτο, οὐκ οἶδ᾽ ὅ τι ἂν ἐποίησεν. ὡς μὲν τοίνυν περιφανῶς ψεύδονται, μάρτυρας ὑμῖν παρεχόμεθα τοὺς παρόντας, ὅτε Δικαιογένης μὲν ἀφίστατο τοῖν δυοῖν μεροῖν τοῦ κλήρου καὶ ὡμολόγει ἀναμφισβήτητα παραδώσειν ταῖς Δικαιογένους ἀδελφαῖς, Λεωχάρης δὲ ἠγγυᾶτο αὐτὸν ἃ ὡμολόγησε καὶ ποιήσειν. δεόμεθα δὲ καὶ ὑμῶν, ὦ ἄνδρες, εἴ τις ἐτύγχανε παρὼν τότε, ἀναμνησθῆναι εἰ λέγομεν ἀληθῆ καὶ βοηθῆσαι ἡμῖν· [21] ἐπεί, ὦ ἄνδρες, εἰ Δικαιογένης ἀληθῆ λέγει, τί ἡμεῖς ὠφελούμεθα νικήσαντες, ἢ τί οὗτος ἐζημιώθη ἡττηθείς; εἰ γὰρ ἀπέστη μόνον (ὥς φησι) τοῖν δυοῖν μεροῖν τοῦ κλήρου, ἀναμφισβήτητα δὲ μὴ ὡμολόγει παραδώσειν, τί ἐζημιοῦτο ἀφιστάμενος ὧν τιμὴν εἶχεν; οὐδὲ γὰρ πρὶν ἡττηθῆναι τὴν δίκην εἶχεν ὧν ἡμεῖς δικαζόμεθα,

testified that our uncle made the will produced by Dicaeogenes were convicted of false testimony. (16) Since both of these wills were going to be invalidated, and it was agreed that no other will existed, no-one had a claim to the estate as a bequest, but the sisters of the late Dicaeogenes, including our mothers, could claim it on the basis of kinship. Because of this we decided to submit a claim on the basis of kinship, and we each claimed a share. And when we were about to make our sworn statements, Leochares here submitted a *diamartyria* declaring that the estate was not adjudicable to us. (17) We then raised an objection, our claim was struck out, and the prosecution for false testimony proceeded. In court, after we had made all the arguments we are making now, and Leochares put forward a long defence, the judges decided that he had testified falsely. And when this became clear, after the ballots had been tipped out, I don't know what I need to say about the appeals Leochares made to us and the judges, or the penalties we could then have imposed, but let me tell you about the agreement we reached. (18) When we agreed with the archon that the ballots should not be counted but mixed together, Dicaeogenes surrendered two thirds of the estate to the sisters of Dicaeogenes, agreeing to hand over these shares to us without further dispute. And Leochares here became his surety, pledging that he would carry out his promise, with Mnesiptolemus of Plotheia as his fellow surety. And I will now produce witnesses of these facts.

WITNESSES

(19) Well now, after being treated like this by Leochares, although we could have had him deprived of civic rights after he was convicted of false testimony, we did not want to do so, but were content to recover what belonged to us and wash our hands of him. Having behaved like this to Leochares and Dicaeogenes, we were deceived by them, gentlemen: for neither did Dicaeogenes hand over two thirds of the estate to us, as he had agreed in court, nor does Leochares agree that he made the pledge as surety. (20) And yet if he had not made his pledge in the presence of the judges – all 500 of them – and the bystanders as well, I don't know what else he could have done. And so to prove to you that they are obviously lying, we bring forward as witnesses those who were present when, on the one hand, Dicaeogenes ceded two thirds of the estate and agreed to hand it over without further dispute to Dicaeogenes's sisters, and, on the other hand, Leochares pledged as surety that he would do what he had agreed. And we beg you, gentlemen, if any of you happened to be there, to remember whether we are telling the truth and help us. (21) Since, gentlemen, if Dicaeogenes is telling the truth, how did we benefit from winning the case, and how was my opponent disadvantaged by losing it? For if, as he says, he merely ceded two thirds of the

ἀλλ᾽ οἱ παρὰ τούτου πριάμενοι καὶ θέμενοι, οἷς ἔδει αὐτὸν ἀποδόντα τὴν τιμὴν ἡμῖν τὰ μέρη ἀποδοῦναι. [22] διὰ ταῦτα γὰρ καὶ τοὺς ἐγγυητὰς παρ᾽ αὐτοῦ ἐλάβομεν, οὐ πιστεύοντες αὐτῷ ἃ ὡμολόγησε ποιήσειν. πλὴν γὰρ δυοῖν οἰκιδίοιν ἔξω τείχους καὶ ἐν Πεδίῳ ἑξήκοντα πλέθρων οὐδὲν κεκομίσμεθα, ἀλλ᾽ οἱ παρὰ τούτου θέμενοι καὶ πριάμενοι. ἡμεῖς δ᾽ οὐκ ἐξάγομεν· δέδιμεν γὰρ μὴ ὄφλωμεν δίκας. καὶ γὰρ Μικίωνα, κελεύοντος Δικαιογένους καὶ φάσκοντος <οὐ> βεβαιώσειν, ἐξάγοντες ἐκ τοῦ βαλανείου ὤφλομεν τετταράκοντα μνᾶς διὰ Δικαιογένην, ὦ ἄνδρες. [23] ἡγούμενοι γὰρ οὐκ ἂν αὐτὸν βεβαιῶσαι οὐδὲν ὧν ἡμῖν ἀπέστη ἐν τῷ δικαστηρίῳ, διισχυριζόμεθα πρὸς Μικίωνα ἐναντίον τῶν δικαστῶν, ἐθέλοντες ὁτιοῦν πάσχειν, εἰ βεβαιώσειεν αὐτῷ Δικαιογένης τὸ βαλανεῖον, οὐκ ἄν ποτε οἰόμενοι αὐτὸν ἐναντία οἷς ὡμολόγησε πρᾶξαι, οὐ δι᾽ ἄλλ᾽ οὐδὲν ἢ διὰ τοὺς ἐγγυητάς, ὅτι καθειστήκεσαν ἡμῖν. [24] ἀποστὰς δὲ Δικαιογένης ταῦτα τὰ μέρη ὧν καὶ νῦν ὁμολογεῖ ἀφεστάναι ἡμῖν, ἐβεβαίωσε Μικίωνι τὸ βαλανεῖον. καὶ ἐγὼ μὲν ὁ ἄθλιος οὐχ ὅπως τι ἐκ τοῦ κλήρου εἰληφώς, ἀλλὰ προσαπολωλεκὼς τετταράκοντα μνᾶς, ἀπῄειν ὑβρισμένος ὑπὸ τοῦ Δικαιογένους. καὶ τούτων ὑμῖν μάρτυρας παρέξομαι.

ΜΑΡΤΥΡΕΣ

[25] Ταῦτα μὲν πεπόνθαμεν ὑπὸ Δικαιογένους, ὦ ἄνδρες· ὁ δ᾽ ἐγγυησάμενος αὐτὸν Λεωχάρης καὶ τῶν πάντων ἡμῖν κακῶν αἴτιος οὔ φησιν ἐγγυήσασθαι ἃ καταμαρτυρεῖται αὐτοῦ, ὅτι ἐν τῷ γραμματείῳ τῷ ἐπὶ τοῦ δικαστηρίου γραφέντι οὐκ ἔνεστι ταῦτα. ἡμεῖς δέ, ὦ ἄνδρες, τότ᾽ ἐπὶ τοῦ βήματος σπεύδοντες τὰ μὲν ἐγράψαμεν, τῶν δὲ μάρτυρας ἐποιησάμεθα· οὗτοι δέ, ἃ μὲν αὐτοῖς συμφέρει τῶν ὁμολογηθέντων τότε, κύριά φασιν εἶναι, εἰ καὶ μὴ γέγραπται, ἃ δ᾽ οὐ συμφέρει, οὐ κύρια, εἰ μὴ γέγραπται. [26] ἐγὼ δ᾽, ὦ ἄνδρες, οὐ θαυμάζω ὅτι ἔξαρνοί εἰσι τὰ ὡμολογημένα· οὐδὲ γὰρ τὰ γραφέντα ἐθέλουσι ποιεῖν. ἡμεῖς δ᾽ ὡς λέγομεν ἀληθῆ, καὶ ἄλλο τι τεκμήριον παρεξόμεθα. Πρωταρχίδῃ γὰρ τῷ Ποταμίῳ ἔδωκε Δικαιογένης τὴν ἀδελφὴν τὴν <τοῦ> ἑαυτοῦ <πατρὸς> ἐπὶ τετταράκοντα μναῖς, ἀντὶ δὲ τῆς προικὸς τὴν οἰκίαν αὐτῷ τὴν ἐν Κεραμεικῷ παρέδωκε. ταύτῃ δὲ τῇ γυναικί, ἣν ὁ Πρωταρχίδης ἔχει, προσήκει τοῦ κλήρου μέρος ὅσον περ τῇ μητρὶ τῇ ἐμῇ. [27] ἐπεὶ δ᾽ οὖν ἀπέστη Δικαιογένης ταῖς γυναιξὶ τοῖν δυοῖν μεροῖν τοῦ κλήρου, ἠξίου ὁ Λεωχάρης τὸν Πρωταρχίδην παραδιδόναι αὐτῷ τὴν συνοικίαν ἣν εἶχεν ἀντὶ τῆς προικός, ὡς ὄντι ἐγγυητῇ αὐτῷ, τὸ δὲ μέρος ὑπὲρ τῆς γυναικὸς τοῦ κλήρου παρ᾽ αὐτοῦ κομίζεσθαι.

estate but did not agree to hand it over without further dispute, what did he lose by ceding property of which he was still holding the value? For even before he lost the case, he did not have the property we are claiming in his possession, but it was held by those who had mortgaged and bought it from him, and he ought to have paid them off and given us our share. (22) And that was why we obtained sureties from him, because we did not believe he would fulfil his promise. For we have received nothing except two small houses outside the walls and 60 plethra in the Plain; the rest is held by those who have mortgaged and bought it from him. We are not trying to evict them, because we are afraid of losing legal cases against them. For when we tried to evict Micion from the bathhouse, at the instigation of Dicaeogenes who said he would not confirm his title to the property, we were fined 40 minas because of Dicaeogenes, gentlemen. (23) For, believing that he would not confirm any title to any of the property he had ceded to us in court, we strongly attacked Micion before the judges, accepting the risk that Dicaeogenes would confirm his title to the bathhouse and not expecting that he would do the opposite of what he had agreed to do; we were relying on the sureties that had been given to us. (24) But Dicaeogenes, despite having given up the shares that he still admits to having ceded to us, confirmed Micion's title to the bathhouse. So I had the misfortune not only to have received nothing from the estate but also to have lost 40 minas, and I went away humiliated by Dicaeogenes. I will produce witnesses of these facts for you.

WITNESSES

(25) That is how we were treated by Dicaeogenes, gentlemen: Leochares, his surety, who is the cause of all our troubles, denies having undertaken to act as surety on the terms stated in the testimony against him, which he says are not in the document drafted at court. But at that time, gentlemen, we hastily wrote down some points while on the rostrum and secured witnesses in support of others, while our opponents are accepting the points of agreement that suit them, even if they are not in writing, but rejecting the points that don't suit them unless they are in writing. (26) I, gentlemen, am not surprised that they are denying their agreements, since they are not even willing to abide by the written points. And to prove that we are telling the truth, we shall produce more evidence. For Dicaeogenes gave his father's sister in marriage to Protarchides of Potamus with a dowry of 40 minas, but instead of a cash dowry he gave Protarchides his house in the Ceramicus. And this woman, whom Protarchides married, is entitled to the same share of the estate as my mother. (27) Now when Dicaeogenes ceded two thirds of the estate to the women, Leochares suggested to Protarchides that he should hand over to him as surety the house

παραλαβὼν δὲ τὴν συνοικίαν τὸ μέρος οὐ παρέδωκε. καὶ τούτων ὑμῖν μάρτυρα τὸν Πρωταρχίδην παρέξομαι.

ΜΑΡΤΥΣ

[28] Περὶ δὲ ἐπισκευῆς τοῦ βαλανείου καὶ οἰκοδομίας καὶ πρότερον εἴρηκε Δικαιογένης καὶ νῦν ἴσως ἐρεῖ, ὡς ὁμολογήσαντες αὐτῷ αὐτῷ ἀποδώσειν τὰ ἀνηλωμένα οὐκ ἀπεδώκαμεν, καὶ ὅτι διὰ τοῦτο οὐ δύναται ἀπαλλάσσειν τοὺς χρήστας, οὐδὲ ἡμῖν παραδοῦναι ἃ δεῖ αὐτόν. [29] ἡμεῖς δέ, ὦ ἄνδρες, ἐπὶ τοῦ δικαστηρίου, ὅτε ἠναγκάζομεν αὐτὸν ἀφίστασθαι τούτων, ἀντὶ τῶν λῃτουργιῶν καὶ τῶν εἰς τὰ οἰκοδομήματα ἀνηλωμένων ἀφεῖμεν αὐτῷ τοὺς καρπούς, οὕτω τῶν δικαστῶν γιγνωσκόντων· ὕστερον δ' οὐκ ἀναγκαζόμενοι ἀλλ' ἑκόντες ἔδομεν αὐτῷ τὴν ἐν ἄστει οἰκίαν ἐξαίρετον προσθέντες τῷ τρίτῳ μέρει τοῦ κλήρου ἔχειν ἀντὶ τῶν ἐπεσκευασμένων, ἣν οὗτος ἀντὶ πεντακισχιλίων δραχμῶν παρέδωκε Φιλονείκῳ. [30] ἔδομεν δὲ οὐ διὰ τὴν τοῦ Δικαιογένους χρηστότητα, ὦ ἄνδρες, ἀλλ' ἐπιδεικνύμενοι ὅτι οὐ περὶ πλείονος χρήματα ποιούμεθα τῶν οἰκείων, οὐδ' ἂν πάνυ πονηροὶ ὦσι. καὶ γὰρ πρότερον ὅτ' ἐφ' ἡμῖν ἐγένετο Δικαιογένην τιμωρήσασθαι καὶ ἀφελέσθαι ἃ εἶχεν, οὐκ ἐβουλήθημεν τῶν τούτου κτήσασθαι οὐδέν, ἀλλὰ τὰ ἡμέτερα μόνον κομίσασθαι ἐξήρκει ἡμῖν. οὗτος δ' ὅτ' ἐκράτησεν ἡμῶν, ἀπεσύλησεν ἃ ἐδύνατο, καὶ ὡς ἐχθροὺς ἀλλ' οὐ προσήκοντας ἀπόλλυσι. [31] τεκμήριον δὲ καὶ τῶν ἡμετέρων τρόπων καὶ τῆς τούτου ἀδικίας μέγα παρεξόμεθα. μελλούσης γὰρ τῆς πρὸς Λεωχάρην δίκης εἰσιέναι, ὦ ἄνδρες, ἐν τῷ Μαιμακτηριῶνι μηνί, ἠξίου Λεωχάρης καὶ Δικαιογένης δίαιταν ἡμᾶς ἐπιτρέπειν τὴν δίκην ἀναβαλλομένους. καὶ ἡμεῖς ὥσπερ μικρὰ ἀδικούμενοι συνεχωρήσαμεν, καὶ ἐπετρέψαμεν διαιτηταῖς τέτταρσιν, ὧν τοὺς μὲν δύο ἡμεῖς ἠγάγομεν, τοὺς δὲ δύο ἐκεῖνοι. καὶ ἐναντίον τούτων ὡμολογήσαμεν ἐμμενεῖν οἷς ἂν οὗτοι γνοῖεν, καὶ ὡμόσαμεν. [32] καὶ οἱ διαιτηταὶ ἔφασαν, εἰ μὲν ἀνώμοτοι δύναιντ' [ἂν] ἡμᾶς διαλλάξαι, οὕτω ποιήσειν, εἰ δὲ μή, καὶ αὐτοὶ ὀμόσαντες ἀποφανεῖσθαι ἃ δίκαια ἡγοῦνται εἶναι. ἀνακρίναντες δὲ ἡμᾶς πολλάκις καὶ πυθόμενοι τὰ πραχθέντα οἱ διαιτηταί, οἱ μὲν δύο οὓς ἐγὼ προὐβαλόμην, Διότιμος καὶ Μελάνωπος, ἤθελον καὶ ἀνώμοτοι καὶ ὀμόσαντες ἀποφήνασθαι ἃ ἐγίγνωσκον ἀληθέστατα ἐκ τῶν λεγομένων, οὓς δὲ Λεωχάρης προὐβάλετο, οὐκ ἔφασαν ἀποφανεῖσθαι. [33] καίτοι Διοπείθης ὁ ἕτερος τῶν διαιτητῶν Λεωχάρει μὲν ἦν τουτῳὶ κηδεστής, ἐμὸς δ' ἐχθρὸς καὶ ἀντίδικος ἐξ ἑτέρων συμβολαίων· Δημάρατος δὲ ὁ μετ' αὐτοῦ Μνησιπτολέμῳ τῷ ἐγγυησαμένῳ Δικαιογένην μετὰ Λεωχάρους ἦν ἀδελφός. οὗτοι μέντοι οὐκ ἠθέλησαν ἀποφήνασθαι, ὁρκώσαντες ἡμᾶς ἦ μὴν ἐμμενεῖν οἷς [ἂν] αὐτοὶ γνοῖεν. καὶ τούτων ὑμῖν μάρτυρας παρέξομαι.

that he possessed in place of a dowry, and receive from him the share of the estate on his wife's behalf. Leochares took possession of the house, but did not hand over the share of the estate. And as witness to these facts I shall now bring forward Protarchides.

WITNESS

(28) About the repairs to the bathhouse and the cost of building, Dicaeogenes has previously said, and will perhaps say again now, that we agreed to reimburse his expenditure but have not done so, and because of that he cannot release his creditors and repay what he owes to us. (29) But we, gentlemen, when we forced him in court to give up the property, excused him from paying the profits in return for the liturgies he had performed and his expenditure on the buildings, as the judges had determined. And later, not under compulsion but willingly, we gave him the house in the city as a gift, in addition to his one third share of the estate, and he sold the house for 5,000 drachmas to Philonicus. (30) And we gave it to Dicaeogenes, gentlemen, not because of his honesty but to show that we do not have a higher regard for money than for our relatives, however villainous they may be. For indeed, on a previous occasion, when we could have punished Dicaeogenes and deprived him of his property, we did not want to acquire anything of his but were satisfied with getting what belonged to us. But he, when he had power over us, robbed us of everything he could and tried to ruin us, as if we had been his enemies and not his relatives. (31) We shall produce firm evidence of both our own character and his. When the case against Leochares was about to come to court, gentlemen, in the month of Maimacterion, Leochares and Dicaeogenes asked us to postpone the trial and go to arbitration. And we agreed, as if we had suffered only a minor injustice, and submitted the case to four arbitrators, two of whom were appointed by us and two by our opponents. And in their presence we took an oath agreeing to abide by their decision. (32) The arbitrators said that if they could achieve a compromise without taking an oath, they would do so; otherwise, they would also take an oath and declare what they considered to be just. After the arbitrators had asked us a lot of questions, and found out what had happened, the two whom I had appointed (Diotimus and Melanopus) were willing to declare either with or without taking an oath what they considered to be the truth in the statements; but the arbitrators appointed by Leochares said they would not make a declaration. (33) And yet Diopeithes, one of the arbitrators, was Leochares's brother-in-law and an enemy of mine, an opponent in other legal actions about contracts. And his colleague Demaratus was a brother of Mnesiptolemus, who was acting with Leochares as surety for Dicaeogenes. Yet

ΜΑΡΤΥΡΕΣ

[34] Οὔκουν δεινὸν εἰ δεήσεται ὑμῶν, ὦ ἄνδρες, Λεωχάρης ἀποψηφίσασθαι ἃ Διοπείθης κηδεστὴς ὢν αὐτοῦ κατεψηφίσατο; ἢ ὑμῖν πῶς καλὸν ἀπογνῶναι Λεωχάρους ἅ γε οὐδ᾽ οἱ προσήκοντες αὐτοῦ ἀπέγνωσαν, δέομαι οὖν ὑμῶν καταψηφίσασθαι Λεωχάρους, ἵν᾽ἃ ἡμῖν οἱ πρόγονοι κατέλιπον κομισώμεθα, καὶ μὴ μόνον τὰ ὀνόματα αὐτῶν ἔχωμεν ἀλλὰ καὶ τὰ χρήματα. τῶν δὲ Λεωχάρους ἰδίων οὐκ ἐπιθυμοῦμεν. [35] Δικαιογένην γάρ, ὦ ἄνδρες, οὔτ᾽ ἐλεεῖν ἐστε δίκαιοι <ὡς> κακῶς πράττοντα καὶ πενόμενον, οὔτ᾽ εὖ ποιεῖν ὡς ἀγαθόν τι εἰργασμένον τὴν πόλιν· οὐδέτερα γὰρ αὐτῷ τούτων ὑπάρχει, ὡς ἐγὼ ἀποφανῶ, ὦ ἄνδρες. ἅμα δὲ καὶ πλούσιον καὶ πονηρότατον αὐτὸν ὄντα ἀνθρώπων ἀποδείξω καὶ εἰς τὴν πόλιν καὶ εἰς τοὺς προσήκοντας καὶ εἰς τοὺς φίλους. οὗτος γὰρ παραλαβὼν τὸν κλῆρον παρ᾽ ὑμῶν φέροντα μίσθωσιν τοῦ ἐνιαυτοῦ ὀγδοήκοντα μνᾶς, καρπωσάμενος αὐτὸν δέκα ἔτη οὔτε ἀργύριον ὁμολογεῖ κεκτῆσθαι οὔτε ὅποι ἀνήλωσεν ἔχοι ἂν ἐπιδεῖξαι, ὦ ἄνδρες. [36] ἄξιον δὲ καὶ ὑμῖν λογίσασθαι. οὗτος γὰρ τῇ μὲν φυλῇ εἰς Διονύσια χορηγήσας τέταρτος ἐγένετο, τραγῳδοῖς δὲ καὶ πυρριχισταῖς ὕστατος· ταύτας δὲ μόνας ἀναγκασθεὶς <τὰς> ληιτουργίας λειτουργῆσαι ἀπὸ τοσαύτης προσόδου οὕτω καλῶς ἐχορήγησεν. ἀλλὰ μὴν τριηράρχων τοσούτων κατασταθέντων οὔτ᾽ αὐτὸς ἐτριηράρχησεν οὔθ᾽ ἑτέρῳ συμβέβληται ἐν τοιούτοις καιροῖς, ἀλλ᾽ ἕτεροι μὲν οὐσίαν κεκτημένοι ἐλάττω ἢ οὗτος μίσθωσιν λαμβάνει τριηραρχοῦσι. [37] καίτοι, ὦ ἄνδρες, οὐχ ὁ πατὴρ αὐτῷ τὴν πολλὴν οὐσίαν κατέλιπεν, ἀλλ᾽ ὑμεῖς ἔδοτε τῇ ψήφῳ· ὥστε εἰ καὶ μὴ πολίτης ἦν, διά γε τοῦτο δίκαιος ἦν τὴν πόλιν εὖ ποιεῖν. εἰσφορῶν τοίνυν τοσούτων γεγενημένων πᾶσι τοῖς πολίταις εἰς τὸν πόλεμον καὶ τὴν σωτηρίαν τῆς πόλεως Δικαιογένης οὐκ ἔστιν ἥντινα εἰσενήνοχε· πλὴν ὅτε Λέχαιον ἑάλω, κληθεὶς ὑπὸ ἑτέρου ἐπέδωκεν ἐν τῷ δήμῳ τριακοσίας δραχμάς, ἔλαττον ἢ Κλεώνυμος ὁ Κρής· [38] καὶ τοῦτο ἐπέδωκεν, οὐκ εἰσήνεγκεν, ἀλλ᾽ ἐπ᾽ αἰσχίστῳ ἐπιγράμματι ἐξετέθη αὐτοῦ τοὔνομα ἔμπροσθεν τῶν ἐπωνύμων, ὅτι οἵδε εἰς σωτηρίαν τῆς πόλεως ὑποσχόμενοι τῷ δήμῳ εἰσοίσειν χρήματα ἐθελονταὶ οὐκ εἰσήνεγκαν. καίτοι πῶς ἄξιον θαυμάζειν, ὦ ἄνδρες, εἰ ἐμὲ ἐξηπάτησεν ἕνα ὄντα, ὃς ὑμᾶς ἅπαντας ἅμα συνειλεγμένους ἐν τῇ ἐκκλησίᾳ τοιαῦτα ἐποίησε; καὶ τούτων ὑμῖν τοὺς μάρτυρας παρέξομαι.

these men refused to make a declaration, although they had made us swear to abide by whatever they decided. And of these facts I will produce witnesses for you.

WITNESSES

(34) Isn't it strange, gentlemen, that Leochares will ask you to acquit him of charges on which his brother-in-law Diopeithes convicted him? Or how can it be right for you to decide in favour of Leochares when even his relatives did not acquit him? I beg you, therefore, to convict Leochares so that we may obtain what our ancestors left to us, and have not only their names but also their property. We have no desire to take Leochares's own property. (35) Dicaeogenes, gentlemen, deserves neither your pity for misfortune or poverty, nor your favour for good services to the city. Neither of these is appropriate for him, as I shall reveal to you, gentlemen. I shall prove that he is simultaneously rich and the meanest of men, both to the city and to his family and friends. After receiving the estate that you adjudicated to him, which produced an annual rent of 80 minas over ten years, he does not admit that he has made money out of it, but neither can he show how he has spent it, gentlemen. (36) This is worth your consideration. For this man served as *chorēgos* for his tribe at the Dionysia, and came fourth, while as *chorēgos* in the tragedies and Pyrrhic dances he was last. These are the only liturgies he has undertaken – under compulsion – and this was how well he performed as *chorēgos*, from such a large income. Indeed, although so many trierarchs have been appointed, he has never undertaken a trierarchy either by himself or in association with someone else in such times of crisis, but others act as trierarchs even though they have less capital than he has income. (37) And yet, gentlemen, his father did not leave him his large fortune, but you gave it to him by your vote, so that even if he had not been an Athenian citizen, it would have been right for him to serve the city well. Although so many contributions have been made by all the citizens for the war and the security of the city, Dicaeogenes has contributed nothing, except that when Lechaeum was captured, someone asked him in the Assembly and he promised 300 drachmas, less than Cleonymus the Cretan. (38) And he promised this, but did not pay, and his name was inscribed on the 'list of shame' in front of the statues of the Eponymous Heroes, which was headed: 'These are the men who voluntarily promised the people to contribute money for the salvation of the city, but have not paid'. Indeed, gentlemen, is it surprising that he deceived me, an individual, when he had treated all of you gathered in the Assembly like this? And I will produce witnesses of these facts for you.

ΜΑΡΤΥΡΕΣ

Εἰς μὲν τὴν πόλιν οὕτω καὶ τοσαῦτα λελῃτούργηκε Δικαιογένης ἀπὸ τοσούτων χρημάτων· [39] περὶ δὲ τοὺς προσήκοντας τοιοῦτός ἐστιν οἷον ὁρᾶτε, ὥστε τοὺς μὲν ἡμῶν ἀφείλετο τὴν οὐσίαν, ὅτι μεῖζον ἐδυνήθη, τοὺς δὲ περιεώρα εἰς τοὺς μισθωτοὺς ἰόντας δι᾿ ἔνδειαν τῶν ἐπιτηδείων. τὴν δὲ μητέρα [τὴν] αὐτοῦ καθημένην ἐν τῷ τῆς Εἰλειθυίας ἱερῷ πάντες ἑώρων, καὶ τούτῳ ἐγκαλοῦσαν ἃ ἐγὼ αἰσχύνομαι λέγειν, οὗτος δὲ ποιῶν οὐκ ᾐσχύνετο. [40] τῶν δ᾿ ἐπιτηδείων Μέλανα μὲν τὸν Αἰγύπτιον, ᾧ ἐκ μειρακίου φίλος ἦν, ὅπερ ἔλαβε παρ᾿ αὐτοῦ ἀργύριον ἀποστερήσας, ἔχθιστός ἐστι· τῶν δὲ ἄλλων αὐτοῦ φίλων οἱ μὲν οὐκ ἀπέλαβον ἃ ἐδάνεισαν, οἱ δ᾿ἐξηπατήθησαν, καὶ οὐκ ἔλαβον ἃ ὑπέσετο αὐτοῖς, εἰ ἐπιδικάσαιτο τοῦ κλήρου, δώσειν. [41] καίτοι, ὦ ἄνδρες, οἱ ἡμέτεροι πρόγονοι οἱ ταῦτα κτησάμενοι καὶ καταλιπόντες πάσας μὲν χορηγίας ἐχορήγησαν, εἰσήνεγκαν δὲ εἰς τὸν πόλεμον χρήματα πολλὰ ὑμῖν, καὶ τριηραρχοῦντες οὐδένα χρόνον διέλιπον. καὶ τούτων μαρτύρια ἐν τοῖς ἱεροῖς ἀναθήματα ἐκεῖνοι ἐκ τῶν περιόντων, μνημεῖα τῆς αὑτῶν ἀρετῆς, ἀνέθεσαν, τοῦτο μὲν ἐν Διονύσου τρίποδας, οὓς χορηγοῦντες καὶ νικῶντες ἔλαβον, τοῦτο δ᾿ ἐν Πυθίου· [42] ἔτι δ᾿ ἐν ἀκροπόλει ἀπαρχὰς τῶν ὄντων ἀναθέντες πολλοῖς, ὡς ἀπὸ ἰδίας κτήσεως, ἀγάλμασι χαλκοῖς καὶ λιθίνοις κεκοσμήκασι τὸ ἱερόν. αὐτοὶ δ᾿ ὑπὲρ τῆς πατρίδος πολεμοῦντες ἀπέθανον, Δικαιογένης μὲν ὁ Μενεξένου τοῦ ἐμοῦ πάππου πατὴρ στρατηγῶν ὅτε ἡ ἐν Ἐλευσῖνι μάχη ἐγένετο, Μενέξενος δ᾿ ὁ ἐκείνου ὑὸς φυλαρχῶν τῆς Ὀλυνθίας ἐν Σπαρτώλῳ, Δικαιογένης δὲ ὁ Μενεξένου τριηραρχῶν τῆς Παράλου ἐν Κνίδῳ. [43] τὸν μὲν τούτων οἶκον σύ, ὦ Δικαιόγενες, παραλαβὼν κακῶς καὶ αἰσχρῶς διολώλεκας, καὶ ἐξαργυρισάμενος πενίαν ὀδύρῃ, ποῖ ἀναλώσας; οὔτε γὰρ εἰς τὴν πόλιν οὔτε εἰς τοὺς φίλους φανερὸς εἶ δαπανηθεὶς οὐδέν. ἀλλὰ μὴν οὔτε καθιπποτρόφηκας· οὐ γὰρ πώποτε ἐκτήσω ἵππον πλείονος ἄξιον ἢ τριῶν μνῶν· οὔτε κατεζευγοτρόφηκας, ἐπεὶ οὐδὲ ζεῦγος ἐκτήσω ὀρικὸν οὐδεπώποτε ἐπὶ τοσούτοις ἀγροῖς καὶ κτήμασιν. ἀλλ᾿ οὐδ᾿ ἐκ τῶν πολεμίων ἐλύσω οὐδένα. [44] ἀλλ᾿ οὐδὲ τὰ ἀναθήματα, ἃ Μενέξενος τριῶν ταλάντων ποιησάμενος ἀπέθανε πρὶν ἀναθεῖναι, εἰς πόλιν κεκόμικας, ἀλλ᾿ ἐν τοῖς λιθουργείοις ἔτι καλινδεῖται, καὶ αὐτὸς μὲν ἠξίους κεκτῆσθαι ἅ σοι οὐδὲν προσῆκε χρήματα, τοῖς δὲ θεοῖς οὐκ ἀπέδωκας ἃ ἐκείνων ἐγίγνετο ἀγάλματα. [45] διὰ τί οὖν ἀξιώσεις σου τοὺς δικαστὰς ἀποψηφίσασθαι, ὦ Δικαιόγενες; πότερον ὅτι πολλὰς λῃτουργίας λελῃτούργηκας τῇ πόλει, καὶ πολλὰ χρήματα δαπανήσας σεμνοτέραν τὴν πόλιν τούτοις ἐποίησας; ἢ ὡς τριηραρχῶν πολλὰ κακὰ τοὺς πολεμίους εἰργάσω, καὶ εἰσφορὰς δεομένῃ τῇ πατρίδι εἰς τὸν πόλεμον εἰσενεγκὼν μεγάλα ὠφέληκας; ἀλλ᾿ οὐδέν σοι τούτων πέπρακται. [46] ἀλλ᾿ ὡς στρατιώτης ἀγαθός; ἀλλ᾿ οὐκ ἐστράτευσαι τοσούτου καὶ τοιούτου γενομένου πολέμου, εἰς ὃν Ὀλύνθιοι μὲν καὶ νησιῶται ὑπὲρ τῆσδε τῆς γῆς ἀποθνῄσκουσι μαχόμενοι τοῖς πολεμίοις, σὺ

WITNESSES

That, then, is the number of public services Dicaeogenes performed from such a large fortune, and how well he did so. (39) And you can see how he behaves towards his relatives: he has robbed some of us of our property because he was stronger, and turned his back on others who took up paid employment because they lacked the necessities of life. And everyone saw his mother sitting in the temple of Eileithyia accusing him of things I am ashamed to talk about but he was not ashamed to do. (40) Among his close friends, he deprived Melas the Egyptian, his friend since they were young men, of money he had received from him, and is now his bitterest enemy. As to his other friends, some did not receive back money they had lent him, while others were deceived by him and did not receive what he had promised to give them if his claim to the estate was successful. (41) And yet, gentlemen, our ancestors who acquired and passed down the property performed all their duties as *chorēgoi*, contributed large sums of money for the city's war expenses, and served continuously as trierarchs. And as testimony to these services, from their remaining property they set up in the temples, as memorials to their virtue, dedications such as tripods they had received for their victories as *chorēgoi* in the temple of Dionysus, or in the shrine of Pythian Apollo. (42) What's more, they dedicated the first fruits of their property on the Acropolis, and so have adorned the temple – out of private wealth – with a large number of bronze and marble statues. And they died fighting for their country: Dicaeogenes (the father of my grandfather Menexenus) while serving as a general at the time of the battle at Eleusis, his son Menexenus commanding the cavalry at Spartolus in the territory of Olynthus, and Dicaeogenes son of Menexenus as trierarch of the Paralus at Cnidus. (43) The inheritance you received from these men, Dicaeogenes, you have wickedly and disgracefully ruined. You converted the property into cash, and now plead poverty, but what did you spend it on? You have clearly spent nothing on behalf of either the city or your friends. And neither, indeed, have you impoverished yourself through horse-rearing, for you never acquired a horse worth more than three minas, nor by keeping racing teams, for you never had so much as a pair of mules on your extensive farms and estates. And, again, you never ransomed a single prisoner of war. (44) Menexenus spent three talents on dedications but died before he could set them up, yet you've never even brought them to the Acropolis; they're still lying around in the sculptor's workshop; so you've claimed money to which you're not entitled, while denying to the gods the statues that are rightfully theirs. (45) What reason will you give for the judges to acquit you, Dicaeogenes? That you have performed many public services for the city, and enhanced its splendour for the citizens by your

δέ, ὦ Δικαιόγενες, πολίτης ὢν οὐδ' ἐστράτευσαι. ἀλλ'ἴσως διὰ τοὺς προγόνους ἀξιώσεις μου πλέον ἔχειν, ὅτι τὸν τύραννον ἀπέκτειναν. ἐγὼ δ' ἐκείνους μὲν ἐπαινῶ, σοὶ δὲ οὐδὲν ἡγοῦμαι τῆς ἐκείνων ἀρετῆς μετεῖναι. [47] πρῶτον μὲν γὰρ εἵλου ἀντὶ τῆς ἐκείνων δόξης τὴν ἡμετέραν οὐσίαν κτήσασθαι, καὶ ἐβουλήθης μᾶλλον Δικαιογένους καλεῖσθαι ὑὸς ἢ Ἁρμοδίου, ὑπεριδὼν μὲν τὴν ἐν Πρυτανείῳ σίτησιν, καταφρονήσας δὲ προεδριῶν καὶ ἀτελειῶν, ἃ τοῖς ἐξ ἐκείνων γεγονόσι δέδοται. ἔτι δὲ ὁ Ἀριστογείτων ἐκεῖνος καὶ Ἁρμόδιος οὐ διὰ τὸ γένος ἐτιμήθησαν ἀλλὰ διὰ τὴν ἀνδραγαθίαν, ἧς σοι οὐδὲν μέτεστιν, ὦ Δικαιόγενες.

generous expenditure? Or that by serving as a trierarch you inflicted great damage on the enemy, and came to the aid of your country when it was in need by paying war taxes? (46) But you have done none of these things. Or because you are a good soldier? But you, Dicaeogenes, although you were a citizen, didn't serve at all throughout the long and critical war in which Olynthians and islanders are dying for the sake of this country at the hands of the enemy. Perhaps you will claim the advantage over me because of your ancestors who killed the tyrant. For my part, I praise them, but I don't think you share in their prowess at all. (47) First of all, you chose to possess our property rather than their reputation, and preferred to be called the son of Dicaeogenes rather than of Harmodius, disdaining the right to dine in the Prytaneum and scorning the presidencies and tax exemptions that were conferred on their descendants. Secondly, the great Aristogeiton and Harmodius were honoured not because of their birth but because of their courage, in which you do not share at all, Dicaeogenes.

# COMMENTARY

*1–4: Introduction*

This is the prosecution speech from an adversarial trial (a *dikē engyēs*, or action to enforce the performance of a surety), so it was the first to be delivered in court. The speaker, Menexenus, represents the interest of his mother, the widow of Polyaratus, in the estate of her brother Dicaeogenes II, who died 22 years before the present trial. The estate has been disputed between Dicaeogenes II's four sisters, on the one hand, and his adopted son, Dicaeogenes III, on the other. After a number of previous trials (discussed in more detail in the introduction to this speech, pp. 16–18), Dicaeogenes III has, according to the speaker, defaulted on an agreement to relinquish two thirds of the estate to the four sisters. The defendant in the case is formally Leochares, a surety for Dicaeogenes III, but much of the speech is directed against Dicaeogenes himself as the speaker's real opponent.

The introduction to the speech (proem) is relatively short, lacking the conventional appeal to the goodwill of the judges. The speaker adduces two items of documentary evidence: an inventory of the property left by Dicaeogenes II and a witness statement. His explanation of the basis of his claim, succinct and businesslike in tone, is inevitably one-sided.

**1 We thought, gentlemen:** Nearly all the forensic speeches in the corpus of the Attic orators begin by soliciting the attention of the judges with a direct address in the vocative case. (One of the rare exceptions is Isaeus 11.) The most common forms of address in private cases, including inheritance claims, were 'gentlemen' (*ō andres*) and 'judges' (*ō andres dikastai*). Isaeus's preferred form was 'gentlemen', which he uses 21 times in this speech. After this conventional introduction, most of the later addresses engage the judges with the speaker's argument (§§13, 20, 21, 25, 26, 34, 35, 38, 41) or direct their attention to a particularly significant point (§§19, 22, 28, 30, 31) while occasionally an address marks the resumption of the speech after the reading of documentary evidence (§§5, 25, 34). The position of an address in its sentence may also be significant: in most instances, as here, it is parenthetic, but sometimes it takes a more emphatic position at the end of a sentence or clause (§§19, 22, 25, and twice in §35).

On addresses to the judges in Isaeus's speeches, cf. Griffith-Williams (2013, 41–42 and 2022, 42); and, in the Attic orators generally, Dickey (1996, 177–81) and Martin (2006).

**our dispute with Dicaeogenes:** Menexenus makes it clear at the outset that he and his associates were involved in a continuing dispute with Dicaeogenes III, even though the defendant in the present trial, was Dicaeogenes's surety, Leochares.

Throughout the speech, Isaeus consistently uses the name Dicaeogenes on its own, or occasionally 'Dicaeogenes here' (§§6, 7, 10, 15) to refer to Dicaeogenes III, the speaker's long-term opponent in the dispute over the estate of Dicaeogenes II. Where there is a need for disambiguation, the Dicaeogenes whose estate is in dispute is distinguished as 'the late Dicaeogenes' (§16), 'the son of Menexenus' (§§ 3, 4, 6, 42), 'our uncle' (§§4, 6, 7, 11, 12, 15), or 'Dicaeogenes who left the property' (§9). Dicaeogenes I is mentioned only once, in §42, where he is identified as the father of the speaker's grandfather Menexenus.

**what was agreed in court:** At a previous trial, the prosecution of Leochares for false testimony, a compromise was reached with Dicaeogenes, and Leochares agreed to act as his surety (§18).

**without further dispute:** According to Menexenus and his associates, Dicaeogenes had promised to restore two thirds of the estate to the sisters of Dicaeogenes II *anamphisbētēta* (lit. 'undisputed'), i.e. free of further claims and liabilities. Leochares and Dicaeogenes will deny that this word (repeated at §§18, 20, and 21) was included in the agreement.

**But, gentlemen:** See on 'We thought, gentlemen', above.

**Leochares, his surety:** Given the significance of Leochares's role as surety for Dicaeogenes, and defendant in the present trial (whose name occurs 25 times in this speech), it seems surprising that he is always identified by his given name alone, with no patronymic or demotic. (See on 'Democles of Phrearrhii', §5, and, for the use of the demotic specifically to designate a legal entity such as a surety, Brock, 2020, 16.) Indeed, Isaeus provides no personal information about Leochares except that he was related by marriage to Diopeithes, one of the arbitrators to whom the dispute was referred (§33). Nevertheless, as noted by Calhoun (1916, 387, n.4), it is safe to assume that he was very rich: 'The estate of Dicaeogenes produced the exceptionally large revenue of 80 minas annually (§§11, 35) and Leochares was accepted as joint surety with one other for the two-thirds interest claimed. He must therefore have been a man of large means'.

**our sworn statement:** The Greek word *antōmosia* is sometimes translated as 'affidavit', a modern legal term which is anachronistic in the Athenian context. The literal meaning of *antōmosia* is 'oath [of two people] against each other' (Todd, 1993, 371), and it refers to the oath sworn by each of the opposing parties at the preliminary hearing (*anakrisis*) before an Athenian trial. According to Harrison (1971, 99–100): 'These oaths seem to have been specifically to the truth of the pleas in the documents handed in [at the *anakrisis*], rather than oaths that everything the litigant was going to say would be true'.

**2 Please read the statement:** The request is addressed to the court clerk, who read out all the documentary evidence produced at an Athenian trial (comprising, in this case, a sworn statement, an inventory, and eight witness statements). For a possible exception, with an excerpt from the laws read by the litigant himself rather than the clerk, see on 'I have read the laws to you', 11.1.

**Cephisodotus here:** Cephisodotus, son of Theopompus (§5), was one of the speaker's cousins, formally mentioned at this point as a joint prosecutor in the action against Leochares. Later in the speech (§§9–11), he is presented as one of the victims of Dicaeogenes's neglect and mistreatment of Theopompus's widow and children.

The deictic pronoun *houtosi* ('this [man] here') is often used by Athenian forensic speakers (and no doubt accompanied by a suitable gesture) to indicate someone present in court, who could be either an associate or an opponent of the speaker. Cf. on 'Dicaeogenes here' (§§6, 7, 10, 15) and 'Leochares here' (§§16, 18).

**Please read the witness testimony:** This is the earliest speech in the corpus of the Attic orators in which there is clear evidence of the use of written testimony; for the scholarly debate on the transition from oral to written testimony in the early fourth century, see the introduction to this speech, pp. 28–30.

Eight items of witness testimony are produced in the course of the speech, only the first of which is introduced with a formula referring unequivocally to written testimony rather than to the witnesses in person. The alternative formulae, which include the words 'I will produce witnesses' (§§6, 13, 18, 24, 33, 38), do not indicate that the witnesses testified orally, but simply that they were present in court and invited to come forward. (Cf. on 'You have heard the witnesses', §3, and 'I shall now bring forward Protarchides', §27.)

**3 You have heard the witnesses:** These words, originally used in cases where the witnesses testified orally, remained appropriate when written testimony was used because the witnesses were still required to come forward and affirm the truth of their statements.

**perhaps he will argue … he will be lying:** Anticipation of the opponent's arguments was a tactic apparently favoured by Athenian prosecutors seeking to prejudice the judges by misrepresenting the defendant's case. On the tentative wording of the prediction, which was almost certainly disingenuous, cf. Dorjahn (1935, 282): 'Speechwriters commonly employed a guarded, cautious manner of expression, qualifying their statement by some word or words. "Perhaps" was a favorite introductory word in such instances'. Other examples (all cited by Dorjahn, in addition to Isae. 5.3) are Isoc. 20.5, 21.16; Lyc. 1.63; Lys. 6.42, 12.5.

**Dicaeogenes (the son of Menexenus):** On the various means by which Isaeus disambiguates the name Dicaeogenes, see on 'our dispute with Dicaeogenes', §1.

**4 our uncle Dicaeogenes:** Again, see on 'our dispute with Dicaeogenes', §1.

*5–18: The history of the dispute (narrative)*

A narrative of this length, uninterrupted by argumentation, is unusual in Isaeus's speeches. It covers events from the death of Dicaeogenes II to the agreement reached between the speaker and Dicaeogenes III, with Leochares as his surety, starting with the division of the estate under the terms of the will produced by Proxenus (§§5–6). 12 years later Dicaeogenes successfully claimed the whole estate, on the basis of a second will (§§7–8). He summarily evicted the sisters of Dicaeogenes II and their families from the property they had occupied for 12 years (§§9–11). Menexenus the son of Cephisophon prosecuted Lycon, one of Dicaeogenes's witnesses, for false testimony but was persuaded by Dicaeogenes to drop his prosecutions of the remaining witnesses and abandon his fellow claimants (§§12–13). After Menexenus the son of Cephisophon was deceived by Dicaeogenes, the cousins joined forces again and submitted a claim for the whole estate as next of kin (§§14–16). Leochares tried to block their claim with a *diamartyria*, but the cousins prosecuted him for false testimony. At the end of the trial, the opposing parties reached a last-minute compromise: Dicaeogenes agreed to return two thirds of the estate to the sisters of Dicaeogenes II, with the backing of Leochares and Mnesiptolemus as sureties (§§17–18).

Apart from the digression at §§9–11, the history of the litigation is narrated in straightforward chronological order, but the presentation is selective and one-sided. Many details are omitted, and the speaker's underlying agenda is to prejudice the judges against Dicaeogenes and Leochares by portraying them in the worst possible light, with himself and his cousins as their innocent (even naïve) victims, who, unlike their opponents, respected the ties of kinship and always behaved more generously than the law strictly required them to. The narrative is prefaced by a brief explanation as to why it is necessary for the speaker to tell the full story.

**5 So, gentlemen:** The address to the judges marks the resumption of the speech after the reading of documentary evidence.

**the only points to be made by Leochares or Dicaeogenes in their defence:** The speaker explicitly links Leochares and Dicaeogenes III, as if they were co-defendants. It is quite likely that Dicaeogenes did speak in court, as a supporting speaker for Leochares, but not (formally, at least) on his own behalf.

**since they are prepared to discuss the inheritance from the beginning:** The speaker's ostensible reluctance to explain the history of the dispute at length is disingenuous. As prosecutor, and therefore first speaker at the trial, he exploits the opportunity to present his own version of events first, repeatedly showing Dicaeogenes and Leochares in an unfavourable light while claiming that he and his associates always acted generously and in good faith. The agreement referred to in §§1–4, the details of which were the real issue at the present trial, is not mentioned again until §18. By that stage, the speaker will have hoped that the judges were already prejudiced against Dicaeogenes and Leochares.

**so that you are not deceived:** To show his respect for the judges, an Athenian litigant had to be careful to avoid any suggestion that they might be mistaken in their decisions. An accusation of (potential) deception against one's opponent was a commonplace way of achieving this. Cf. on 'the judges were deceived by them', §8, and, for discussion, see Kremmydas (2013).

The verb 'deceive' (Gk. *exapatan*) occurs seven times in this speech, always with Dicaeogenes III or his associates as the agent(s). Cf. Edwards (2020, 73): 'Five of the seven instances in [Isae. 5] contribute to the picture of unreliability that is the *ēthos* of the opponents and the previous behaviour of the cousin, as opposed to the reasonable behaviour of the speaker and his supporters'.

**Our grandfather, Menexenus:** Menexenus I, the maternal grandfather of Menexenus the speaker (and, after the adoption, of Dicaeogenes III), was killed while in command of the cavalry at Spartolus in 429 BC (§42).

**four daughters:** Menexenus's daughters are not named in the speech, but always identified as the wife, daughter, mother, or sister of one of the male protagonists. Cf. on 'Eubulides's daughter', 11.9.

**My father, Polyaratus:** Polyaratus of Cholargus, a small city deme of the tribe Acamantis in the northern Athenian plain (represented by four members of the Boule), had died before the present trial (§9). He was reputedly very rich ([Dem.] 40.24), and held the offices of Assessor (Paredrus) of the Hellenotamiae (public treasurers) in 410/09 BC and Secretary of the Boule in 405/4. He had two daughters and three sons: Menexenus, Bathyllus, and Periander ([Dem.] 40.6). In accordance with Greek naming customs, a second son was commonly named after his maternal grandfather, but modern scholars have generally assumed that Menexenus was Polyaratus's oldest son and the speaker of Isaeus 5.

Mantitheus, the speaker of Dem. 39 and [Dem.] 40 *Against Boeotus*, was a grandson of Polyaratus, one of whose daughters married Mantitheus's father, Mantias of Thoricus, as her second husband. Since Polyaratus had already died before her second marriage, she was given to Mantias by her brothers, Menexenus and Bathyllus, while their younger brother Periander was still a child. According to Mantitheus, Menexenus and Bathyllus had large fortunes of their own ([Dem.] 40.25; cf. on 'we … lost our property', §9).

**Democles of Phrearrhii:** Phrearrhii was one of the 20 demes of the tribe Leontis, located in the south of Attica. It sent nine representatives to the Boule, indicating that it was among the larger demes. (Several demes sent only one member, while Acharnae, the largest, sent 22.)

In most contexts an Athenian would be identified simply by his given name, but his full formal identity also included a patronymic and demotic. Marriage, as Brock (2020, 17) points out, is 'one context in which demotics are commonly specified'. Their use, however, is not consistent, and it is not clear why Isaeus chose to identify only three of the men who married Dicaeogenes's sisters, Democles and Cephisophon (including Protarchides of Potamus, §26) by their demotics. One possibility is to avoid confusion with others of the same name.

We have no information about the children (if any) of Democles and his wife, and there is no indication that she or her representatives were directly involved at any stage of the dispute with Dicaeogenes.

**Cephisophon of Paeania:** Upper and Lower Paeania were rural demes of the tribe Pandionis, lying to the east of Mount Hymettus. Lower Paeania sent 11 representatives to the Boule, and Upper Paeania one.

Cephisophon was Secretary of the Boule in 403/2 BC and one of the Treasurers of Athena and the other gods in 398/7. His son, Menexenus, had been an active participant in earlier litigation against Dicaeogenes and Leochares (§§12–14), but it is not clear whether he was a joint prosecutor in the present case. The manuscript text of §9 suggests that Cephisophon and his wife also had a daughter, but there is no evidence for her existence if the emendations proposed by Edwards (2002) are accepted (see on 'the wife of Cephisophon …', §9).

Cephisophon had another son, Callibius (*PAA* 555420), not mentioned in this speech, who is likely to have been the offspring of a different marriage and therefore had no interest in the estate of Dicaeogenes II (cf. Cobetto Ghiggia, 2002, 70).

**Theopompus, the father of Cephisodotus:** Theopompus had a house next door to that of Dicaeogenes III in the city (§11). Like Polyaratus, he had died by the time of the present trial; he was survived by his widow and, apparently, at least two children (§10). Nothing further is known about him, but see on 'guardian', §10, for the suggestion that he might have been related to Dicaeogenes III. Theopompus was a relatively common name in ancient Greece; *LGPN* cites 232 instances, including 87 in Attica.

**6 trierarch of the Paralus:** The trierarchy was the most expensive and prestigious of the liturgies (public services) required of the wealthiest Athenians as a form of taxation; the minimum financial qualification for membership of the 'liturgical class' was probably at least three talents. By the late fifth century, a trierarch's functions included the payment of the ship's running costs for a year, which could amount to as much as a talent, as well as commanding it in the fleet (Rhodes, 1981, 680).

The trierarchs of Athens's two sacred state triremes, the Salaminia and the Paralus, enjoyed a special status as elected officials, not appointed through the regular procedure under the supervision of the generals (Gabrielsen, 1994, 73–74).

**died in action:** This wording (Gk. *machomenos*, lit. 'fighting') excludes any possibility of a natural or accidental death in the course of a military campaign. The judges would have understood from this that Dicaeogenes was entitled to a state funeral, although the burial arrangements are not mentioned in the speech. (Cf. Isae. 6.27, with Griffith-Williams, 2022, where Philoctemon died 'at the hands of the enemy'.)

**at Cnidus:** Cnidus was a Greek city and port in the southwest of Asia Minor (modern Turkey). Athens and her allies won a significant victory there against Sparta in August 394 BC, and some nineteenth-century scholars argued that this was the battle in which Dicaeogenes was killed. Since the present trial took place about 22 years after his death (see on 'one long ago and the other much later', §15), that would date the speech to 372 BC. That view has, however, long been discredited (cf. on 'when Lechaeum was captured', §37). According to the more recent scholarly consensus, Dicaeogenes II was killed in a sea battle in early 411 BC, when 20 Athenian triremes were defeated by the Peloponnesian fleet near Syme, an island southeast of Cnidus (Thuc. 8.42), and the speech was delivered in 389. Wyse (1904, 413) points out that 'at Cnidus' (Gk. *en Knidō*) is an odd way of referring to the battle near Syme, and suggests a slightly earlier date: 'it is possible that Dicaeogenes II was killed in the late autumn of 412 BC, when the Athenians made two unsuccessful attempts to storm Cnidus (Thuc. 8.35)'. The reference to Cnidus may, in any event, have evoked the more recent battle in the judges' minds (cf. Thomas, 1989, 116, n.68). For further discussion of chronology and dating, see the introduction to this speech, pp. 18–19.

**died childless:** This is a significant detail because only an Athenian with no legitimate natural son was entitled by Solon's law to adopt a son, either *inter vivos* or, as in the case of Dicaeogenes II, by nominating his adopted son in a will to come into effect after his death.

**Proxenus ... produced a will:** The fact that it was not Dicaeogenes III himself who produced the will, but his father, suggests (but does not definitively prove) that Dicaeogenes was a minor at the time.

Proxenus of Aphidna, a descendant of the tyrant-slayer Harmodius (see on 'your ancestors who killed the tyrant', §46), was a Hellenotamias (public treasurer) in 410/09 BC. The assumption that he was married to a daughter of Dicaeogenes I (and sister of Menexenus I), accepted by most modern scholars, is supported by the naming of his son Dicaeogenes III, whose adoption by Dicaeogenes II would be explained by their relationship as cousins. Davies (1971, 476–77, cited by Edwards, 2007, 76) suggests that the daughter of Dicaeogenes I was Proxenus's mother rather than his wife.

Proxenus's deme, Aphidna (not mentioned in the speech), belonged to the tribe Aeantis and sent 16 representatives to the Boule. It was located in the northeast of Attica.

**Dicaeogenes here:** See on 'Cephisodotus here', §2, and 'Dicaeogenes (the son of Menexenus)', §3.

**our fathers ... divided the estate:** Menexenus was speaking on behalf of his cousins (as legal representatives of their mothers) as well as his own branch of the family, so 'our fathers' refers to Polyaratus, Diocles, Cephisophon, and Theopompus, and presumably also includes Proxenus, the father of Dicaeogenes III. The property rights of Athenian women were limited, so although two thirds of Dicaeogenes's estate went to his sisters as next of kin (closest collateral relatives), it was their husbands who controlled the property and acted on their behalf in legal proceedings. (Cf. on 'legal representative', §10.)

**was to become:** In the Greek text, the imperfect tense of the verb 'to become' (*egigneto*) indicates that this was the intention of the document, not the result of the court's judgment, for which the aorist (*egeneto*) would have been appropriate. The same wording is used with reference to the second will at §15 (cf. Wyse, 1904, 413).

**with a third of the estate:** This is the only attested case of an Athenian will in which an adopted son was not given the whole of his adoptive father's estate. Some scholars (e.g. Cox, 1998, 15–16) have questioned the legality of the arrangement, or suggested that it was a compromise intended to remain in effect only while Dicaeogenes III was still a minor (Wyse, 1904, 414). But although such a will was probably not common, the wording of Solon's law, which allowed a childless Athenian to 'dispose of his property as he wishes', was certainly broad enough to accommodate it. Cf. Harrison (1968, 95–96): 'While the normal effect of any adoption was to make the adopted son or daughter heir to the whole of the estate of the adopter it was certainly possible in the classical period, though probably even then not common, to adopt a child and leave it only a proportion of one's estate'.

**awarded by the court:** The Greek verb, *epedikaseto* (translated here as 'was awarded by the court'), relates to *epidikasia*, the procedure (probably administrative rather than judicial) by which an uncontested claim to an estate – either from the next of kin or from the beneficiary of a will – was approved by the court. It is not entirely clear from this narrative whether Dicaeogenes specifically bequeathed the remaining two thirds of his estate to his sisters in his will (cf. on 'what her brother Dicaeogenes had given her', §9). There was, however, no need for him to do so, since he would have known that they would receive the property in any event as his next of kin. So it is perhaps more likely that after Dicaeogenes III had taken one third of the estate in accordance with the will, the sisters submitted a separate claim to the court for the remainder of the estate.

**I will produce witnesses who were present at the time:** For the formula 'I will produce witnesses', see on 'Please read the witness testimony', §2, and 'You have heard the witnesses', §3. Witnesses in the Athenian courts were often identified as 'those who were present' (cf., e.g., Isae. 2.33, 6.7, 37, 9.4) or 'those who know the facts' (e.g. Isae. 2.37; 8.6, 29, 42; 9.29; cf. Andoc. 1.69, [Dem.] 33.16, Lys. 26.8).

**7 after swearing to observe the agreed terms:** The parties had to decide which parts of the estate each of them should receive, in the proportions determined by the will. In this case the agreement is presented as amicable, but quarrels over the division of an estate were not unknown in classical Athens (e.g. Isae. 9.17).

**each possessed the share:** The Greek word 'each' is in the masculine form (*hekastos*), making it clear that although the property had been nominally inherited by Dicaeogenes I's sisters, it was really their husbands who had control of it. Cf. on 'our fathers … divided the estate', §6.

**although cases were being heard:** If Dicaeogenes II and his friends had wanted to submit a legal claim to the whole estate, they could have done so at any time while cases were being heard (Gk. *ousōn dikōn*), i.e. before the democratic business of the law courts was disrupted under the rule of the so-called 'Thirty Tyrants', the oligarchic government that came into power in April 404, after the defeat of Athens in the Peloponnesian War. Cf. Lys. 17.3, where the speaker says that he was unable to recover money owed to him during the war because no cases were being heard (*dioti ouk ēsan dikai*), and Isoc. 21.7 (trans. Whitehead, 2022): 'Besides, when conditions in the polis were unstable and no lawsuits were being heard (*kai dikōn ouk ousōn*) the complainant had nothing to gain and the misappropriator had nothing to fear'. As Bonner (1926, 216) points out, this 'does not necessarily mean that there was no provision for the trial of private suits (*dikai*) during the whole period of the tyranny; it may simply mean that toward the end of their rule the city was distracted by civil war and the courts could not sit'.

**disorder and civil war in the city:** Cf. on 'because of the city's misfortune', §8. The Thirty presided over a brutal regime during which many Athenians were executed, others fled the city, and the institutions of the democracy, including the courts, no longer functioned properly. (Cf. Wolpert, 2002, 129: '[The Thirty] compelled others to commit wrongs (Isoc. 18.17), and they created such a state of lawlessness that even individuals with private disputes were unable to go to court to settle them'.) In May 403 BC, the oligarchs were defeated in battle by an army led by

Thrasybulus, and democracy was finally restored in September 403. On the implications of this allusion to the turmoil of 404–403 for the dating of the speech, see the introduction, pp. 18–19.

Cf. Jebb (1876, 351, n.1) on the wording of §7: 'This does not say that the *stasis* was going on at the time the false claim was made. No doubt a slip of three years would not be impossible for what Schoemann calls "oratoria magis quam historica fides"; but the apology is not needed here'.

**persuaded by Melas the Egyptian:** Nothing is known about this man, who was presumably a metic (resident alien) in Athens. His Greek name, meaning 'black' or 'dark-skinned', was probably a nickname acquired in Athens. The ethnic, repeated with every occurrence of the name (cf. §§8, 40) is a deliberate slur. Cooper (2003, 62) comments that: 'To dub someone an Egyptian was to imply certain recognizable physical and moral traits', and points out that the verb *aigyptiazein* (Ar. *Thesm.* 922) meant 'to be villainous or mischievous'. Cf. Hall (2006, 203–04) on the 'cunning Egyptian tradesman' as a stereotype that could be exploited by Athenian speechwriters: 'In Isaeus' fifth oration, Melas (whose name, 'the black one', may also be ethnically significant) is labelled 'The Egyptian' every time he is mentioned in order to ensure that the jury never forgets that they are not dealing with an Athenian Greek'. Cf. Dem. 21.163 and Hyp. *Athenog.* 3 (with Whitehead, 2000, 287–88).

By blaming Melas for persuading Dicaeogenes III to claim the whole estate, Isaeus might appear to be trying to shield Dicaeogenes himself from responsibility for the litigation (cf. the roles of Diocles in Isaeus 8 and Hierocles in Isaeus 9) but that can hardly have been his intention, since he loses no opportunity to blacken the character of Dicaeogenes III. Probably the reference to Melas was intended as an indirect criticism of Dicaeogenes III for relying on such a disreputable source of advice.

**our uncle's son:** On the designation of Dicaeogenes II as 'our uncle', see on 'our dispute with Dicaeogenes', §1.

**8 We thought he was mad:** Isaeus, understandably, ridicules Dicaeogenes's claim to the whole estate, giving no details of the evidence or arguments he put forward. So it is impossible to assess the strength of the claim, which, on the face of it, does seem far-fetched; it is particularly difficult to imagine how he explained the appearance of a second will 12 years after the first. For further discussion, see the introduction to this speech, pp. 21–23.

**the claim:** *Lēxis*, the Greek word for 'claim', is the legal term for the document which a claimant to an estate under a will or as next of kin had to submit to the archon. If the claim was contested, as in this case, the dispute would go to court for determination in a *diadikasia* (the special, non-adversarial procedure used for competing claims to a benefit or to avoid performing a duty).

**when we came to court:** It was the speaker's father, Polyaratus, who was defeated in the court action by Dicaeogenes III (§9), so 'we' here refers to the speaker's immediate family, not including the cousins with whom he later joined forces to defend their mothers' shares of the estate.

**not by the judges but by Melas the Egyptian and his friends:** The speaker avoids criticizing the judges for their decision at the earlier trial by placing the blame on Melas and his friends (cf. on 'Melas the Egyptian', §7). The reference to 'friends', who are not further identified, conveys the impression of a conspiracy of shady characters around Dicaeogenes III.

**because of the city's misfortune:** Cf. on 'disorder and civil war in the city', §7. For a modern reader, it is not clear how the 'misfortune' of Athens could have enabled Dicaeogenes to have a false will ratified by the court. 'What did [Isaeus] wish the judges to understand? That the trial took place before the restoration of order? or that Dicaeogenes III was an oligarch? or that he was an unprincipled democrat who denounced his opponents as enemies of the people and made capital out of political prejudices?' (Wyse, 1904, 415).

**take possession of other people's property:** Litigants in Athenian inheritance disputes often accuse their opponents of taking or claiming 'other people's property' (Gk. *ta allotriōn*); cf. Isae. 4.11, 29; 8.1, 4. The wording is obviously tendentious, because it prejudges the outcome of the case. In this context, it could also be taken as an allusion to the confiscation of property by the oligarchs – perhaps an indication that Dicaeogenes III or some of his associates were indeed supporters of the Thirty (see previous note).

**support one another with false testimony:** Another slur on Dicaeogenes III and his associates, anticipating the result of the *dikē pseudomartyriōn* against Lycon (§12).

**the judges were deceived by them:** See on 'so that you are not deceived', §5.

*9–11: Dicaeogenes's callous treatment of his aunts and cousins*

At this stage of the narrative Isaeus introduces a digression, turning attention away from the litigation to focus on the allegedly callous way in which Dicaeogenes III, after his victory in court over Polyaratus, reclaimed the two thirds of the estate which had previously been adjudicated to the sisters of Dicaeogenes II. The inevitably one-sided account is uncorroborated by witness testimony, and – although at least one of Dicaeogenes's witnesses at the *diadikasia* was later convicted of false testimony (§13) – there is no real evidence that he was acting illegally at the time, when he had the judgment of the court in his favour. The intended effect of the passage was, apparently, to prejudice the judges against Dicaeogenes rather than to provide them with information material to the case; but Dicaeogenes's behaviour towards his family is also part of Isaeus's argument from probability, aiming to show that he was likely to have reneged on the agreement (cf. the introductory note to §§35–47).

**9 victims of false testimony:** This, again, anticipates the result of the *dikē pseudomartyriōn* (cf. on 'support one another with false testimony', §8), and explicitly identifies Menexenus and his associates as victims. (In the Greek text they are described with the aorist passive participle *katapseudomartyrēthentes*, lit. 'having been testified falsely against'. On compound verbs beginning with *kata-*, cf. on 'neither … impoverished yourself through horse-rearing', §43.)

**lost our property:** Polyaratus having died (see following note), 'our' refers to the speaker Menexenus and his mother, two brothers, and two sisters. As Wyse (1904, 416) points out, what they lost was only one sixth of the property of Dicaeogenes II, and the substantial estate the children inherited from Polyaratus was not affected by the intervention of Dicaeogenes III, so they were hardly left destitute. Even one sixth of the property of Dicaeogenes II would, nevertheless, have been worth a significant amount, and must have been enough to make the pursuit of the troublesome (and no doubt expensive) litigation worthwhile. In any case, the monetary value of the estate was not necessarily the only concern of the rival branches of the family; they may also have been anxious to retain and consolidate the property they held in particular localities (cf. on 'in the Plain', §22).

**for our father died … the witnesses to whose evidence he had objected:** Polyaratus raised an objection to Dicaeogenes's witnesses at the *diadikasia* (see on 'objection', below), but died before he could carry out his intention of prosecuting them for false testimony, and the speaker and his brothers were evidently not old enough to pursue the case on their own behalf. (The minimum age for initiating a legal action was 20.)

Isaeus does not mention the appointment of a guardian for Menexenus and his siblings. This responsibility is most likely to have been assumed by a relative or friend of Polyaratus, but the possibility that Dicaeogenes was the guardian of Polyaratus's children, as well as those of Theopompus, cannot be ruled out. (See on 'guardian', §10.)

**proceed against the witnesses:** The verb translated as 'proceed against' (*epexelthein*) is not a precise legal term, so it is not clear at what stage of the process Polyaratus died; it is possible, though not certain, that he had already started an action for false testimony but died before the case came to court.

**objected:** In this technical usage, the Greek verb *episkēptesthai* means 'to give formal notice of an intention to prosecute a witness' (Harrison, 1971, 192). Isaeus 5 is our earliest evidence for *episkēpsis*; the date when the procedure was introduced is not known. A litigant who intended to prosecute one or more of his opponent's witnesses for false testimony had to raise his objection orally during the trial, before the judges had voted. There was no obligation to proceed with the prosecution, and, presumably, no point in doing so if the litigant who had objected to the testimony actually won the case. So the immediate effect of the denunciation was rhetorical rather than legal, casting doubt into the minds of the judges about the reliability of the opponent's witnesses. (See Harrison, 1971, 192–93, for further discussion.)

**against us:** For the significance of this, see on 'without waiting for a judgment', §10.

**the wife of Cephisophon of Paeania (sister of Dicaeogenes who left the property):** According to the manuscripts, the woman in question was the *daughter* (θυγατέρα) of Cephisophon and *niece* (ἀδελφιδῆν) of Dicaeogenes II. For discussion of the textual problems this raises, see the introduction to this speech, pp. 32–33.

**the former wife of Democles:** It is unclear whether Democles had died, or whether his marriage to one of the daughters of Dicaeogenes II had ended in divorce. No children of theirs are mentioned in the speech. Pythodorus, son of Democles of Phrearrhii, who was an ephebe in 324/3 BC, was presumably a descendant of the Democles who married a sister of Dicaeogenes II, but possibly by a later wife (Edwards, 2002, 597, n.23).

On the possibility that the former wife of Democles married Protarchides of Potamus as her second husband, see the introduction to this speech, pp. 34–35. It is unclear whether she had already remarried when she was 'robbed' by Dicaeogenes III, or whether he was her *kyrios* (Wyse, 1904, 417).

**what her brother Dicaeogenes had given her:** The verb 'to give' (Gk. *didonai*) is commonly used by Isaeus with reference to a bequest in a will. So, as noted by Roussel (1926, 92), this wording might be taken to mean that

Dicaeogenes II had made a bequest in favour of the wife of Democles, but it is more likely that two thirds of the estate had gone to the four sisters as next of kin, in accordance with the normal rules of succession (§6). Cf. on 'had given them', §10.

**robbed both Cephisodotus and his mother of everything:** Theopompus, husband of one of Dicaeogenes's sisters, had died, leaving a widow and (as it appears from the subsequent narrative) at least two children, although only Cephisodotus is named. The significance of 'everything' will soon become clear: like her three sisters, the widow of Theopompus lost her share in her brother's estate; but in addition (according to the speaker), Dicaeogenes deprived her children of their paternal inheritance. (See on 'handed over to their enemies', §10.)

**10 guardian:** When an Athenian died leaving children who were still minors, a guardian or guardians (*epitropos*, plur. *epitropoi*) would be appointed to manage their father's estate on their behalf until they came of age. The guardian(s) might be nominated in the father's will; otherwise, the duty probably fell to the father's brother or closest male relative (Harrison, 1968, 99–100). Isaeus does not specify how Dicaeogenes was qualified to be the guardian of Theopompus's children, so he may have been appointed by will, but it is also possible that he was in some way related to Theopompus (Wyse, 1904, 417); cf. on 'next of kin', below.

**legal representative:** The Greek word *kyrios* (lit. 'lord' or 'master') designates the adult male who had legal authority to act on behalf of a child or woman. In the case of a male child, the authority of the *kyrios* would end when the child came of age, but a female was, in principle, subject to the authority of a *kyrios* throughout her life. A woman's *kyrios* would normally be her father until she married, and then her husband, but if circumstances required it (e.g. because of the death of her husband or father) the role could be taken on by a brother or adult son, or any other male relative.

**legal opponent:** The contrast with 'guardian' and 'legal representative' is pointed: Dicaeogenes, the very man who ought to have been defending the interests of Theopompus's widow and children in any court proceedings, in fact opposed them in pursuit of his own interests.

**did not have the slightest pity:** There are numerous accounts in the Attic orators of guardians who did not properly carry out their duties to their wards, either through negligence or deliberate fraud (for examples, see the General Introduction, pp. 4–5). If a guardian failed to hand over the full value of the estate when his ward came of age, the ward could prosecute him in a *dikē epitropēs*, as Demosthenes famously did (Dem. 27–31). By the time of the present trial, Theopompus had been dead for over 10 years, and Cephisodotus was old enough to participate in the litigation (§2), yet there is no suggestion that he had prosecuted Dicaeogenes or even contemplated doing so. Nor is there any hint of a public action for maltreatment of an orphan (*eisangelia kakōseōs orphanou*, the procedure used by the prosecutor in Isaeus 11), which would have been open to any volunteer prosecutor while the wards were still minors under the tutelage of the negligent guardian. As always, there must have been another side to the story, and it is probably safe to assume that Dicaeogenes would have been able to give a satisfactory account of his guardianship (cf. on 'handed over to their enemies', below).

**orphans, alone and destitute, lacking all the everyday necessities:** Even without the qualifying adjectives, the Greek word *orphanos* (which refers to any child whose father has died, whether or not the mother is still alive) was an emotive one. Dicaeogenes's alleged neglect of Theopompus's children is reminiscent of the allegations against Diogeiton in Lys. 32 (cf. on 'cheap shoes and a threadbare cloak', §11). In Isaeus 11, where the speaker aims to minimize any sympathy the judges might feel for his orphaned nephew, the word *orphanos* is generally avoided; see on 'the boy', 11.1.

**next of kin:** If Dicaeogenes III's mother was a sister of Menexenus I, he and the sisters of Dicaeogenes II were cousins. He did not lose that relationship after Dicaeogenes II adopted him (Isae. 7.25, with Griffith-Williams, 2013), but he became, in addition, their nephew and a cousin of their children. Thus he was 'next of kin' to the orphaned children of Theopompus because (unlike their other cousins, the sons of Polyaratus and Cephisophon) he was related to them through his (adoptive) father, not his mother. (For the alternative possibility that Dicaeogenes III was a blood relation of Theopompus, see on 'guardian', above.)

**handed over to their enemies:** The allegation is vague and unsubstantiated. Its effect is to emphasize both the callousness of Dicaeogenes III and the extreme poverty to which he condemned the widow and children of Theopompus. If there was any truth in the allegation, it seems most likely that the estate of Theopompus was in debt at the time of his death and the 'enemies' were his creditors (cf. Wyse, 1904, 418; Roussel, 1926, 92; Cudjoe, 2000, 435–36). For the Athenian conception of personal enmity, see on 'by friends and enemies alike', §13, and for the notion that children could 'inherit' enemies, like property, from their fathers, cf. Lys. 32.22 (cited by Alwine, 2015, 49, with n.168).

**their maternal uncle and their grandfather:** The property that Theopompus's children inherited from Dicaeogenes II (their maternal uncle) had been left to him by his father (and their grandfather), Menexenus I. The translations of both Forster (1927) and Edwards (2007) have 'my maternal uncle and my grandfather', which is possible because the Greek text uses definite articles rather than possessive adjectives, and Menexenus the speaker stood in the same relationship to Dicaeogenes II and Menexenus I as did his cousins, the children of Theopompus. In the context, however, their relationship to their uncle and grandfather is more significant than the speaker's. (Cf. Roussel, 1926: 'leur oncle maternel et leur grand-père'.)

**without waiting for a judgment:** This implies that Dicaeogenes III had acted illegally by taking possession of property that had not been adjudicated to him by a court. A similar accusation is made by the speaker of Isaeus 9, who says that Cleon, as soon as he heard about Astyphilus's death, took possession of the estate 'before you [judges] had the opportunity to vote' (9.3). In this case, Dicaeogenes III did submit a claim to the court, which voted in his favour (§8), but it appears that Polyaratus (acting on behalf of his wife) was the only rival claimant. Technically, therefore, it is possible that the judgment did not entitle Dicaeogenes III to take immediate possession of the property held by the other sisters of Dicaeogenes II, but it is not clear what further formalities he ought to have completed.

**11 bought the house they had inherited from their father:** The house was, presumably, put up for sale by Theopompus's creditors. A conscientious guardian might have taken the opportunity to buy it back and restore it to the orphans, but Dicaeogenes allegedly used the land for purely selfish purposes. By way of contrast, the speaker of Isaeus 1 says that his uncle Cleonymus (who was probably also his guardian at the relevant time) 'rescued our property from creditors seeking to deprive us of it' (1.12) and 'gave more help [to us] from his own means than to any of his other relatives' (1.27).

**his own house in the city:** The precise location of Dicaeogenes's house in the city is not mentioned; it may have been in his own deme, Cydathenaeum (cf. Osborne, 1985, 48).

**80 minas in rent:** See on 'an annual rent of 80 minas over ten years', §35.

**sent ... Cephisodotus to Corinth as an attendant for his brother Harmodius:** Harmodius was apparently serving in the Athenian army during the Corinthian War (395–386 BC). The 'attendant' (Gk. *akolouthos*) who accompanied a soldier would normally have been a slave, so it was demeaning for a citizen to be put in that position. Cudjoe (2000, 432) describes Dicaeogenes II's alleged treatment of Cephisodotus as the 'single worst personal offence alleged against a guardian of which we know'.

Harmodius, son of Proxenus, was alive in 371 BC, when he attacked as illegal a resolution to grant certain honours to the general Iphicrates. A speech in Iphicrates's defence was attributed by some late antique writers to Lysias, although the attribution was questioned by, among others, Dionysius of Halicarnassus (Lys. frr. 41a–45, 49 *OCT*).

The name was not common (*LGPN* lists only ten individuals in Attica), and it is also possible that this Harmodius is to be identified with the friend and neighbour mentioned by Euxitheus, the speaker of Lys. 1, delivered at some time between 403 and 380 (Lys. 1.41, with Todd, 2007, 140–41).

**cheap shoes and a threadbare cloak:** Cf. Lys. 32.16, where Diogeiton is accused of ejecting his wards from their house in worn-out clothes, with no shoes, bedding, or cloaks. Such details as these add to the pathos of the speaker's account, soliciting the indignation of the judges.

*12–13: The prosecution of Lycon for false testimony*

Isaeus now resumes the main narrative, beginning with the successful prosecution of one of Dicaeogenes's witnesses by the speaker's cousin Menexenus. Isaeus gives no indication of how much time had elapsed since the death of Polyaratus, but it is unlikely to have been 'many years' (as suggested by Calhoun, 1916, 381, n.1). Indeed, given that there must have been a time limit for starting a prosecution for false testimony after the *episkēpsis* at the original trial, the interval is likely to have been a few months at most, and may have been only a matter of days if Menexenus was already old enough to take legal action. The dispute then dragged on for a further ten years (§35), during which Dicaeogenes remained in possession of the whole estate – allegedly through deception and delaying tactics.

Menexenus's role as prosecutor shows that, at least in some circumstances, it was possible for someone other than the litigants at the original trial to prosecute the witnesses. Calhoun (1916, 381, n.1) reasonably infers from this passage that 'in an inheritance case the impeachment of a witness by a single claimant would secure to the other claimants also the right to prosecute', but, as he acknowledges, the complexity of the case and the obscurity of the details preclude any firm conclusions.

**12 now I'll get back to the point:** These words mark the end of the digression, which started at §9, about Dicaeogenes's callous treatment of the sisters of Dicaeogenes II and their families.

**Menexenus the son of Cephisophon:** This is the first reference to the speaker's cousin Menexenus, whose patronymic differentiates him from his and the speaker's grandfather. Cephisophon's son was presumably the oldest of the cousins, while some or all of the others were still minors. In §§13 and 14, where his identity is unambiguous, he is referred to simply by his given name.

**my cousin and the cousin of Cephisodotus:** These details explain the status of Menexenus in the litigation against Dicaeogenes.

**entitled to the same share of the estate as I was:** Menexenus the speaker and his cousin Menexenus the son of Cephisophon were 'entitled to the same share of the estate' only in the sense that both of them were claiming on behalf of their mothers, each of whom was entitled to one sixth. After the death of the speaker's mother, her share would have had to be further subdivided among her three sons (cf. on 'My father, Polyaratus', §5), whereas Cephisophon and his wife had only two sons (see on 'Cephisophon of Paeania, §5), who would have divided her share equally after her death. Menexenus the speaker's use of the first person singular is, nevertheless, a reminder that when an Athenian woman inherited property from a male relative, the ultimate (and often intended) beneficiary was always a man.

**proceeded against:** See on 'proceed against the witnesses', §9; the same verb is used here, in this instance evidently to indicate that Menexenus formally initiated legal proceedings.

**who had testified falsely against him and us:** Polyaratus, at the *diadikasia*, had represented the interests not only of his own wife and sons but also his sisters-in-law and their children. Again, this clarifies Menexenus's status as prosecutor of the witnesses.

**the first man he took to court:** Each of the witnesses prosecuted by Menexenus would have been subjected to a separate trial, but the speaker does not say how many there were. (Cf. on 'the witnesses who had not yet been convicted', §13, and 'since the witnesses had been convicted', §14.)

**Lycon, who had testified that Dicaeogenes had been adopted by our uncle with the whole estate:** This is Isaeus's only reference to Lycon, about whom nothing further is known. The name is quite common: *LGPN* lists a total of 169 individuals, of whom 33 are in Attica. The issue to which Lycon had testified was the validity of the second will, so his conviction would have been seriously damaging to the credibility of Dicaeogenes's claim to the estate. (Cf. on 'the witnesses who had not yet been convicted', §13.)

**our uncle:** Dicaeogenes II (see on 'our dispute with Dicaeogenes', §1).

**I will produce witnesses on these matters for you:** See on 'Please read the witness testimony', §2, and 'You have heard the witnesses', §3.

**13 And when, gentlemen, Dicaeogenes was no longer able to deceive you:** Dicaeogenes and his friends had 'deceived' the judges who awarded him the entire estate (§8); cf. on 'so that you are not deceived', §5. Having previously blamed Melas the Egyptian for the supposed miscarriage of justice, Isaeus now places Dicaeogenes III in the central role. Melas is not mentioned again as playing any active part in the litigation, so perhaps he and Dicaeogenes had already fallen out (see §40).

**I'm ashamed:** Menexenus's embarrassment (real or feigned) forestalls any hostile reaction from the judges to his disclosure of facts that reflect badly on his family.

**to do what?:** Rhetorical questions (of which there are 11 in this speech) are a characteristic feature of Isaeus's style, especially when combined with irony to ridicule his clients' opponents for their behaviour or arguments. (For discussion and further examples, see Hatzilambrou, 2018a, 37–39.) In this instance, where I have tried in the translation to reproduce the unusual and somewhat fractured syntax of the Greek sentence, the short question following the speaker's parenthesized embarrassment is particularly striking.

**the witnesses who had not yet been convicted:** According to a law cited by the speaker of Isaeus 11, 'if anyone is convicted of false testimony, the claims for an estate must start again from the beginning'. Thompson (1976, 55) accepted this at face value (see on 'the law prescribes …', 11.46), but earlier scholars had questioned whether the conviction of a single witness would be sufficient to trigger a retrial. Calhoun (1916, 391) argued persuasively that the significant factor was not the number or proportion of witnesses convicted but 'the refutation of some definite portion of the evidence presented to the jury, by the conviction of the witnesses who had attested it'. But it is not necessary to assume, as Calhoun apparently does, that such a conviction would automatically annul the court's original decision, at least in an inheritance case. The court's decision in a *diadikasia* was not final, but could be challenged either by a new claimant or the previous loser, on payment of a deposit and provided he could satisfy the archon that he had reasonable grounds for a new claim ([Dem.] 43.19). In this case, as Harrison

(1968, 161, n.2) observes, 'from the narrative it would not seem that the sentence for perjury automatically overturned the previous adjudication, but that it would provide valuable evidence in support of the claims of those who reopened the case'.

**by friends and enemies alike:** An Athenian would expect to be treated badly by his enemies (Gk. *echthroi*) but supported by his friends (Gk. *philoi*), so, while the deceitful behaviour of Dicaeogenes and his coterie was unsurprising, that of Menexenus (the speaker's cousin) was a disappointment. Enmity, in Athenian terms, was more than just a relationship of mutual dislike; it 'entailed expectations of the participants, not simply an emotional state … Just as friends were expected to help each other and to share in each other's victories, enemies were expected to seek each other's harm and to rejoice at each other's failures' (Alwine, 2015, 26–27).

Alwine (2015, 96, n.10) cites Isaeus 5 in support of the proposition that 'In private prosecution speeches that primarily concern disputes about ownership, speakers usually affirm enmity'. In fact, Isaeus's rhetorical strategy is more subtle than this suggests: Menexenus accuses Dicaeogenes of treating his relatives *as if* they were enemies (§30), but on the whole he takes great care to avoid any suggestion that the relationship was one of reciprocal enmity, insisting that he and his cousins always responded with magnanimity. Whatever the truth of the relationship, it seems reasonable to infer from this that he feared the judges would be unsympathetic if they thought the prosecutors' motivation was vindictive.

**And I will produce witnesses on these matters for you:** See on 'Please read the witness testimony', §2, and 'You have heard the witnesses', §3.

*14–16: Menexenus and his cousins claim the estate as next of kin*

**14 deceived by Dicaeogenes:** It was not only the judges who were liable to be deceived by Dicaeogenes III (see on 'so that you are not deceived', §5) but also his relatives and friends – specifically, at this point, Menexenus son of Cephisophon. Deceitfulness now becomes a significant character trait of Dicaeogenes III.

**since the witnesses had been convicted:** Only one witness, Lycon, had been convicted of false testimony when Dicaeogenes III persuaded Menexenus (son of Cephisophon) to drop his prosecutions of the rest (§13). There is at least a remote possibility that the remaining witnesses were convicted at a later stage, after Menexenus the son of Cephisophon had again joined forces with his cousins, and that Isaeus omitted this from the narrative for the sake of brevity, but this reference to 'witnesses' in the plural appears to be a rhetorical exaggeration. For the legal effect of a conviction for false testimony, see on 'the witnesses who had not yet been convicted', §13.

**any part of the estate ... the whole estate:** The Greek word *klēros* ('estate', 'property', 'inheritance') occurs 26 times in this speech (§§1, 2, 3, 5, 6, 7, 8, 12(x2), 13, 14(x2), 15, 16 (x2), 17, 18, 19, 20, 21, 24, 26, 27(x2), 29, 40). In this sentence, presumably for the sake of variation, Isaeus uses first *klēros* and then *oikos*, which is used only three times in the speech (§§14, 15, 43). While the two words are often interchangeable (MacDowell, 1989, 11), *oikos* also has broader connotations, for which see on 'the inheritance you received ...', §43.

**on grounds of kinship:** The Greek word translated here as 'kinship' is *anchisteia*, which has a more precise legal meaning than other kinship terminology such as *genos* or *syngeneia* (cf. Griffith-Williams, 2022, 44). Only the members of a dead man's *anchisteia* – that is, his closest collateral relatives – were entitled to inherit his estate if he left no natural or adopted legitimate son. The order of succession is discussed in more detail in the introduction to and commentary on Isaeus 11, where the precise extent of the *anchisteia* is a central issue.

**15 one long ago and the other much later:** It was apparently about 22 years since the death of Dicaeogenes II: the terms of the original will were observed for 12 years before Dicaeogenes III produced the second one (§7), and by the time of the present trial he had been in possession of the whole estate for ten years (§35).

**was to become:** See on 'was to become', §6.

**one third of the estate ... the whole of the estate:** Again, the Greek words *klēros* and *oikos* are used interchangeably for 'estate' (see on 'any part of the estate ...', §14).

**Dicaeogenes persuaded the judges:** Once again, Menexenus avoids criticizing the judges in the earlier trial, this time by blaming Dicaeogenes III for 'persuading' them (cf. on 'so that you are not deceived', §5). It was, of course, the aim of all litigants, including Isaeus's clients, to persuade the judges in their favour, but when a speaker's opponent is the subject, the verb 'persuade' often has pejorative connotations, amounting almost to a synonym of 'deceive'. Cf., e.g., Isae. 1.26, 48; 3.77; 8.3, 43.

**not the true one:** The original will produced by Proxenus was 'not the true one' in the sense that it had been superseded by another produced at a later date. We do not know exactly how Dicaeogenes III persuaded the court to annul the first will, but (as discussed in the introduction to this speech, pp. 21–22) he may have argued that it was unusual for a testator to give only part of his estate to an adopted son.

**the witnesses ... were convicted of false testimony:** Again, the plural seems to be a rhetorical exaggeration; see on 'since the witnesses had been convicted', §14.

**our uncle:** Dicaeogenes II.

**16 Since both of these wills were going to be invalidated:** Not 'both wills had been invalidated'. The logic of the cousins' decision to claim the entire estate as next of kin to Dicaeogenes II was that there was no longer a valid will in existence, since the first had been annulled by the decision of a court and the second was discredited by the conviction for false testimony. (Cf. Wyse, 1904, 422.)

**the late Dicaeogenes:** Dicaeogenes II.

**on the basis of kinship:** Again, and also in the next sentence, the Greek word is *anchisteia*; see on 'on grounds of kinship', §14.

**Leochares here:** See on 'Cephisodotus here' §2. 'Leochares here' is repeated at §18.

**a *diamartyria* declaring that the estate was not adjudicable to us**: The *diamartyria* was a procedural device that enabled a deceased Athenian's legitimate son (natural or adopted *inter vivos*) to assert his right to the paternal estate in the face of a claim from a collateral relative. Either the son himself or a witness on his behalf testified in a formal declaration that the estate was 'not subject to adjudication' by the court because the deceased had left a legitimate son. Once the *diamartyria* had been submitted, the rival claim from the collateral relative was automatically struck out. If the collateral relative still wanted to proceed, he or she could only do so by prosecuting the son or his witness for false testimony. (Cf. the General Introduction, p. 8, and see Harrison, 1971, 124–31, for a fuller account of the *diamartyria*.)

A son who had been (or claimed to have been) adopted by will could not enter on the estate until the court had approved his claim, but on the evidence of this passage (and of a similar situation in [Dem.] 44) a testamentary adoptee was also entitled to make use of the *diamartyria* once the formalities of the adoption had been completed (cf. Rubinstein, 1993, 54). Whether the procedure was really intended for use by someone in Dicaeogenes III's position is, however, questionable, and the *diamartyria* seems to have been an evasive tactic on his part. If the case had been tried in a *diadikasia*, he would have had to defend his entitlement to the estate on the same grounds as in the previous *diadikasia*, but after the conviction of Lycon it would have been difficult – perhaps impossible – for him to find witnesses who were willing to risk prosecution by testifying to the validity of the second will. (Cf. Calhoun, 1916, 391, n.2: 'The fact that Dicaeogenes thought it advisable to employ a *diamartyria*, instead of again putting forward the witnesses to the will, is of itself a strong indication that the witnesses were unwilling to face the conviction which was certain after the condemnation of Lycon'.) Leochares, in the *diamartyria*, would not have had to give detailed reasons for his assertion that Dicaeogenes II had left a legitimate son.

*17–18: The prosecution of Leochares for false testimony and the agreement with Dicaeogenes II*

**17 raised an objection:** Gk. *episkēpsamenōn* (cf. on 'objected', §9). Isaeus's account of the legal proceedings at this point is very condensed.

**our claim was struck out:** The annulment of the claim was an automatic effect of the *diamartyria* (not, as this sentence might suggest, of the *episkēpsis*). For discussion, see Harrison (1971, 125).

**a long defence:** Isaeus gives no details of Leochares's defence against the charge of false testimony, but presumably he relied on the original will, arguing that it had been validated again by the annulment of the second will (cf. on 'not the true one', §15).

**the judges decided that he had testified falsely:** As the following narrative explains, the judges' vote appeared to be going against Leochares, but the court did not formally reach a decision in the case because of the parties' agreement to compromise.

**after the ballots had been tipped out:** The ballots, or 'pebbles' (Gk. *psēphoi*) were the tokens used by Athenian judges to cast their votes at the end of a trial by putting them into urns. At an adversarial trial, under the voting system used in the late fifth century (and evidently still in operation at the time of the *dikē pseudomartyriōn* described here), there were two urns, one for conviction and one for acquittal, and each judge had a single ballot which he put into the urn of his choice. So a significant majority in favour of one litigant would immediately become apparent when the urns were emptied, before the votes were actually counted. That would not have been the case under the new system introduced later in the fourth century, whereby each of the judges had two ballots, one for the litigant who spoke first and the other for the second speaker. The judge put the ballot for his favoured litigant into a bronze urn, and discarded the other one into a wooden urn. When all the judges had voted, the ballots were emptied from the bronze urn and counted on a specially constructed voting board.

For the system of voting in a *diadikasia*, which must always have been different from that used in an adversarial trial, see on 'a separate voting urn', 11.21; and, for a more detailed account of the system as a whole, Harrison (1971, 164–65).

**the appeals Leochares made to us and the judges … the penalties we could then have imposed:** Leochares was evidently desperate to avoid conviction for false testimony, which could have led to his disfranchisement (see on 'deprived of civic rights', §19).

In a *dikē pseudomartyriōn* (prosecution for false testimony), as in all private actions, any financial penalty would have been payable to the prosecutor as damages. But, reflecting the seriousness with which the Athenians regarded false testimony, a third conviction automatically incurred *atimia* or loss of civic rights (Andoc. 1.74). Although it would have been impossible to prevent all witnesses from lying, that must have been a powerful deterrent.

On the *dikē pseudomartyriōn* as a 'hybrid action' – a private action with some features of a public one – see Carey (2018, 89–90), and cf. on 'all 500 of them', §20.

**the agreement we reached:** Menexenus has explained at some length (§§15–16) that he and his associates considered themselves entitled to the whole estate on grounds of kinship, because both wills had been invalidated. He now presents their willingness to compromise as an example of their magnanimity towards their opponents, but they may have been less than fully confident of their entitlement to the whole estate.

**18 Dicaeogenes surrendered two thirds of the estate to the sisters of Dicaeogenes:** The agreement thus had the effect of restoring the terms of the original will, perhaps the best result that Menexenus and his associates could realistically have expected.

**without further dispute:** The crucial term of the agreement, disputed by Dicaeogenes and Leochares, was first mentioned in the opening section of the speech (see on 'without further dispute', §1). Isaeus now repeats it here, and at §§20 and 21, to ensure that it stays in the minds of the judges.

**Mnesiptolemus of Plotheia:** Plotheia, of the tribe Aegeis, was one of the smallest Attic demes, situated to the northeast of the city and sending only one representative to the Boule.

According to Brock (2020, 16) one reason for the use of a demotic in a forensic speech is 'the evocation of the individual in question as a legal personality'. Examples cited by Brock include the sureties identified by demotic at [Dem.] 33.15, 22. In the present instance, as Brock suggests, the demotic was used 'perhaps to underline the official status of an adjudgment which in the event was not adhered to'.

**I will now produce witnesses of these facts:** See on 'Please read the witness testimony', §2, and 'You have heard the witnesses', §3. The testimony of those who witnessed Dicaeogenes's agreement and Leochares's pledge as surety will have been crucial for Menexenus's version of the terms.

*19–24: Problems in recovering the property (narrative and argumentation)*

Following the agreement they reached with Dicaeogenes III at the false testimony trial, Menexenus and his cousins have managed to recover no more than two small houses and 60 plethra (about 13 acres or 5.26 hectares) of land (§22). At this stage, about ten years have elapsed (§35) since the *diadikasia* of ca. 402–401 BC, when Dicaeogenes gained control of the whole estate. Some of the property he then took from the sisters of Dicaeogenes II has fallen into disrepair (§28), and some of it is now in the possession of creditors or mortgagees because he has used it as security for loans (§21). According to Menexenus, Dicaeogenes agreed to return the property 'without further dispute' (§§1, 18, 20, 21) so he ought to have paid off the creditors and returned all the property in its original condition. But, true to his mean and dishonest character, Dicaeogenes disputes the terms of the agreement and obstructs his opponents' attempts to recover the remaining property from his mortgagees.

**19 deprived of civic rights:** The fact that Leochares, if convicted, would have lost his civic rights indicates that he already had two convictions for false testimony (see on 'the appeals Leochares made to us and the judges …', §17). It is possible that *atimia* could be imposed for a single offence in certain types of cases, such as false testimony in a *diamartyria*, but the evidence (discussed by MacDowell, 1962, 66) is inconclusive. If, as seems most likely, Leochares did have two previous convictions, there would have been no need for Isaeus to spell this out because the implication would not have been lost on the judges (cf. Calhoun, 1916, 386–87).

By the time of Hyperides's prosecution of Philippides (ca. 337 BC), someone with two previous convictions for false testimony could not be compelled to testify again (Hyp. *Phil.* 12; for discussion, see Harrison, 1971, 138–39). It is not known when this provision came into force.

**we did not want to do so:** By emphasizing that he and his associates were prepared to treat Leochares leniently by allowing him to escape conviction for false testimony, the speaker makes the point that their real opponent is not Leochares but Dicaeogenes. Cf. on 'We have no desire to take Leochares's own property', §34.

**content to recover what belonged to us:** Menexenus implies that he and his friends demonstrated their magnanimity by accepting the share of the estate that they had previously held rather than insisting on a count of the votes, which would (on his account) have led to disfranchisement for Leochares. Cf. on 'when we could have punished Dicaeogenes', §30.

**we were deceived by them, gentlemen:** Now Menexenus the speaker includes himself among the victims of Dicaeogenes's (and Leochares's) deceit. (Cf. on 'deceived by Dicaeogenes', §14.) The address to the judges, in an emphatic position at the end of the sentence, invites them to share in the experience of the victims.

**20 all 500 of them:** The number of judges at an Athenian trial varied according to the type of case. A panel of 500 appears to have been standard for public cases, and this passage shows that there were also 500 judges in a *dikē pseudomartyriōn*, although the number in private cases was normally smaller. In practice, there would most probably have been 501, with an extra judge added to create an uneven number and thus avoid a tied vote, so Isaeus was using the round figure for convenience.

The fact that Leochares made his pledge in the presence of the judges, after the archon had agreed not to proceed with the vote, implies that it carried the authority of the court; cf. on 'while on the rostrum', §25 (and see Christ, 1998, 266, n.48).

**bystanders:** Gk. *hoi periestēkotes*: the 'audience' of spectators who stood around the edges of an Athenian courtroom to observe the trial. Although they had no formal role in the proceedings, Lanni (1997, 183) argues that 'the spectators played a crucial role in the social dynamic of the courts and had an important effect both on the litigants' arguments and on the jurors' decisions'. In this context the presence of the bystanders would, in the Athenian mind, have conferred greater legitimacy on the settlement between the parties and the pledge made by Leochares.

**I don't know what else he could have done:** Leochares put himself at considerable financial risk in undertaking the suretyship, which he might have been reluctant to do if he had not been under threat of conviction and punishment for false testimony (cf. on 'deprived of civic rights, §19). The speaker implies that Leochares had no other means of escaping that threat.

**we bring forward as witnesses those who were present:** This apparently refers to the witnesses produced after §18. For 'those who were present', see on 'I will produce witnesses who were present at the time', §6.

**without further dispute:** Again, Isaeus repeats the crucial term of the agreement, which was contested by Dicaeogenes and Leochares (cf. on 'without further dispute', §§1, 18, 21).

**we beg you, gentlemen:** On the whole, the language of this speech is relatively restrained and unemotional, but the combination of an address to the judges with a verb of pleading (Gk. *deomai*) intensifies the speaker's appeal for their assistance (cf. on 'I beg you, therefore, to convict Leochares', §34). In other speeches by Isaeus it is not uncommon to find appeals involving two or more verbs of pleading or supplication, e.g. 'I beg, entreat and beseech you all to receive my speech with goodwill', Isae. 2.2; cf. Isae. 2.44, 6.57, 9.37.

**if any of you happened to be there:** It is possible that some of the judges in the current trial were also present in court, either as judges or as bystanders, when the compromise was made after the conviction of Leochares for false testimony. So the speaker appeals to them, as informal additional 'witnesses', to support his version of events. Cf. on 'you are all my witnesses', 11.48.

**21 Since, gentlemen … how was my opponent disadvantaged by losing it?:** The rhetorical question, introduced with a direct address to the judges, engages them in the speaker's argument and invites them to discredit his opponent.

**winning the case … losing it:** Technically, neither party had won or lost the *dikē pseudomartyriōn* against Leochares because the votes had not been counted. Moreover, Menexenus and his associates had not won their claim to the whole estate, but had accepted Dicaeogenes's offer of two thirds by way of compromise. At this stage, nevertheless, they were in some sense entitled to consider themselves moral victors.

**without further dispute:** Another reminder to the judges of the crucial, disputed term in the agreement (cf. §§1, 18, 20).

**mortgaged and bought:** Not 'mortgaged *or* bought', which would imply that Dicaeogenes had sold some of the property outright while some of it was mortgaged, as in most translations (Roussel 1926, Forster 1927, Edwards 2007). Carey (2018, 86) explains: 'I take [the men who mortgaged and bought the property from Dicaeogenes] as a single group of people … so we have a reference not to outright sale but to *prasis epi lysei*, a form of borrowing'. Inscribed boundary stones (Gk. *horoi*) were erected on mortgaged property as a warning that the person in possession did not have an unencumbered right of disposal (Todd, 1993, 379).

**he ought to have paid them off and given us our share:** This confirms that Dicaeogenes had 'sold' the property *epi lysei*. Cf. Carey (2018, 86, n.31): 'If this was outright sale, Dikaiogenes had no right simply to buy back the property from the purchasers and it is difficult to believe that any of the audience could take the suggestion seriously. But he could recover property held by creditors against a loan simply by paying off the capital and any outstanding interest'.

**22 because we did not believe he would fulfil his promise:** Menexenus and his associates have learnt from experience that Dicaeogenes is not to be trusted, so they are not willing to accept the agreement without sureties.

**60 plethra:** About 13 acres (5.26 hectares).

**in the Plain:** This could refer either to the plain of agricultural land south of the city, or more probably to the upper Cephissus valley in the northern plain, where many elite families owned land in the fifth century. In the latter case, according to Cox (1998, 13): 'it would not have been a coincidence that Menexenus contracted a marriage for a daughter to Polyaratus of Cholargus'. (See on 'My father, Polyaratus', §5.)

**We are not trying to evict them:** The Greek verb translated as 'evict' (*exagein*, lit. 'lead out') relates to *exagōgē*, a 'self help' procedure available in certain circumstances to an Athenian wishing to assert his claim to property occupied by someone else. As Harrison (1968, 314) points out, Menexenus 'seems to think it almost essential to explain why he has not used *exagōgē*', which indicates that 'in the situation in which the speaker was, *exagōgē* was the method by which he would have been expected to assert his right'.

**losing legal cases:** As Menexenus goes on to explain, he and his associates had been successfully prosecuted by one of Dicaeogenes's creditors in an action for ejectment (*dikē exoulēs*), so they were afraid that the other creditors would take similar action.

**we tried to evict Micion:** According to Harrison (1968, 314), this does not necessarily mean that Micion was actually in possession of the bathhouse: 'If, as seems probable, Mikion's rights were those of a creditor-purchaser by *prasis epi lusei*, it would be quite possible, normal in fact, for the debtor, Dikaiogenes, still to be in occupation, in which case the *exagōgē* might perhaps have consisted in a formal removal from the bath of a *horos* stone'. (Cf. on 'mortgaged and bought', §21.)

Nothing further is known about Micion, whose name was fairly common in Attica (51 individuals listed in *LGPN*, from a total of 126).

**would not confirm his title to the property:** Micion, as mortgagee of the bathhouse who was being threatened with eviction by a third party, had a right to prosecute the potential evictor in a *dikē exoulēs* (see on 'attacked Micion before the judges', §23). If he did so, he was entitled to expect that Dicaeogenes, the mortgagor, would confirm (Gk. *bebaioun*) his title to the property. But Dicaeogenes had promised Menexenus that he would not confirm Micion's title, thus allowing Menexenus and his associates to take possession. If, in the event, Dicaeogenes did not confirm Micion's title (and did not pay him off for the value of the property), Micion would be able to sue him in an 'action for confirmation' (*dikē bebaiōseōs*). Cf. Harrison (1968, 314).

**fined 40 minas:** In a private action the penalty would normally have been damages payable to the winning party, but in a *dikē exoulēs* a penalty equivalent to the assessed value of the disputed property was also payable to the state (Harrison, 1968, 219). Cf. Carey (2018, 78–79) on the 'hybrid' nature of the *dikē exoulēs*.

**because of Dicaeogenes, gentlemen:** The address to the judges, placed in an emphatic position at the end of the sentence, reinforces Menexenus's point that it was Dicaeogenes who was to blame for the penalty imposed on Menexenus and his associates.

**23 believing that he would not confirm …:** Menexenus and his associates are now relying on the sureties they obtained to deter Dicaeogenes from deceiving them again (cf. on 'because we did not believe he would fulfil his promise', §22).

**attacked Micion before the judges:** Although Isaeus does not specify the nature of the proceedings, the context suggests that Micion prosecuted Menexenus and his associates in an 'action for ejectment' (*dikē exoulēs*), a procedure which 'serves to allow execution of a legally recognised right' (Carey, 2018, 84). The right to prosecute in a *dikē exoulēs* was, in the main, restricted to litigants whose claim to the property in dispute was based on a court judgment or who were the legitimate offspring of the deceased former owner. Another category was those who were prevented from fulfilling a function (such as extraction of minerals) they had leased from the state. Apart from this passage, the only evidence that the right to prosecute also extended to mortgagees comes from the lexicographers Harpocration and Pollux. See Carey (2018, 82–85) for a full discussion of qualifications to prosecute in a *dikē exoulēs.*

**not expecting that he would do the opposite of what he had agreed to do:** As Menexenus now recognizes, he and his associates were naïve in their confidence that Dicaeogenes would keep his word because of the sureties.

**relying on the sureties:** The repeated reference to sureties (cf. §22) was perhaps intended as a reminder to the judges that Leochares, the defendant in the present case, was liable for Dicaeogenes's default.

**24 I had the misfortune … to have lost 40 minas:** Cf. on 'fined 40 minas', §22. The switch from the first person plural 'we' to the singular 'I' is striking: having previously implied that he and his associates were acting jointly in their efforts to recover the property from Dicaeogenes, Menexenus now seems to suggest that he alone suffered the consequences of Dicaeogenes's deception, including the financial loss.

**received nothing from the estate:** This overlooks the two small houses and 60 plethra of land mentioned at §22.

**humiliated by Dicaeogenes:** The Greek verb is *hybrismenos*, a strongly condemnatory term suggesting an attitude of contempt on the part of the agent as well as harm to the victim. In the context, it does not imply that Dicaeogenes was guilty of *hybris* in the sense of physical violence or assault, but rather that he had gravely insulted Menexenus. Forster (1927) misses the point with 'fooled', while Edwards (2007) conveys the sense more effectively with 'thoroughly abused'. The semantic range of *hybris* and its cognates has been a rich source of scholarly debate; see, e.g., MacDowell (1976), Fisher (1990), Cairns (1996).

**I will produce witnesses of these facts for you:** The testimony produced at this point evidently confirmed Menexenus's account of the failed attempt to evict Micion from the bathhouse.

*25–30: The agreement (narrative and argumentation)*

Menexenus claims that in addition to the written agreement, which was drafted in haste, some supplementary points were agreed orally in the presence of witnesses. Leochares and Dicaeogenes, he says, are now accepting the points of the agreement that suit them (written or oral) and rejecting the rest. Modern scholars have often taken a sceptical view of this argument, especially given that Isaeus never sets out the terms of the agreement in full, and deals with them only briefly at this relatively late stage in the speech. (See, e.g., Forster, 1927, 156: 'This argument would hardly recommend itself to a court of law and constitutes a great weakness in the case'.) As others have recognized, however, the absence of a full agreement in writing would not necessarily have been decisive in the Athenian courts, 'given the greater importance of witnesses over documents in most legal transactions' (Edwards, 2007, 79, n.7). Indeed, it is worth pointing out that oral agreements are (with certain exceptions) legally binding under modern English law. Nowadays, as in the Athenian courts, the source of disputes is not the legal validity of an oral agreement *per se* but the scope it provides for misunderstanding and misrepresentation, leading to difficulties of proof and enforcement.

Five of Menexenus's 21 addresses to the judges occur in §§25–30, apparently reflecting the intensity of his efforts to persuade them that his version of the agreement is the correct one (or, as a sceptical commentator might say, his desperation).

**25 That is how we were treated by Dicaeogenes, gentlemen:** Again, the address to the judges is placed in an emphatic position, at the end of a clause, inviting them to share in the experience of the speaker and his associates. (Cf. on 'we were deceived by them, gentlemen', §19.)

**Leochares ... the cause of all our troubles:** Leochares will no doubt argue that Dicaeogenes has done his best to return the two thirds of the estate to his opponents, and that the written agreement drawn up in court did not stipulate that the property was to be handed over free of further claims and liabilities ('without further dispute').

**on the terms stated in the testimony against him:** The testimony presumably confirmed that Dicaeogenes had agreed to surrender the property 'without further dispute'.

**but at that time, gentlemen:** The repeated address to the judges emphasizes the importance that the speaker attaches to this part of his narrative.

**hastily wrote down some points while on the rostrum:** When the agreement was drawn up, the parties were still on the raised platform (Gk. *bēma*) from which litigants and witnesses addressed the court. Menexenus's account conveys a sense that the parties were under pressure to complete their agreement in a short time, presumably because it had to be approved by the archon before they could leave the court.

**secured witnesses in support of this:** Cf. on 'we bring forward as witnesses those who were present', §19. It would have been essential to secure witnesses who could attest to the oral points of the agreement. The veracity of witnesses could of course be challenged, but in principle their testimony would have carried at least as much weight as a document (the authenticity of which could also be called into question).

**even if they are not in writing:** Leochares and Dicaeogenes are being selective about which points of the agreement they accept, but it is significant that (if Menexenus's account is accurate) they do not deny that some points were agreed orally, and actually accept the orally agreed points that go in their favour.

**26 I, gentlemen, am not surprised:** With another direct address to the judges, following shortly after the two in §25, the speaker invites them to agree with his account of his opponents' behaviour.

**to prove that we are telling the truth:** The formulaic phrase, in this specific context, creates an expectation that the speaker is about to adduce further evidence to prove that his version of the agreement reached in court is the true one. That expectation does not appear to be met by the testimony of Protarchides (cf. on 'as witness to these facts', §27).

**more evidence:** The Greek word translated here as 'evidence' is *tekmērion* (lit. 'sign', 'token' or 'proof'), which in rhetorical theory denotes a fact or piece of evidence from which a speaker invites the judges to draw inferences in support of the proposition he wants to prove. (As noted by Griffith-Williams, 2022, 48, 'Arist. *Rhet.* 1.2 defines it as a "necessary sign", in the sense that it forms the basis of a syllogism leading to a logically irrefutable conclusion'.) In practice, as the present context illustrates, a *tekmērion* is often no more than an indication that a particular conclusion is probable rather than necessary.

**Dicaeogenes gave his father's sister in marriage:** The ms. text has 'his sister' (τὴν ἀδελφὴν τὴν ἑαυτοῦ), which is problematic. For discussion, see the introduction to this speech, pp. 33–36.

**Protarchides of Potamus:** Isaeus does not specify whether the deme to which Protarchides belonged was Upper or Lower Potamus. These were small demes of the tribe Leontis, lying on the east coast north of Thoricus, which sent a total of three representatives to the Boule. On the use of the demotic in the context of marriage, see on 'Democles of Phrearrhii', §5.

**a dowry of 40 minas:** There was a strong expectation, though not a legal requirement, that an Athenian woman would be married with a dowry. According to Foxhall (1989, 32): 'A dowry is the property which goes with a woman when she is married. Fundamentally, it is the basis of her maintenance and livelihood … In fact, dowries served as a woman's patrimonial inheritance, received at marriage … Girls' dowries are the equivalent of (though not usually equal in value to) what their brothers receive as inheritance on their father's death'.

**instead of a cash dowry:** 'Dowry property among upper-class Athenians normally consisted of money, furniture and other moveable goods' (Foxhall, 1989, 33).

**Ceramicus:** Originally the potters' district, in the northwest of the city, Ceramicus became known as the red-light district of Athens. (Euctemon, in Isaeus 6, owned a brothel in Piraeus and another house in Ceramicus which may also have been a brothel; see Griffith-Williams, 2022, 212–14.) The city's main burial area was located in the outer Ceramicus.

**entitled to the same share of the estate as my mother:** These words show conclusively that the woman married to Protarchides was a sister of Dicaeogenes II (see on 'cousin', above).

**27 Leochares suggested to Protarchides … did not hand over the share of the estate:** Another difficult passage: the legal basis for the transaction between Leochares and Protarchides is obscure. On the face of it, the passage implies that an Athenian woman was not entitled to keep her dowry in addition to the share she inherited of her father's (or brother's) estate (cf. Forster, 1927, 179, n; Foxhall, 1989, 32). Yet there is no independent evidence of a legal requirement for the dowry to be returned in these circumstances, and if such a requirement did exist, why did it apply to only one of the four sisters? (cf. Wyse, 1904, 443). Perhaps the best explanation is that Protarchides succumbed to unfair pressure from Leochares because he was short of money – only to become yet another victim of the duplicity of Dicaeogenes and Leochares (cf. Edwards, 2002, 596, n.17).

**as witness to these facts:** The evidentiary value of Protarchides's testimony about his dealings with Leochares may have been less than Isaeus wanted the judges to think (cf. on 'to prove that we are telling the truth', §26). If the testimony is true, it proves that Leochares was indeed acting as surety for Dicaeogenes (cf. Jebb, 1876, 353), and that Protarchides was swindled by Leochares and Dicaeogenes, but what is less clear is how it supports the speaker's contention that Dicaeogenes agreed to return the property in question 'without further dispute'.

**I shall now bring forward Protarchides:** Protarchides is the only witness to be identified by name in any of Isaeus's extant speeches. That does not necessarily indicate that his testimony was more important than that of other witnesses, but rather that he was testifying about a private matter of which he knew more than anyone else. (Cf. Isae. 9.19, where a witness is identified as 'the husband of Astyphilus's aunt'.)

**28 the repairs to the bathhouse and the cost of building:** Although Menexenus does not discuss the full terms of the agreement, these details give an indication of their complexity and of the difficulty of assessing the value of the estate, which must inevitably have changed over the 22 years since the death of Dicaeogenes II.

**and will perhaps say again now:** On anticipation of the opponent's argument, qualified by 'perhaps', see on 'perhaps he will argue …', §3. At this point, Menexenus apparently expects Dicaeogenes himself to speak in court (cf. on 'the only points …', §5).

**29 But we, gentlemen …:** Menexenus's reply to the question he anticipates from Dicaeogenes is evasive: instead of addressing directly the point about the repairs to the bathhouse and the cost of building, he takes the opportunity to expand on his own and his associates' generosity towards Dicaeogenes.

**in return for the liturgies he had performed:** At this point, although the value of the liturgies is not quantified, Menexenus acknowledges that Dicaeogenes III had used some of the wealth he inherited for the benefit of the city. When he reverts to Dicaeogenes's record of public service, at §36, he is scathing about the inadequacy of the liturgies he performed.

**later, not under compulsion but willingly:** Menexenus seeks to convey the message that he and his cousins treated Dicaeogenes more generously than he deserved, because they were not required by the court to give him the house but did so of their own volition. This contrasts with the stance taken by Theopompus, the speaker of Isaeus 11, who insists that he has always behaved in accordance with the law but who never shows any willingness to go beyond what he is legally required to do. (See the introductory note to 11.20–26.)

**sold the house for 5,000 drachmas to Philonicus:** Menexenus produces no evidence of this transaction, but he adds credibility to his account by specifying the price and naming the purchaser.

**30 we gave it to Dicaeogenes, gentlemen:** The repeated address to the judges (cf. on 'But we, gentlemen', §29) suggests that Menexenus is particularly anxious to persuade them at this point.

**to show that we do not have a higher regard for money than for our relatives:** Citing this passage as a reflection of the popular Athenian prejudice against litigation between kin, Christ (1998, 169) observes: 'One concern of disputing kin is that they may appear to value money and property, which are commonly at the root of their disputes, over kinship. They therefore often represent themselves as interested only in their due, even willing to accept a financial loss in the interest of preserving good relations. They point out that their opponents, by contrast, subordinate even the bonds of kinship to the pursuit of gain'. Cf. Dover (1974, 275): 'Injustice committed against a relation incurred greater reproach than the same injustice committed against a stranger, and litigation within the family was a matter of great embarrassment'. Other examples (cited by Dover) include Ant. 1.1, Isae. 1.6, 9.25, and Lys. 32.2.

Menexenus, significantly, does not say that he and his associates gave the house to Dicaeogenes *because* they valued the ties of kinship more highly than money, but *to show* that they did so. This illustrates the importance attached by the Athenians to reputation; cf. on 'if it were shown that …', 11.38.

**when we could have punished Dicaeogenes:** This implies that, if Menexenus and his associates had insisted on having the votes counted after the trial of Leochares for false testimony, instead of agreeing to compromise, they could have taken the whole estate and left Dicaeogenes III with nothing. Cf. on 'content to recover what belonged to us', §19.

**when he had power over us:** This refers to the period after the court ruled in favour of the second will, and Dicaeogenes recovered the property previously held by the sisters of Dicaeogenes II (§§9–11).

**as if we had been his enemies and not his relatives:** Blood kinship is no guarantee of friendly relations (otherwise, there would be fewer inheritance disputes) but Dicaeogenes has transgressed Athenian norms by treating his relatives as enemies (whereas they, for their part, have refrained from entering into a relationship of mutual hostility; see on 'by friends and enemies alike', §13).

*31–34: The failed arbitration (narrative and argumentation)*
When the prosecution of Leochares as surety was about to come to court, Menexenus and his associates, at the request of Dicaeogenes and Leochares, agreed to postpone the trial and go to private arbitration. Four arbitrators were appointed (two by each side) and the litigants swore an oath agreeing to abide by their decision. The arbitrators questioned the parties at length, but the attempt to settle the dispute was a failure because the two appointed by Leochares and Dicaeogenes declined to announce a decision. As in his account of the trial of Leochares for false testimony (§§17–18), Isaeus exploits this situation to present his client as behaving more reasonably and magnanimously than the opponents deserved, and from the arbitrators' refusal to announce a decision he invites the judges to infer that Leochares was guilty.

Arbitration, as a means of settling a dispute without a formal trial, was an established feature of the Athenian legal system. Two forms of arbitration were available: private and (from around 400 BC) public. Litigants in any type of case could, by agreement, submit their dispute to private arbitrators, while in certain types of cases the authorities could impose public arbitration. See MacDowell (1978a, 203–11) for an overview of the system, and, for a more nuanced discussion of the advantages and disadvantages of both forms of arbitration, Harris (2018).

The only other confirmed example of arbitration (also private) in Isaeus's speeches is at Isae. 2.29–33, on which see Griffith-Williams (2022, 114–15).

**31 firm evidence:** See on 'more evidence', §26.
**Maimacterion:** The fifth month of the Athenian year (October-November).

**asked us to postpone the trial and go to arbitration:** Normally, one of the advantages of private arbitration was speed: a case could be disposed of without the need to wait for trial, which could take several months to come to court (cf. Harris, 2018, 220–21). In this case, however, it appears that there would not have been much longer to wait for the trial, so the request for arbitration was probably a delaying tactic on the part of Dicaeogenes and Leochares.

**we agreed:** Private arbitration was voluntary and had to be acceptable to both parties. Harris (2018, 221) identifies the requirement for the consent of both parties as 'the main disadvantage of private arbitration', and discusses several cases where one of the parties withheld consent.

**as if we had suffered only a minor injustice:** Menexenus implies that arbitration was only suitable for relatively trivial disputes. Whether or not that was true, it enables him to present himself and his associates as magnanimously accepting their opponents' proposal against their own interests.

**four arbitrators:** The number and identity of private arbitrators was a matter for the parties to decide, but the appointment of two by each party seems like a recipe for deadlock; it would have been an obvious precaution to appoint an odd number. In fact, in the majority of attested arbitrations there was either a single arbitrator acceptable to both sides, or one chosen by mutual agreement in addition to those nominated by each side (cf. Harris, 2018, 217). In this case, it may be that the opposing parties could not agree on a neutral arbitrator, or perhaps no-one who would have been acceptable to them was willing to take on the duty.

**an oath agreeing to abide by their decision:** Although private arbitration was not compulsory, once the arbitrators had reached a decision, it was binding, and the case could not subsequently be taken to court (Isoc. 18.11; for detailed discussion, see Harris, 2018, 214).

**32 achieve a compromise:** The first stage in a private arbitration was an attempt to reconcile (Gk. *diallattein*) the opposing litigants.

**what they considered to be just:** Unlike the judges at a formal trial, arbitrators were not obliged to observe the strict requirements of the law, but could make any decision they considered to be fair to both parties.

**asked us a lot of questions:** Unlike judges, again, private arbitrators could ask questions if they needed more information than the litigants had already given them (cf. Harris, 2018, 221).

**found out what had happened:** The wording is tendentious, implying that the arbitrators accepted the version of events put forward by Menexenus and his associates.

**would not make a declaration:** Athenian judges cast their votes in a secret ballot, but arbitrators voted openly; and, since they were likely to be known to the litigants, there was a risk that they might be unwilling to announce a decision for fear of giving offence to one of the parties. In this case, it was the arbitrators appointed by Leochares who refused to announce a decision, so the implication is that they would have found in favour of Menexenus. A similar situation arose in a dispute between Chrysippus and Lampis about a maritime loan in Dem. 34 (discussed by Harris, 2018, 222–23).

**33 Leochares's brother-in-law:** The Greek word *kēdestēs*, here translated as 'brother-in-law', could in fact be used of any male affine (relative by marriage). Thompson (1971, 110) cites examples from Attic prose where *kēdestēs* certainly refers to a sister's husband, a daughter's husband, a wife's father, a wife's brother, or even a non-specific 'connection by marriage'. In this instance, 'brother-in-law' seems most likely, but the exact relationship between Leochares and Diopeithes is neither verifiable nor especially significant; the important point is that Diopeithes, as a member of Leochares's wider family circle, was not an impartial arbitrator. So, according to Menexenus, the obvious inference to be drawn from his refusal to announce his decision is that it would have gone against Leochares.

**an enemy of mine:** For the Athenian conception of personal enmity as a reciprocal social relationship, see on 'by friends and enemies alike', §13. The enmity between Diopeithes and Menexenus of course makes it all the more likely that Diopeithes would favour Leochares.

**an opponent in other legal actions about contracts:** It was not surprising that someone described as an enemy would have been an opponent in litigation, but Menexenus also reveals through this detail that he himself was an experienced litigant, not only in the earlier stages of the dispute with Dicaeogenes. It is possible that his opponents were able to exploit his experience by suggesting he had used it to gain an unfair advantage.

**a brother of Mnesiptolemus:** See on 'Mnesiptolemus of Plotheia', §18.

**And of these facts I will produce witnesses for you:** The most credible witnesses to what had happened at an arbitration would have been one or more of the arbitrators themselves; cf. [Dem.] 59.47, 70 (cited by Harris, 2018, 216–17), where arbitrators are called as witnesses. So the fact that Menexenus does not identify these witnesses implies strongly that none of the arbitrators had been willing to testify on his behalf. For the formula 'I will produce witnesses', see on 'Please read the witness testimony', §2, and 'You have heard the witnesses', §3.

**34 Isn't it strange, gentlemen … convicted him?:** The first of two successive rhetorical questions, both designed to prejudice the judges against Leochares by ridiculing the inconsistency of his behaviour. It is obviously an exaggeration to say that Diopeithes had 'convicted' Leochares, but the refusal of the arbitrators appointed by Leochares to announce a decision enables the speaker to draw the inference that they would have found in his (the speaker's) favour.

**Or how can it be right …?:** Menexenus could have made his point with a direct statement, 'It cannot be right for you to decide in favour of

Leochares when even his relatives did not acquit him', but the rhetorical question invites the judges to agree with his point of view.

**I beg you, therefore, to convict Leochares:** Using a verb of pleading (Gk. *deomai*) for only the second time (cf. on 'we beg you, gentlemen', §20), Menexenus at this point explicitly recognizes that Leochares is the defendant in the trial.

**what our ancestors left to us:** As discussed by Thomas (1989, 123–31), Athenian family memory often seems to extend for no more than three generations, as far as the speaker's grandfather. So this speech is unusual in that the earliest ancestor mentioned is the speaker's great-grandfather, Dicaeogenes I (who, before the adoption, was also the maternal grandfather of Dicaeogenes III).

**not only their names but also their property:** Both Menexenus the speaker and his cousin, the son of Cephisophon, were named after their maternal grandfather Menexenus I. According to the traditional pattern of Greek naming, the first son takes the name of his father's father and the second that of his mother's father. But practice was flexible, and in this case it seems that the maternal grandfather's name was given to two first sons, perhaps as a reflection of his distinction. The wording of this sentence implies an expectation that the transmission of names should be linked with the inheritance of property, but in a predominantly patrilineal inheritance system an Athenian would not necessarily expect to inherit property from his maternal ancestors.

**We have no desire to take Leochares's own property:** By agreeing to act as surety, Leochares had accepted the risk that he might have to pay from his own resources if Dicaeogenes failed to honour the agreement. The speaker wants to convey the impression that he and his associates regarded that as a last resort; their aim in prosecuting Leochares was not to punish him, but to recover the property owed to them from Dicaeogenes himself. Cf. on 'we did not want to do so', §19.

### *35–47: Family history and the character of Dicaeogenes III*

The final 13 paragraphs of the speech focus entirely on Dicaeogenes III. In stark contrast with the patriotic exploits of Dicaeogenes I and Menexenus I (§§41–43), he is characterized as mean and untrustworthy, despite his great wealth, both in his public conduct as a citizen and in his private relations with friends and family. As observed by Griffith-Williams (2025, 229): 'This is the longest and most vitriolic character assassination in all Isaeus' speeches, but it is not mere invective. It not only condemns Dicaeogenes as a useless citizen and neglectful family member, but also reflects a pattern of behaviour – especially in terms of broken promises – that makes his alleged failure to honour his agreement with Menexenus all the more credible'. (Cf. the introduction to this speech, pp. 24–27, on the relevance of character evidence.)

**35 Dicaeogenes, gentlemen:** The speaker makes it clear that his target is now Dicaeogenes, not Leochares, addressing the judges directly to mark the start of a new division of the speech. The frequency of addresses to the judges in §§35–41 (six in all, more than a quarter of the total number in the speech) reflects the intensity of Menexenus's efforts to engage them in his condemnation of Dicaeogenes.

**as I shall reveal to you, gentlemen:** Menexenus wants to arouse the judges' expectations of some scandalous revelations.

**the estate that you adjudicated to him:** Athenian litigants frequently conflated the judges hearing a trial with those who had acted at an earlier one (cf. on 'you adjudicated in my favour', 11.18), or with the Assembly, or even with the citizen body as a whole, past as well as present (cf. Wolpert, 2003). So 'you', in this context, is a rhetorical fiction, not to be taken literally as an indication that the judges at the trial of Leochares were the same men as those who awarded the estate to Dicaeogenes at the *diadikasia* ten years earlier.

**an annual rent of 80 minas over ten years:** This refers to the ten-year period immediately before the present trial, during which Dicaeogenes had been in possession of the whole estate. Even so, 80 minas (a talent and a third) was a very substantial amount; Edwards (2007, 90, n.53) describes it as a 'suspiciously high sum'.

**neither can he show how he has spent it, gentlemen:** The implication that Dicaeogenes has concealed his wealth in order to avoid performing liturgies is elaborated at §§43–47.

**36 served as *chorēgos*:** Acting as a *chorēgos* (plur. *chorēgoi*), the producer of a play at one of the annual dramatic festivals in Athens, was, like the trierarchy, one of the public services performed by the wealthiest citizens (cf. on 'trierarch of the Paralus', §6).

**the only liturgies he has undertaken – under compulsion:** Dicaeogenes's public services were, according to Menexenus, the minimum that was required of him. In the fourth century, liturgies which had previously been voluntary increasingly became compulsory, so those who performed them were less able to claim credit for their public spirit. (On 'compulsory philanthropy', see Christ, 1990, 155–57.)

**how well he performed as *chorēgos*:** Isaeus implies that Dicaeogenes's undistinguished performance was due to his reluctance to spend more money on the liturgy. Cf. Christ (1990, 157–58): 'Wealthy men who were unable to avoid assignment to public service … might show their displeasure by spending the bare minimum necessary to carry out their obligations. This was not without its risks, since poor performance might expose a liturgist to ridicule or criticism and jeopardize his future claim to *charis*'. This passage is one of three cited by Christ as 'attacks on cheap *choregoi*'. The others are from comedy: Ar. *Ach.* 1150–52 and Eupolis fr. 329 (Kassel-Austin).

**so many trierarchs have been appointed … in such times of crisis:** The trierarchs were appointed by the generals (*Ath. Pol.* 61.1). Presumably a larger number than usual were needed for service in the Corinthian War (395–386 BC), which was in progress at the time of the trial.

**either by himself or in association with someone else:** The system of 'syntrierarchy', which was probably introduced in the late fifth century, allowed the heavy financial burden of a trierarchy (cf. on 'trierarch of the Paralus, §6) to be shared by two or more people. According to Gabrielsen (1994, 175): 'it seems certain that whether to serve as sole trierarch or as syntrierarch was a choice that lay with the individual'. Thus in a rhetorical context an Athenian could be either criticized (as here) for failing even to share the responsibility of the trierarchy, or praised for performing the service 'not jointly with another, but by himself' (Isae. 7.38).

**less capital than he has income:** This appears to be an exaggeration. Dicaeogenes's annual income from the estate was 80 minas (§§11, 35), a substantial sum but still less than half the likely qualification for the performance of liturgies (cf. on 'trierarch of the Paralus', §6).

**37 And yet, gentlemen, his father did not leave him his large fortune:** Isaeus draws a distinction between an inheritance passed directly from father to son (in which the court did not intervene) and one that was given to an adopted son or other claimant by the adjudication of the court, implying that an award from the court placed a stronger obligation on the recipient to use his wealth for the public good. There is no legal basis for this argument, but it may have carried some weight with the judges.

**by your vote:** This should obviously not be taken literally as implying that the judges sitting at the trial of Leochares were the same men as those who awarded the estate to Dicaeogenes 22 years previously; see on 'property that you adjudicated to me', 11.14, and cf. on 'the estate that you adjudicated to him', §35.

**when Lechaeum was captured:** Lechaeum, a Corinthian harbour, was captured by the Spartans in 392 BC. The speaker's reference seems casual, implying a recent event that would be fresh in the judges' minds. For Jebb (1876, 352, n.1) this was the decisive factor in convincing him that the date of the speech could not have been as late as 372 BC: 'Clearly the details set forth [in §§37–38] are comparatively *recent.* They could not have been used thus effectively after 21 years'. (On the dating of the speech, cf. on 'at Cnidus', §6, and see the introduction, pp. 18–19.)

**less than Cleonymus the Cretan:** The purpose of the ethnic is not to denigrate Cleonymus himself (cf. on 'Melas the Egyptian', §7), but to shame Dicaeogenes because the amount he promised to contribute was less than that offered by someone who was not even an Athenian citizen. Nothing further is known about Cleonymus the Cretan, who, like Melas, probably lived in Athens as a metic (resident alien). By naming him, whether or not he was likely to be known to the judges, Isaeus makes his barb about Dicaeogenes's meanness more vivid and plausible.

**38 And he promised this, but did not pay:** In the Greek text there is no conjunction between the two clauses: an example of asyndeton (for which, see on 'not given an answer …', 11.6).

**the 'list of shame':** Even if some of Isaeus's allegations against Dicaeogenes were exaggerated or unprovable, this is a detail that he could hardly have invented.

**the statues of the Eponymous Heroes:** The statues of the Eponymous Heroes, who gave their names to the ten tribes, stood near the Boule (Paus. 1.5.1).

**Indeed, gentlemen, is it surprising that he deceived me, an individual …?:** At this point the argument from probability, which was implicit throughout much of the narrative, becomes explicit: Dicaeogenes's consistently dishonest and deceitful behaviour, in both public and private matters, makes it all the more likely that he would have cheated on his agreement with Menexenus. This argument could have been expressed more simply as a direct statement in the indicative ('it is not surprising that …') but Isaeus enhances its persuasiveness with an address to the judges followed by an ironic rhetorical question.

**And I will produce witnesses of these facts for you:** See on 'Please read the witness testimony', §2, and 'You have heard the witnesses', §3.

**That, then, is the number of public services Dicaeogenes performed from such a large fortune, and how well he did so:** Once again, Isaeus uses irony to ridicule his clients' opponents; cf. on 'to do what?', §13.

**39 towards his relatives:** Menexenus now turns from Dicaeogenes's undistinguished record of public service to his allegedly stingy treatment of his family.

**robbed some of us of our property because he was stronger:** Dicaeogenes 'robbed' Menexenus and his family of 'their' property when he won the entire estate on the basis of the second will (§§7–8) and they were unable to prosecute his witnesses for false testimony because of the death of Polyaratus (§9).

**paid employment:** Menexenus has already described in detail (§§9–11) how Dicaeogenes reduced the children of Theopompus to poverty. It was the position of subordination to an employer, not the performance of manual labour in itself, that was demeaning to the status of Athenian citizens, putting them on the level of slaves or metics.

**Eileithyia:** The goddess of childbirth.

**accusing him of things I am ashamed to talk about but he was not ashamed to do:** By refusing to be more specific, Isaeus encourages the judges to exercise their imagination and think the worst. Some modern scholars have adopted the suggestion, originally made by the eighteenth-century scholar Reiske, that Dicaeogenes was accused of incest with his mother, resulting in the birth of a child. (See, e.g., Edwards, 2007, 92, n.65; Hatzilambrou, 2011, 46.) Wyse (1904, 465) records Reiske's 'opinion', but does not explicitly endorse it. Cobetto Ghiggia (2002, 219 and 2012, 212, n.68) suggests that Dicaeogenes had simply neglected his filial duty to maintain his mother (a duty that would have continued even after his adoption out of his paternal *oikos*). This, although the more sensational allegation cannot be ruled out, appears more likely in the context of Isaeus's other accusations of meanness and financial wrongdoing (cf. Griffith-Williams, 2025, 227).

**40 bitterest enemy:** On the Athenian conception of personal enmity, see on 'by friends and enemies alike', §13.

**deceived by him:** Once again, Dicaeogenes III is accused of deceiving his personal associates.

**41 And yet, gentlemen, our ancestors:** The speaker, Menexenus, now turns briefly to the civic and military achievements of his own ancestors, going back to his maternal great-grandfather Dicaeogenes I (cf. on 'what our ancestors left to us', §34). His aim is to show that Dicaeogenes III (who was also descended by birth from Dicaeogenes I but not from Menexenus I or Dicaeogenes II) does not deserve to share in their material heritage because he has shown none of their courage or public spirit.

**performed all their duties as *chorēgoi*:** See on 'served as *chorēgos*', §36.

**served continuously as trierarchs:** Cf. on 'trierarch of the Paralus', §6. In recognition of the heavy financial burden imposed by the trierarchy, a concession was introduced (possibly near the beginning of the Peloponnesian War) allowing a respite of one or two years from the performance of the service (Gabrielsen, 1994, 85–87). So, according to Menexenus's account of his ancestors' liturgical service, they went beyond the call of duty in this respect. Christ (1990, 146, n.41) observes that relatively few liturgists could apparently claim to have carried out their services voluntarily, 'and fewer still could boast that they did not take advantage of the respite permitted them by law after performing a public service (Lys. 19.29, 21.3, Is. 5.41 and 7.38)'.

**tripods:** A tripod would be erected in honour of the winning *chorēgos* at a dramatic festival, standing as a public symbol of his wealth and virtue (cf. Isae. 7.40, with Griffith-Williams, 2013).

**42 Dicaeogenes (the father of my grandfather Menexenus):** This is the only reference in the speech to Dicaeogenes I, who was not only the great-grandfather of Menexenus the speaker but also (before the adoption) the grandfather of Dicaeogenes III.

**serving as a general:** An Athenian general (Gk. *stratēgos*, plur. *stratēgoi*) was a military commander both on land and at sea, and the office also had political importance. Unlike other public officials who were appointed by lot, the *stratēgoi* were elected on merit. From the early fifth century, ten *stratēgoi* were appointed annually, one for each tribe (*phylē*).

Thomas (1989, 116–17) suggests that family tradition sometimes exaggerated the status of a speaker's ancestors, but 'No one has questioned the accuracy of the speaker of Is. v 41f. who gave his ancestors' posts with detail that suggests he was telling the truth'.

**at the time of the battle at Eleusis:** Eleusis was an Attic deme known chiefly for the annual celebration of the mysteries at the sanctuary of

Demeter and Kore. During the regime of the Thirty (see on 'disorder and civil war in the city', §7) it was a haven for the oligarchs and the scene of some of their worst atrocities.

From the sixth century, Eleusis became one of the three main fortresses for the defence of western Attica, but there is no record of a battle there. Dobree's suggested emendation to 'Halieis', a port town at the mouth of the Argolic gulf where a battle took place in 460/59 BC (Thuc. 1.105), has been adopted by Edwards (2007). Wyse (1904) retains 'Eleusis' in his text with the comment: 'The emendation has much to recommend it'. But, as Thomas (1989, 116, n.66) points out: 'there is ample room for an incident at Eleusis and it sounded impressive: perhaps in the Corinthian invasion of Megara (Thuc. 1.105) in 458/7, or at the time of the revolt of Euboia, *c.* 466, when the Peloponnesians advanced to Eleusis and Thria (Thuc. 1.114) … Insignificant "battles" are precisely what family tradition remembered'. Cf. Thomas (1989, 118): 'A family had an interest in remembering details which the general tradition did not (and we should not emend their testimony to a better-known battleground)'.

**commanding the cavalry at Spartolus:** In the summer of 429 BC, the third year of the Peloponnesian War, Athens sent a force of 2,000 hoplites and 200 cavalry against the Chalcidians based on Olynthus and the Bottiaeans. In a battle outside the city of Spartolus, the Athenians defeated the Chalcidian hoplites and some mercenaries, but the Athenian cavalry and light-armed troops were defeated by the Chalcidians (Thuc. 2.79). In the Greek text, Menexenus I was a 'phylarch', i.e. leader of his *phylē* (tribe) in the battle.

**trierarch of the Paralus at Cnidus:** See on 'at Cnidus', §6.

**43** From this point until the end of the speech, Menexenus speaks to Dicaeogenes III directly. Apostrophe (direct address to an opponent in the vocative case) is relatively rare in Isaeus's speeches, but in this passage he uses it four times: §§43, 45, 46, and 47. (Cf. Isae. 3.40, 69, 70, 71; 6.25, 53; 9.23; 11.4, all cited by Denommé, 1974, 137–38.)

**The inheritance you received … wickedly and disgracefully ruined:** The Greek word *oikos*, here translated as 'inheritance', is sometimes used interchangeably with *klēros* (see on 'any part of the estate …', §14) but it has a wider semantic range including 'house' (in the sense of 'lineage' or 'line of descent') and 'family'; an *oikos*, in the sense of 'household' or 'family', was an essential constituent of the Athenian *polis*. In the present context, it seems that Isaeus chose the word deliberately to evoke these connotations in the minds of the judges. Dicaeogenes III has 'ruined' his inheritance by selling off property and thus breaking up the ancestral estate, and brought dishonour to the family by his conduct. For the various meanings of *oikos*, see MacDowell (1989), and on its significance in this passage, Cobetto Ghiggia (2002, 222–23).

**you converted the property into cash:** Menexenus implicitly accuses Dicaeogenes of selling off property in order to conceal his wealth and thus avoid public services (cf. Gabrielsen, 1994, 56): 'One could convert realty into cash through sale (*exargyrosis*), and then see to it that no one could keep track of this. However, those opting for this arrangement might have had to face public resentment …'). By suggesting that Dicaeogenes is wealthier than he admits, Menexenus is also trying to forestall a claim from Dicaeogenes that he cannot afford to redeem the mortgaged property and hand it over to Menexenus and his associates.

**but what did you spend it on?:** Of the 11 rhetorical questions in this speech, five are directed personally at Dicaeogenes in these concluding paragraphs.

**neither … impoverished yourself through horse-rearing:** The breeding of horses was not only a military necessity for Athens, but also a luxury in which the wealthy indulged for sport (satirized by Aristophanes in *Clouds*, where Strepsiades is nearly driven to financial ruin by his son's extravagant expenditure on horses). This created tensions between democratic ideology and the values of the elite; 'The horse remained a status symbol long after cavalry service ceased to be the privilege of the rich' (*OCD*, 'horses').

The phrase 'impoverished yourself through horse-rearing' translates a single word in the Greek text: *kathippotrophēkas*; in compound verbs beginning with *kata-*, the prefix often has a pejorative sense, denoting excessive expenditure on a particular activity. (For further examples and discussion, see Griffith-Williams, 2013, 244.)

**never ransomed a single prisoner of war:** In other passages from the Attic orators (cited by Cobetto Ghiggia, 2002, 223, n.412), the ransoming of prisoners of war is mentioned as a philanthropic gesture (Lys. 12.20, 19.59) or, in a specific case, as a sign of the close friendship between the prisoner and his benefactor (Isae. 7.8). Here, Menexenus implies that a wealthy and public-spirited Athenian would have been expected to provide ransom money, but he is evidently unable to specify any particular prisoner(s) of war for whom Dicaeogenes ought to have assumed responsibility.

**44 Menexenus spent three talents ... in the sculptor's workshop:** This passage is problematic. If the dedicator of the statues was Menexenus I, who died in 429 BC (see on 'commanding the cavalry at Spartolus, §42), responsibility for completing the dedication would have passed to his son, Dicaeogenes II, who lived for at least 15 more years (see on 'at Cnidus', §6). It seems hardly credible that the latter could have neglected the duty for so long – or, even if he did, that the statues were still in the sculptor's studio at the time of the present trial 22 years after his own death. As discussed by Wyse (1904, 475–76), the passage makes even less sense if the dedicator is taken to be Menexenus son of Cephisophon (who was almost certainly still alive at the time of the present trial). Others (Roussel, 1926, 102, n.1), Forster (1927, 190, n.d) have raised the possibility of textual corruption, but without proposing an emendation.

**money to which you're not entitled ... the statues that are rightfully theirs:** Whatever the truth behind the anecdote about the abandoned statues, it enables Isaeus to make the rhetorical point that Dicaeogenes III's personal avarice is matched by his disrespect of the gods. (Wyse, 1904, 476, puts this in characteristically exaggerated terms: 'In vituperation Greek pleaders are absolutely reckless, and Isaeus was a man who would stick at nothing; the broadside of invective here is too furious for the judges to reflect on the justice of each accusation'.)

**45 What reason will you give for the judges to acquit you, Dicaeogenes?:** Menexenus now openly addresses Dicaeogenes as if he, not Leochares, were the defendant (cf. on 'to convict Leochares', §34). With a cluster of four ironic rhetorical questions in §§45 and 46, Menexenus exposes Dicaeogenes's failure to support the state either through civic or military service or by financial contributions. An Athenian litigant seeking the favour of the judges would often refer to his record of public service, but Menexenus predicts that Dicaeogenes will be unable to do so.

**the enemy:** Here and at §46, the Greek word is not *echthros* (for which, see on 'by friends and enemies alike', §13), but *polemios*, designating an enemy of the state rather than a personal enemy.

**war taxes:** Special war taxes (Gk. *eisphorai*) were levied on the 300 richest Athenians in times of need.

**46 the long and critical war:** Another allusion to the Corinthian War of 395–386 BC, which was in progress when the speech was delivered. (Cf. on 'sent ... Cephisodotus to Corinth', §11; 'in such times of crisis', §36, 'when Lechaeum was captured', §37.)

**although you were a citizen ... Olynthians and islanders:** Again (cf. on 'less than Cleonymus the Cretan', §37), Dicaeogenes's neglect of his civic duties is contrasted with the commitment of others who were not even Athenian citizens.

**your ancestors who killed the tyrant:** Harmodius, one of the two celebrated Athenian 'tyrant-slayers' (the other being Aristogeiton), was an ancestor of Dicaeogenes III on his father's side. In 514 BC Harmodius and Aristogeiton killed Hipparchus, younger brother of the tyrant Hippias, and were executed, four years before the Athenian tyranny was brought to an end by the expulsion of Hippias. Popular tradition credited them with a more central role in the ending of the tyranny, and they were elevated to the status of heroes (Thuc. 1.20, 6.53–59).

Hatzilambrou (2011, 46) points out that an Athenian of such distinguished ancestry as Dicaeogenes III was a 'difficult opponent', and Isaeus was 'taking a risk' with regard to the judges' tolerance of such a strong attack on his character.

**I don't think you share in their prowess at all:** Isaeus makes this point, elaborated in §47, in order to deflect any admiration or respect the judges might feel towards Dicaeogenes III because of his ancestry.

**47 you chose to possess our property rather than their reputation:** The reputation of a family, like its property, was transmitted from generation to generation, but an adopted son lost his legal relationship with his natural family, relinquishing his inheritance rights in his father's *oikos*. Menexenus tendentiously presents the adoption as an active choice on the part of Dicaeogenes III, for materialistic reasons, with the words 'our property' implying that Dicaeogenes was not entitled to the inheritance.

**preferred to be called the son of Dicaeogenes rather than of Harmodius:** Again, the wording is tendentious, but Menexenus makes the valid point that after the adoption, Dicaeogenes III is no longer entitled to claim any credit for the distinguished ancestry of his birth family.

**the right to dine in the Prytaneum:** The Prytaneum, the symbolic centre of the Athenian state, was supposedly founded by Theseus (Thuc. 2.15). It housed the city's communal hearth, eternal flame, and public dining-room, and the right to dine there for life, at public expense, was among the highest civic honours. A fifth-century decree (possibly dating from the

430s) conferred the right on descendants of the tyrannicides Aristogeiton and Harmodius, but it was confined to the oldest living male descendant of each. So if Dicaeogenes III was the younger son of Proxenus (as seems probable, given that he was named after his maternal grandfather), he would not have been likely to benefit from the dining rights even if he had not been adopted out of the family. (Cf. Wyse, 1904, 481–82; Edwards, 2007, 94; Blok, 2017, 137, n.144.)

**tax exemptions:** Exemption from a tax or liturgical obligation (Gk. *ateleia*) was 'one of the rarest and most prestigious honours and privileges available in Athens' (Kremmydas, 2007, 43); its significance, as Kremmydas explains, was that the honorand's benefactions to the city were considered more valuable than any future contribution he (or his descendants, if the exemption was hereditary) might make. The exemptions did not extend to military liturgies or war taxes.

**in which you do not share at all, Dicaeogenes:** For the concept of 'sharing' in an abstract quality such as courage, see on 'I don't think you share in their prowess at all', §46.

The speech comes to an abrupt and unexpected conclusion, lacking the conventional epilogue and ending with a final apostrophe to Dicaeogenes. This has led to some speculation that the speaker ran out of time in court, or that the manuscript text is incomplete, but it seems more likely that the abruptness of the ending was a deliberate tactic on Isaeus's part: a powerful and dramatic expression of the speaker's contempt, after which anything further would have come as an anti-climax (cf. Avramovič, 1997, 116–17).

# ISAEUS 11

# ON THE ESTATE OF HAGNIAS

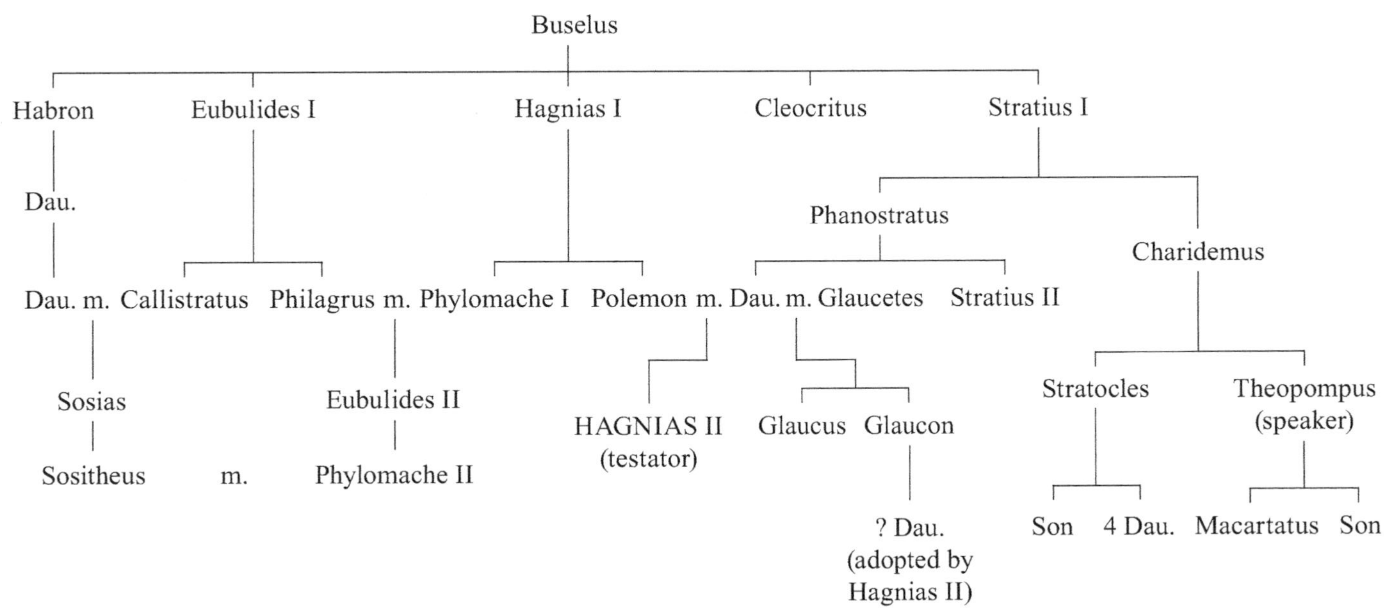


The Family of Hagnias: Partial stemma

# INTRODUCTION

Isaeus 11 is the defence speech from a public action for mistreatment of an orphan (*eisangelia kakōseōs orphanou*). Theopompus, the speaker, was one of the guardians of his nephew and nieces, the children of his deceased brother Stratocles. He had recently inherited the estate of a second cousin, Hagnias, which was worth about two talents. The prosecutor in the *eisangelia,* another guardian of Stratocles's children, claimed that half of the estate should go to Stratocles's son, from whom Theopompus was wrongfully withholding it. We do not know the names of either Theopompus's orphaned nephew or his fellow guardian and prosecutor, but the latter, who was evidently not a blood relation of Theopompus, may have been a brother of Stratocles's wife (that is, the boy's maternal uncle).[1] There had been previous litigation over Hagnias's estate, and the trial at which this speech was delivered took place some years after his death.

## THE DISPUTE OVER HAGNIAS'S ESTATE: SUMMARY

Hagnias left a will in which he adopted a niece, with the proviso that if she died childless the estate should pass to Glaucon, a half-brother of Hagnias by the same mother. The will was apparently uncontested during the adopted daughter's lifetime; she died unmarried, and Glaucon duly took over the estate. Hagnias's cousin Eubulides had been preparing to claim the estate as next of kin, but died before the claim came to court. It was then pursued by his daughter Phylomache II (acting through her husband Sositheus), who succeeded in having the will annulled and took over the estate from Glaucon.

After this trial (the first *diadikasia*) Theopompus, his brother Stratocles, and their cousin Stratius, who had not previously contested the estate, decided to challenge Phylomache's tenure. They each submitted a claim to one third of the estate, but both Stratius

1 Cf. MacDowell (1978a, 106).

and Stratocles died before the dispute came to court. Theopompus proceeded on his own account, won the second *diadikasia*, and took over the whole estate from Phylomache. Some of his witnesses were prosecuted for false testimony, but it is not clear whether the case against them went to court. If it did, Theopompus was evidently vindicated, since the estate remained in his possession until his death, when it passed to his son Macartatus. Later, Macartatus was faced with a challenge from Sositheus (speaking on behalf of his son, who, as he claimed, had become the closest surviving relative of Hagnias as the result of a posthumous adoption)[2], in a speech that survives in the Demosthenic corpus as [Dem.] 43.

## DATING AND CHRONOLOGY

Despite some ambiguity in the sources, it seems most likely that Hagnias died in the late 370s, and that Isaeus 11 was delivered around 359 BC. The starting point for the dating of the speech is a statement by one of Sositheus's witnesses ([Dem.] 43.31) that Phylomache won the estate 'in the archonship of Nicophemus' (i.e. the year 361/60). On that basis, although the authenticity of the witness testimony is uncertain,[3] it is generally accepted that Isaeus 11 was delivered at some time in the early 350s. Wevers's stylometric method of dating also supports a date around 360.[4]

Although Isaeus does not explicitly say so, Hagnias presumably died on the embassy mentioned at 11.8. Earlier scholars, linking him with the man of that name mentioned by the lexicographer Harpocration, thought that he was killed in the course of an embassy to Sparta during the Theban War (378–371 BC).[5] But according to *Hellenica Oxyrhynchia* (first published in 1908), an ambassador named Hagnias was among those killed on an Athenian embassy to Persia in 396 BC.[6] This earlier

---

2 On posthumous adoption, see General Introduction, p. 4.

3 For discussion, see Scafuro (2011, 137, n.25).

4 Wevers (1969, 19).

5 Blass (1874, 531); Jebb (1876, 358–59); Wyse (1904, 684).

6 *Hell. Oxy.* (ed. McKechnie and Kern) VII.1.

date, adopted by some commentators,[7] creates a dilemma: if we agree, we must either reject the evidence of [Dem.] 43 on the dating of the speech, or accept an implausibly long interval of 35 years between the death of Hagnias and the trial in which Isaeus 11 was delivered.[8] The solution advocated by Sally Humphreys after a thorough review of the evidence, and now generally accepted,[9] is to revert to a date in the late 370s for Hagnias's death, possibly on an embassy to Macedon in 375 or 373. As Humphreys concludes:

> the identification with the embassy of 396 is not obligatory, creates serious chronological difficulties, and does not even fit with Isaeus' text in 11.8. We should therefore return to a date in the 370s for Hagnias' death and assume that his adopted daughter died, before reaching marriageable age, in the late 360s, after which the claim to the estate by Glaucon, the opposition of Eubulides II, his death, the attack on the will by Sositheus and Phylomache, and the *diadikasia* in which the estate was awarded to Theopompus, all followed in fairly rapid succession.[10]

## HAGNIAS'S FAMILY AND THE ORDER OF SUCCESSION

If an Athenian died leaving no legitimate descendants, and without leaving a will – or if, as in the case of Hagnias, he did leave a will which was later overturned by the court – his estate went to his next of kin, that is his closest surviving collateral relative(s). Isaeus 11 begins with a reading of the law setting out the order of succession. The text of the law is not preserved with the speech, but Isaeus's paraphrase (11.1–3) may be compared with the law cited at [Dem.] 43.51.[11] That text is

---

7 Roussel (1926, 193, n.1); Forster (1927, 382); Thompson (1976, 12).

8 For other difficulties with chronology, see commentary on 'that embassy which turned out so well for the city', §8.

9 Humphreys (1983), followed by Edwards (2007, 178) and Scafuro (2011, 137–38).

10 Humphreys (1983, 225).

11 See General Introduction, pp. 3–4.

itself defective, and some of the details are uncertain, but the essential features, insofar as they are relevant to Isaeus 11, are clear enough. Priority was given to the dead man's relatives on his father's side: first brothers and their children, then sisters and their children, down to 'the children of cousins'. If there was no-one close enough on the father's side, the succession passed to the dead man's closest relatives on his mother's side, in the same order. An Athenian's closest relatives, as defined by this law, formed his *anchisteia*,[12] whose mutual rights and obligations included a duty of care in old age as well as rights of inheritance. Membership of Hagnias's *anchisteia* is the key legal issue in Isaeus 11. Theopompus has already established his membership, at the *diadikasia* where he won the estate from Phylomache, and he now seeks to refute a claim from his opponent that his nephew (Stratocles's son) is also a member.

Under the terms of Hagnias's will, his half-brother, Glaucon, took over the estate after the death of his adopted daughter. But Hagnias and Glaucon were half-brothers through the same mother, so, once the will was annulled, Hagnias's relatives on his father's side had priority in the order of succession. As can be seen from the stemma on p. 110, Hagnias II and his patrilineal kinsmen were descendants of Buselus of Oeum, who had five sons: Hagnias I, Eubulides I, Stratius I, Cleocritus, and Habron. Isaeus identifies their sons – Hagnias II (son of Polemon and grandson of Hagnias I), Eubulides II (son of Philagrus and grandson of Eubulides I), Stratius II (son of Callistratus and grandson of Stratius I), and Stratocles and Theopompus (sons of Charidemus and grandsons of Stratius I) – as 'children of cousins' in the sense that their fathers were first cousins (§8). Theopompus himself, when he submitted his claim to the estate at the second *diadikasia*, gave his relationship to Hagnias as 'cousin's son' (§18).

In modern English terms, Hagnias II, Eubulides II, Theopompus, Stratocles, and Stratius II were all second cousins, because they were descended from the same great-grandfather. We learn from [Dem.] 43 that Hagnias II and Eubulides II were also first cousins (descendants

12 On the wider meaning of *anchisteia*, see p. 133.

of the same grandfather), because Eubulides's mother, Phylomache I (the wife of Philagrus) was a daughter of Hagnias I and sister of Hagnias II's father Polemon. But the identity of Phylomache I as a full legitimate sister of Polemon – which, according to Sositheus, was successfully but wrongly disputed by Theopompus at the second *diadikasia* – is never mentioned by Isaeus.

Modern scholarship on Isaeus 11 and [Dem.] 43 has, rightly, identified the ambiguity of *anepsios* ('cousin') and the meaning of *anepsiōn paides* ('children of cousins') as a problem. But the question is not, as commentators have tended to assume, the legitimacy of Theopompus's own claim to Hagnias's estate as a 'cousin's child' (*anepsiou pais*, §11). Rather, the point in dispute between Theopompus and the prosecutor was the status of Stratocles's son, and whether his relationship to Hagnias (second cousin once removed) also entitled him to a share in the estate.

## ISAEUS 11 AND [DEMOSTHENES] 43

After her defeat at the second *diadikasia*, Phylomache and her husband Sositheus did not give up their aspirations to Hagnias's estate, although it appears that they did not challenge Theopompus's possession during his lifetime. Some time after his death, Sositheus instigated a new claim to the estate on behalf of his son, after having him posthumously adopted as Eubulides III, the son of Phylomache's father Eubulides. The speech delivered in court on his behalf by Sositheus, which survives as [Dem.] 43, enables us – unusually – to see some aspects of the case from the opposing side. Sositheus, in [Dem.] 43, continues to maintain that his wife Phylomache was Hagnias's legitimate next of kin, and asserts that she was deprived of the estate through the trickery of her opponents.

Sositheus's speech *Against Macartatus* is the work of an inferior speechwriter, certainly not Demosthenes but either a second-rate logographer or perhaps Sositheus himself.[13] The speech not only

13 Modern scholars almost unanimously reject the attribution to Demosthenes, though according to MacDowell (2009, 87): 'there is no strong reason to deny that

reveals a lack of rhetorical skill and limited understanding of Athenian inheritance law, but – in sharp contrast with Isaeus's highly economical style – it is also overloaded with unnecessarily detailed information more likely to confuse or distract the judges than to help them understand the complexities of the case. From a modern commentator's perspective, this has some advantages: [Dem.] 43 includes the names of many family members who are either not named or not mentioned at all by Isaeus, and it also gives an account of the earlier litigation which includes some information omitted by Isaeus (while itself omitting some details that Isaeus includes). But both speakers had their own reasons for focusing on different aspects of the litigation, and, as we shall see, critics who are suspicious of Isaeus's integrity have sometimes been over-eager to accept Sositheus's version of events. Above all, it needs to be remembered that the two speeches do not in any straightforward sense represent two sides of the same case. They originate from two separate trials, several years apart, in which the issues were different: Theopompus's speech, unlike that of Sositheus, is not a claim to the estate of Hagnias but a defence against a charge of mistreatment of an orphan.

Sositheus does not mention Hagnias's testamentary adoption of his niece; his account begins with the first *diadikasia*, at which Phylomache won the estate from Glaucon. At this first *diadikasia*, according to Sositheus ([Dem.] 43.4), Glaucon produced a will which he had concocted with his brother Glaucus, and Theopompus testified in support of it. But Phylomache successfully proved that the will was a forgery, so she won the case, the will was annulled, and she took possession of the estate. Isaeus, in contrast, refers only very briefly to the first *diadikasia*, saying merely that Phylomache and her associates 'won the case against those who claimed on the basis of the will' (11.9), without mentioning that Theopompus was involved in any capacity.

The two speeches also diverge significantly in their accounts of the second *diadikasia*, at which Phylomache lost the estate to Theopompus. We know from [Dem.] 43 that Phylomache claimed

Demosthenes is the author'. For a reasoned view to the contrary, see, e.g., Scafuro (2011, 138).

Hagnias's estate as the granddaughter of Phylomache I (that is, Hagnias's first cousin once removed) and that Theopompus defeated her by proving that Phylomache I was not a full legitimate sister of Hagnias's father Polemon. (It is unclear whether Theopompus argued that Phylomache I was an illegitimate daughter of Hagnias I or his legitimate daughter by a different mother from Polemon, or not his daughter at all. Sositheus, in any event, accuses him of a 'monstrous lie'.[14]) Isaeus gives an equally tendentious but vaguer account, saying only that Phylomache and her associates 'were lying when they tried to explain her kinship [to Hagnias]' and 'easily convicted' by Theopompus of submitting a false claim.[15] By omitting to refer specifically to Phylomache's relationship to Hagnias as a first cousin once removed, he focuses the judges on her identity as a second cousin once removed, which places her in the same relationship to Hagnias as Stratocles's son and thus, as he repeatedly says, outside the *anchisteia*.

Apart from Theopompus and Phylomache, Isaeus mentions only one other claimant at the second *diadikasia*, Hagnias's mother (11.16–17), who is not mentioned at all in [Dem.] 43. According to Sositheus, however, Phylomache's tenure of the estate was challenged by four rival claimants: Theopompus, Glaucus, Glaucon, and a 'friend' of theirs called Eupolemus ([Dem.] 43.7). All of these, according to Sositheus, were acting in collusion to deprive Phylomache of the estate, so it was four against one at the trial: five claimants, each with an equal share of the time allocation, but four of them telling the same concocted story, and not allowing Sositheus enough time to refute them and put Phylomache's case effectively. The judges, he says, were confused by his opponents' fraudulent tactics, and in the event, Theopompus won only three or four more votes than Phylomache ([Dem.] 43.10).[16]

Attempts to reconcile the conflicting accounts are inevitably speculative and inconclusive, but it is worth examining some of the

---

14 [Dem.] 43.29; see commentary on 'what was not true', §17.

15 11.17.

16 See commentary on 'those who were then acting as judges … gave their vote to me', §18, and 'a separate voting urn', §21.

discrepancies in more detail. A point to note at the outset is that Isaeus never explicitly says that Hagnias's mother and Phylomache were Theopompus's *only* opponents at the second *diadikasia*, and neither (unlike Sositheus) does he specify the total number of claimants to the estate. In fact, he does not purport to give a full account of the litigation; rather, he focuses on those aspects of it that were most relevant to his argument that Stratocles's son was outside the legal order of succession to Hagnias.

Why, in particular, does Isaeus not mention that Glaucon and Glaucus were claimants to the estate? One possibility is that they were not involved in the second *diadikasia* as litigants, but as representatives of their (and Hagnias's) mother.[17] But if they did claim the estate for themselves, the fact that they were related to Hagnias only through their mother would have put them at a disadvantage, so they would have needed to convince the judges on two points: first – in agreement, but not necessarily in collusion, with Theopompus – that Phylomache (I) was not a full legitimate sister of Polemon and therefore Phylomache (II) had no claim to the estate as Hagnias's first cousin once removed. Secondly, they would have had to prove that Theopompus himself was outside the *anchisteia* – by arguing, presumably, that 'children of cousins' did not include second cousins.[18] That, of course, is a point that Isaeus would not have wanted to bring to the attention of the judges at the *eisangelia*, and there is the further point that – if Sositheus's account is correct – Theopompus had supported Glaucon at the first *diadikasia* but then switched sides to oppose him at the second. As we have seen from the example of Menexenus (son of Cephisophon) in Isaeus 5, such changes of allegiance were not unknown in Athenian inheritance disputes, but neither Theopompus's involvement in the first *diadikasia* nor Glaucon's in the second was strictly relevant to Theopompus's case in Isaeus 11. The omission of such details, although it has been

17 An alternative conjecture is that Hagnias's mother was represented by Eupolemus (see p. 119).

18 As discussed by Scafuro (2011, 131–32); cf. commentary on 'it is agreed by everyone', §11.

seen by some scholars as suspicious,[19] may be taken as an example of Isaeus's skill in making the best case for his client:

> In any case, Theopompos does not want to bring up old issues that have been settled, so he explains his position as succinctly as possible. That way he does not confuse the question at hand and does not raise doubts about the justness of his previous victory.[20]

Another topic of scholarly speculation is the identity of Eupolemus and his relationship to Hagnias, about which nothing definite is known. One conjecture is that he could have been a grandson of Hagnias I, claiming the estate of Hagnias II as the child of a first cousin.[21] That seems improbable, however, given that as a first cousin once removed he would have had a stronger claim to the estate than Theopompus. According to an alternative hypothesis,[22] he did not claim the estate on his own account but represented Hagnias's mother at the trial, either as her current husband or some other male relative. This, although impossible to prove, is plausibly consistent with both Isaeus's narrative, where Eupolemus could be the unnamed 'legal representative' (*kyrios*) and that of Sositheus, who may have had his own reasons for not wanting to disclose that Hagnias's mother was a party to the litigation.

It is, in fact, difficult to understand how Hagnias's mother could have sustained a credible claim to the estate, given that she had no legal standing as mother of the deceased and, as a female second cousin, was not his next of kin.[23] Scholars have speculated that the real reason for her claim may have been the need for evidence about the status of Phylomache I, which was crucial to the defeat of Phylomache II. Hagnias's mother, as the (former) wife of Polemon,

19 Notably by Wyse (1904, 689); see the introductory note to §§15–19 in the commentary.

20 Thompson (1976, 27).

21 Broadbent (1968, 96–97).

22 See Scafuro (2011, 129) and cf. commentary on 'the legal representatives of Hagnias's mother', §16.

23 See commentary on 'excluded by the law because it gives preference to males', §17.

would have been in the best position to know whether Phylomache I was her husband's full and legitimate sister, but being a woman she could not testify as a witness. Perhaps the most obvious way of using her knowledge would have been for a male witness to testify on her behalf, but witnesses were vulnerable to prosecution for false testimony, so the safest way of introducing her 'evidence' to the court was by making her a party to the case. If that hypothesis is correct, it adds some credence to Sositheus's claim of collusion against Phylomache II; but on the other hand, if the 'evidence' of Hagnias's mother was true, the strategy was not necessarily unfair. The intervention of Hagnias's mother, in whatever capacity, could have been highly damaging to Phylomache, and that probably explains why Sositheus does not mention her.[24]

## ISAEUS 11 IN MODERN SCHOLARSHIP

This speech has probably contributed more than any other to Isaeus's reputation as a devious and unscrupulous advocate and an unreliable source of Athenian law.[25] The scholarly debate on Isaeus 11 has been largely concerned with the meaning of 'children of cousins' (*anepsiōn paides*), and whether Theopompus correctly described himself as a 'cousin's son' (*anepsiou pais*, §18) in relation to Hagnias. In the nineteenth and early twentieth centuries it seemed obvious to eminent scholars such as Friedrich Blass, R. C. Jebb,[26] and William Wyse that *anepsios* must mean 'first cousin', so that *anepsiōn paides* are 'first cousins once removed'. So the earlier court's decision to award the estate to Theopompus – a second cousin of Hagnias – was, in Jebb's words, 'manifestly unjust'.[27] And according to Wyse: 'All critics are now of opinion that [the award of the estate to Theopompus at the second *diadikasia*] was a blunder'.[28] Wyse's commentary, valuable

24 For fuller discussion, see Scafuro (2011, 129–31).

25 Cf. Avramovič (1997, 236).

26 Blass (1874, 530); Jebb (1876, 357).

27 Jebb (1876, 357); see commentary on 'a cousin's son', §10.

28 Wyse (1904, 673).

as it remains in some respects, is deeply flawed by his underlying assumption that the Athenian judges were an ignorant rabble, easily taken in by an unscrupulous speechwriter such as Isaeus. Theopompus, according to Wyse, was a rogue; he and Stratocles knew that their claim to the estate of Hagnias was 'unfounded'; in reality 'Isaeus has suppressed facts indispensable to a proper understanding of the situation'. Although he credits Isaeus with 'a technical power comparable with the mature art of Demosthenes', Wyse believes that technical skill was used 'to cloak the fact that [Theopompus] was excluded by the very law which he invokes against his opponent'.[29]

This restrictive interpretation of Athenian inheritance law, translating *anepsios* only as 'first cousin' and so denying Theopompus's right to the estate, was followed by some later twentieth-century commentators, including Pierre Roussel in the introduction to his French translation of Isaeus 11.[30] J. K. Davies took a similar view, describing Theopompus as 'a thorough-paced scoundrel'.[31] But E. S. Forster, in his introduction to the speech in the Loeb edition, takes a markedly different stance (without reference to earlier scholarship):

> In this speech the word *anepsios* is translated as 'cousin'. But it covers not only 'first cousin' but also 'first cousin once removed' and 'second cousin'. It does not however cover 'second cousin once removed'. Theopompus was a second cousin, and as such had a claim to the estate. But his nephew (ward) had not.[32]

Both Harrison (1947) and Miles (1950) agree that *anepsios* could mean 'first cousin once removed'. As Harrison points out:

> If … the orthodox view is right, we are bound to rate very low the competence of the jury system in cases of this kind. It is not merely that a verbal quibble has misled a jury (and we must remember that presumably at the original trial Theopompus' opponents had the opportunity of exposing the quibble), but we should have to suppose

29 Wyse (1904, 674–76).

30 Roussel (1926, 188–89).

31 Davies (1971, 84).

32 Forster (1927, 387).

> that the preliminary proceedings before the archon were quite ineffective for preventing errors of this kind.[33]

The 'orthodox view' is firmly opposed by Wesley Thompson in his 1976 work *De Hagniae Hereditate*, a running commentary on both Isaeus 11 and [Dem.] 43. As he explains in his preface to the book, Thompson adopts a 'heterodox standpoint', accepting that Theopompus's claim to the estate was legally valid, and 'attempting to correct Wyse's malicious treatment of Isaeus and his client'.[34] Although some of Thompson's detailed comments on Athenian legal procedure are questionable, his overall method is sound and the book remains a valuable corrective to Wyse's scepticism.[35]

An alternative view, somewhere between the extremes of orthodoxy and heterodoxy, is that the wording of the law was ambiguous even in fourth-century Athens, so that Isaeus, although he was not unquestionably right, did at least have an arguable point.[36]

## THE *EISANGELIA KAKŌSEŌS ORPHANOU*

Whatever view one takes of Isaeus's interpretation of the law, it is not Theopompus's claim to the estate of Hagnias that is in dispute in Isaeus 11, but that of his nephew. It is worth repeating that the case for which Isaeus 11 was written was (despite the misleading title given to the speech in the manuscripts, 'On the estate of Hagnias') a prosecution for mistreatment of an orphan (*eisangelia kakōseōs orphanou*), not a claim to the estate of Hagnias.[37]

---

33 Harrison (1947, 42).

34 Thompson (1976, x).

35 As MacDowell (1978b, 381) points out, the book would be more accessible if it included a general introduction and an index. MacDowell finds Thompson's argument that *anepsiou pais* means 'second cousin' 'not … fully convincing'. He concludes that Thompson 'has made a contribution which will be of interest to specialists in Athenian prosopography'.

36 MacDowell (1978a, 107), Scafuro (2011, 132); see commentary on 'It is agreed by everyone', §11.

37 That point has not always been properly understood by modern scholars.

Theopompus had already established his right to inherit the estate when he defeated Phylomache at the second *diadikasia*. As we have seen, his status as a 'cousin's son' was probably disputed by Glaucus and Glaucon, but Theopompus won the case, and (leaving aside the failed prosecutions for false testimony) his right to the estate was never, so far as we know, challenged in his lifetime. The legal issue between him and the prosecutor in the *eisangelia* is not his own right to inherit the estate but that of his nephew. His fellow guardian, the prosecutor in the present trial, accuses him of keeping the whole of the estate for himself, depriving his nephew of his rightful share. It would not have been in the prosecutor's interest to question Theopompus's relationship to Hagnias as a 'cousin's son', or deny the validity of his claim to a share in the estate: if Theopompus did not have a legitimate claim to the estate of Hagnias, then neither, *a fortiori*, did his nephew, Stratocles's son.[38]

According to the prosecutor's interpretation of the law, after the death of Stratocles, what would have been his share of the estate should have gone to his son. The prosecutor says that Theopompus had promised Stratocles he would share the estate with the boy, so it seemed unnecessary to submit a formal claim to the court on the boy's behalf, but Theopompus is now refusing to honour his agreement with Stratocles. Both Theopompus and his opponent, then, accept that he was entitled to claim the estate as a 'cousin's son', and that if Stratocles had survived, he and Theopompus would each have been entitled to half of the estate. The legal issue between them is whether, now that Stratocles has died, what would have been his share of the estate legally belongs to his son.

---

See, e.g., Harris (2013, 385), where the issue in Isae. 11 is incorrectly defined as 'Does Theopompus have the right to inherit the estate of Hagnias?', and cf. Usher (1999, 154), where the prosecutor is said to be 'indirectly challenging [Theopompus's] title to the estate by prosecuting him for the mistreatment of an orphan'.

38 What may be a more significant point in Theopompus's favour is that his status as a 'cousin's son' is never explicitly denied by Sositheus, the speaker of [Dem.] 43. For details, see commentary on 'a cousin's son', §10.

There are three interconnected strands to Theopompus's defence:

> Stratocles's son has no legal claim to the estate, because he is not within the recognized degrees of relationship (the *anchisteia*) to Hagnias; Theopompus himself is the only surviving relative of Hagnias with a legitimate claim.
>
> Theopompus did not make a private agreement with Stratocles about the division of the estate.
>
> Theopompus is the victim of a malicious prosecution by his fellow guardian, arising from a quarrel between them about the management of the orphans' estate.

### *a) The legal order of succession*

Theopompus accuses the prosecutor of 'twisting' the law by arguing that after Stratocles died, his right to inherit half of the estate of Hagnias descended to his son. As he implies at the beginning of the speech, that would have been correct if Stratocles and Hagnias had been brothers, since the law gave precedence to 'brothers and nephews' on the father's side (§1). In other words, the patrilineal brothers of a deceased Athenian were considered to be his closest collateral relatives, but if one of them was already dead, his share could be claimed by his son(s), the nephew or nephews of the deceased.[39] But after the 'children of cousins' on the father's side, the right of inheritance does not pass to *their* children, but to the relatives of the deceased on his mother's side (§11).

The prosecutor may well have pointed out that if Stratocles had survived to take his share of the estate, that share, along with the rest of his property, would have passed to his son when Stratocles himself died, and (as the prosecutor may have argued) it was unfair to deprive the boy of his share just because Stratocles had happened to die at the wrong time. There is certainly some force in the argument that Stratocles's son was unlucky, but Theopompus (or rather Isaeus on his behalf) was undoubtedly right in his interpretation of the law.

39 In modern legal terminology, this is known as the 'principle of representation', because the nephew in this situation takes a share of the estate as the representative of his deceased father.

***b) The possibility of a private agreement***

When it comes to the second point in Theopompus's defence, his denial that he and Stratocles made a private agreement about the division of Hagnias's estate, Isaeus and his client seem to be on much shakier ground. Since it was impossible to prove conclusively that no such agreement existed, Isaeus has to rely on arguments from probability. He continues to frame the argument in legal terms, aiming to show that Theopompus has acted throughout in accordance with the law (and, at least by implication, that it would have been *illegal* for him to act in any other way). As Theopompus points out, an agreement between him and Stratocles to share the estate, if either of them won, would have been pointless: they were both in the same relationship to Hagnias, each of them was claiming half of the estate, and their claims (if Stratocles had survived) would have stood or fallen together.

The argument is perfectly sound, as far as it goes, but it overlooks the possibility of a different (and more likely) form of agreement: that if either Theopompus or Stratocles died before their claims came to court, and the survivor won the whole estate, he would share it with his deceased brother's offspring. The two brothers probably understood the law and knew that, if one of them died before the conclusion of the court case, his son would not be legally entitled to a share in the estate. So they might well have agreed that, if that happened, the survivor would simply give half of the estate to his nephew as a gift. Isaeus does not address this possibility until after the less plausible scenario has been excluded, and he continues to frame the argument in strictly legal terms. Why, on the one hand, should Theopompus have made a private agreement if the boy was legally entitled to half the estate, which could have been claimed on his behalf (§24)? If, on the other hand, the boy had no legal claim to the estate, why should Theopompus agree to share it with him when he was legally entitled to keep the whole estate himself (§25)?

It must surely have occurred to at least some of the judges that Theopompus could have acted more generously out of affection for his brother and nephew, or a sense of fairness. Isaeus evidently wrote the concluding part of the speech, where Theopompus enumerates his own property and that of Stratocles, in anticipation of such a response.

Ostensibly a rebuttal of 'slanderous' allegations from the opponent, this part of the speech continues the probability argument from a different angle, seeking to convey the impression that there was no need for Theopompus to share Hagnias's estate with his nephew, who was already amply provided for by the property that Stratocles had left to him. We shall, of course, never know for certain whether Theopompus had reneged on an agreement with his brother, or whether the whole idea of an agreement was a fiction invented by his opponent.[40] But it seems clear that this, rather than Isaeus's interpretation of Athenian inheritance law, was the weak point in Theopompus's case.

If the judges in the *eisangelia* were persuaded that Theopompus was trying to get out of an obligation (albeit moral rather than legal) they could justifiably convict him of *kakōsis orphanou* (mistreatment of an orphan). That verdict would not have led directly to the restoration of the property to Stratocles's son, but perhaps that was not the prosecutor's real aim in bringing the case; it is possible that he simply wanted to punish Theopompus, in particular by having him removed from the guardianship. That leads us to the third strand in Theopompus's defence.

### c) A malicious prosecution: Theopompus's counter-attack on the prosecutor

Attacks on the credibility of a prosecutor (or attempts by the prosecutor himself to anticipate and deflect such an attack) are a feature of Athenian forensic speeches that surprises modern readers. At least in the context of criminal (as distinct from civil) justice, we think of the prosecutor as an impartial figure, vested with the authority of the state and with no personal interest in the case. But in a legal system

---

40 According to Sositheus ([Dem.] 43.6–7), Theopompus made a written agreement with his 'co-conspirators' at the second *diadikasia*, which was deposited with Medeius of Hagnus (*PAA* 648005). Although nothing further is known about Medeius, the reference to a named depositary, including his demotic, adds credence to this (cf. Brock, 2020, 17); but the allegation is not supported by witness testimony, and it seems to relate to a general 'conspiracy' to defraud Phylomache rather than a specific arrangement between Stratocles and Theopompus.

with no public prosecution authority, where the role of the 'volunteer prosecutor'[41] was open to abuse, undermining the credibility of the prosecutor is likely to be a useful strategy for a defendant, and it was certainly one with which Athenian judges were familiar. Athenian litigants, prosecutors as well as defendants, routinely accused their opponents of lying or trying to deceive the judges, but for a defendant there were additional possibilities. A prosecutor could be accused of 'sykophancy' or malicious prosecution: pursuing the case for personal motives of greed or revenge rather than in the interests of justice.[42] Or he could be characterized as a 'criminal double', someone who has himself committed a similar offence to the one with which he has charged the defendant.[43] Or his choice of procedure could be called into question, conveying the impression that he is abusing the system.

Isaeus deployed all of these tactics in the defence speech that he wrote for Theopompus. The prosecutor is repeatedly accused not only of misrepresenting the law (§§4, 36) but also of lying about the facts of the case (§§20, 23, 38, 47), and the same accusation is levelled against Phylomache and her supporters at the second *diadikasia* (§17). The prosecutor is 'trying to deceive' the judges in the present trial (§4), and he prepared his whole case on the basis of fabricated stories 'in the expectation that he could easily deceive' them (§22). According to Theopompus, moreover, his fellow guardian's true motive for bringing the case was personal malice, because Theopompus had previously accused him of mismanaging the orphan's estate (§§14, 16), so he is pursuing a malicious or 'sykophantic' prosecution (§§4, 13, 31); what he really wants is not to secure justice for the orphan but to remove Theopompus from the guardianship, so that he can continue to 'squander the boy's property with impunity' (§31).

Theopompus's fellow guardian chose to prosecute him in a public action for mistreatment of an orphan (*eisangelia kakōseōs orphanou*). Isaeus condemns that choice as inappropriate and disproportionate to

41 See General Introduction, pp. 6–7.

42 For the modern scholarly debate on 'sykophancy', see, e.g., Osborne (1990) and Harvey (1990).

43 Kucharski (2020, 179–82).

the alleged offence: in an *eisangelia* the penalty was not fixed by law but had to be assessed by the judges, and (unlike other forms of public action) there was no penalty for the prosecutor in the event of failure. So the prosecutor in this case has subjected Theopompus to unnecessary personal risk (§§13, 35), with no risk at all to himself (§31). Moving from the specifics of the case to a more general statement of policy, Theopompus urges the judges not to 'encourage the bringing of public actions about matters for which the laws have created private actions' (§§32, 35). But Isaeus does not merely criticize the prosecutor's choice in general terms; he adds plausibility to the complaint by explaining what legitimate options were available to the prosecutor if he really had a good case against Theopompus (§§33–35).[44] If the prosecutor thinks that Stratocles's son was legally entitled to a share of the estate, he should have submitted a claim (*lēxis*) to the archon, and then accepted the court's decision. Alternatively, if he thinks that Theopompus had defaulted on an agreement, he should have sued him in a 'private action' – by which he probably means a *dikē blabēs*, an action for damages. Or, if he thinks that the property in question already belongs to the boy, he should register it with the archon as part of the orphan's estate.

It would be difficult to argue (and Isaeus does not attempt to do so) that the prosecutor's choice of procedure was actually illegal. The literal meaning of *eisangelia* is 'denunciation', and the term was used for a range of legal procedures initiated by the denunciation of an alleged wrongdoer.[45] As in all public actions, any citizen – not just one with a direct personal interest in the case – could bring a prosecution by way of *eisangelia*, and that apparently reflects the Athenians' recognition of orphans as a vulnerable category in need of protection from society. Once an orphan came of age, he could prosecute his guardian in a *dikē epitropēs* (a private action that enabled him to recover any property lost through the guardian's fraud or maladministration); but while he

44 Cf. Thompson (1976, 43): 'In fact … the more options he presents, the fairer he seems. For in that way he does more than complain about his opponent's choice of proceeding, he actually shows what other recourse he had'.

45 Cf. Hansen (1991, 212–13).

was still a minor he could not bring a legal action himself and would have been dependent on his guardians to represent him in any private action against another individual.[46] (In this case, as Theopompus points out, it would have been open to the other guardian to undertake a private action on the orphan's behalf.) As to the meaning of *kakōsis* ('maltreatment') and the scope of the offence, the evidence is sparse,[47] but we may reasonably assume that it would have covered mismanagement of the orphan's estate as well as physical mistreatment or neglect, and there is no reason to think that it would have been considered inappropriate for the prosecution of a guardian who was allegedly withholding property that legitimately belonged to the orphan. In any event, the archon who received the denunciation clearly thought it was appropriate to allow the case to proceed (although his criteria may not have been particularly rigorous).[48]

The Athenian legal system offered considerable flexibility to litigants in their choice of procedure, and complaints that a speaker's opponent has made the 'wrong' choice – along with more general attacks on the character or motivation of the prosecutor – are not uncommon. In other cases, though, the flexibility of the system is praised as a positive feature,[49] and the argument can easily be turned against the defendant. For example, Demosthenes, in his prosecution speech against Meidias, anticipates an objection from Meidias that it would have been more appropriate to use private actions, and a public action (*graphē*) for *hybris* than the form of public action that

46 Cf. Carey (2004, 124) on the *eisangelia kakōseōs orphanou* as an alternative to the *dikē epitropēs*: 'Here the rationale, as far as one can divine it by conjecture, seems to be to allow a mechanism for third parties to intervene both to protect orphans from physical mistreatment and to check gross financial irregularity which could not be left until the victim reached maturity'.

47 Apart from Isae. 11, our only other evidence for a public action for mistreatment of an orphan is an obscure reference at Dem. 58.32 (where the procedure is described as a *graphē* rather than an *eisangelia*).

48 Cf. Harris (2013, 196): 'When it came to deciding whether to accept cases … magistrates were willing to let an accuser bring a case that relied on a remarkably broad interpretation of statute'.

49 Notably at Dem. 54.1, 8–9, discussed by Carey (2004, 116–19).

Demosthenes has actually chosen (a *probolē*). But, Demosthenes says, 'if I had brought a private case and not a *probolē* against him, I should immediately have been faced with the converse argument, that … I ought to have brought a *probolē*'.[50] Tellingly, he also condemns Meidias's expected complaint as a rhetorical ploy, pointing out that it has no relevance to the question of the defendant's guilt or innocence:

> An offender on trial, I suppose, will try to evade the method of justice which is being used and say that the one which is not ought to have been; yes, but sensible judges will pay no attention to that, and will punish anyone they catch bullying. So don't let him say that the law permits me private cases and a *graphē* for *hybris*. It does permit them, but what he has to show is that he hasn't done the things of which I've accused him … and on that you will cast your votes today.[51]

How, then, would the 'sensible judges' who tried Theopompus's case have reacted to his counter-attack on the prosecutor? They could, on the one hand, simply have dismissed it as a rhetorical ploy, irrelevant to their deliberations – as the prosecutor, like Demosthenes, would have wanted them to do. But if, on the other hand, they were impressed by the plausibility of Theopompus's story about a quarrel between two guardians that led to a malicious prosecution, they might at least have been willing to give him the benefit of the doubt and acquit him of the substantive allegation.

## THE STRUCTURE AND STYLE OF THE SPEECH

Ancient rhetorical theory recognized four divisions of a forensic speech: the proem, or introduction (Gk. *prooimion*, Lat. *proemium*), narrative (Gk. *diēgēsis*), proof (Gk. *pistis*), and epilogue (Gk. *epilogos*). According to Aristotle (*Rhet.* 3.13.4) both the proem and the epilogue served as an *aide-mémoire* for the audience, but neither was essential, especially in a short speech.

---

50 Dem. 21.25, trans. MacDowell (1990).

51 Dem. 21.27–28, trans. MacDowell (1990), slightly adapted.

Isaeus, compared with the earlier Athenian speechwriters, shows considerable flexibility in his approach to the structure of speeches,[52] often dispensing with the proem or epilogue, or both, and breaking his narratives down into short sections interspersed with proofs instead of a single, longer narrative followed by proofs. The structure of each of his speeches is different, part of a rhetorical strategy reflecting the legal needs of the case. The highly unconventional structure of Isaeus 11, in particular, seems calculated to focus the judges' attention on the strength of Theopompus's case (his interpretation of Athenian inheritance law) and divert it from his weakness (his denial that he made a private agreement with Stratocles about the division of Hagnias's estate). There is no formal proem, and the opening of the speech, which begins with a reading from the law, is unparalleled in the extant corpus of the Attic orators. Throughout the introductory sections (§§1–7) and the narrative and argumentation about the order of succession to Hagnias, the emphasis is entirely on the law; the prosecutor's allegations about the private agreement are not even mentioned until §20, which immediately follows an emphatic conclusion to the section dealing with the legal issue: 'what further information do you need, and what more do you want to hear about these matters? I think that what I have said is enough for you, as men of good sense' (§19).

The manuscript text of the speech breaks off before the end, so we do not know whether there was a formal epilogue, but (as is further explained in the commentary) §§32–36 could be seen as a quasi-epilogue, concluding Theopompus's formal defence to the charge of mistreating an orphan and marking the transition to his rebuttal of the prosecutor's allegations of wealth concealment.

Rhetorical questions and answers, a characteristic feature of Isaeus's style, occur frequently in this speech (see the commentary on §§11, 12, 19, 24, 26, 33, 44, 46, and 47) as a means of both discrediting Theopompus's opponent and engaging the judges in his argument.

---

52 Cf. Usher (1999, 128): 'An increasingly flexible attitude to the conventional division of a speech, already to be seen occasionally in Lysias, is adopted by Isaeus as a matter of course'.

Repetition of key phrases, another characteristic of Isaeus's prose, is used to hammer home the message that only Theopompus is legally entitled to the estate 'according to the order of succession' (Gk. *kat' anchisteian* §§19 (twice), 22, 33), and that all the other claimants, including Stratocles's son, are 'outside the order of succession' (Gk. *exō tēs anchisteias*, §§7, 12, 13, 16, and 30).

A distinctive feature of this speech is Isaeus's use of 'logical conditions' in the argumentation. Conditional clauses, of which three or more are sometimes strung together (§§3–4, 19, 24–26, 33, 38) enable the speaker to create an impression of fairness by appearing to keep an open mind about the arguments put forward by his opponent.[53]

Theopompus repeatedly uses verbs and pronouns in the second person plural to address the judges, but the formal address in the vocative, 'gentlemen' (Gk. *ō andres*), is relatively rare in comparison with its frequency in Isaeus's other speeches.[54] This, together with an absence of supplications or pleas for goodwill, contributes to the businesslike tone of the speech, conveying an impression of Theopompus as a confident speaker who is respectful of the judges but not unduly deferential to them. And he is unusual among Isaeus's speakers in his repeated use of imprecations: 'by Zeus' (twice in §35) and 'by the gods' (§36), which add to the intensity of his attack on the prosecutor's choice of procedure.

## A NOTE ON THE TRANSLATION OF GREEK KINSHIP TERMINOLOGY

In describing the relationships of those who have asserted a claim to Hagnias's estate, Isaeus uses a range of terms (*anchisteia*, *genos*, *syngeneia*) that present problems for the translator because they have no direct equivalents in modern English. They are also difficult to translate consistently because the same word may convey different shades of meaning in different contexts.

---

53 See commentary on 'If he is shown to be related in some way', §3.

54 See commentary on 'gentlemen', §8.

According to context, I have translated *anchisteia* as either 'right of succession' or 'order of succession'.[55] Edwards (2007) translates it as 'the prescribed degree(s) of kinship' when someone is described as being 'inside' or 'outside' the *anchisteia* of Hagnias.

Except in the phrase *engutata genous* ('next of kin', §§8, 10, 19), the word *genos* has a less precise legal significance than *anchisteia*. Its basic meaning is 'kinship' or 'blood relationship', and a claim to an estate could be made on the basis of kinship (*kata genos*), in contrast to one based on a will (§§25, 26).

The general term for '(blood) relationship', *syngeneia*, occurs only twice in this speech: at §3, where Theopompus says that his nephew is 'outside the [legally prescribed] relationship' to Hagnias, and at §10, where he says that when he challenged Phylomache for the estate, he alone had a legitimate claim because all the others 'in the same relationship' to Hagnias had already died.

In her translation of [Dem.] 43, Adele Scafuro uses 'kin circle' or 'inheriting circle' for *genos* (when it is used in the context of inheritance or succession), explaining that 'These "circles" of kin are collectively known as the *anchisteia* (which is sometimes equivalent in meaning to "the order of succession")'.[56] Scafuro's approach thus has the advantage that it conveys the idea of the *genos* and *anchisteia* as groups of people with a specific membership, but this leads to translations such as 'nearest by kin circle' (for *genei engutatō*), which for an English reader makes the meaning less clear than 'next of kin'.

## CONCLUSION

At the heart of this case is a bitter dispute between two guardians of a family of orphaned children, each accusing the other of exploiting his position of trust for his own financial gain. Modern scholarship, in its preoccupation with the meaning of 'cousin's children' and the validity of Theopompus's claim to the estate, has diverted attention from this

55 See commentary on 'the right of succession', §2, and 'outside the order of succession', §7.
56 Scafuro (2011, 30).

dispute, and from Theopompus's real vulnerability on the question of a private agreement with Stratocles.

We are in no position to know which of the two guardians was the true villain, or whether there was in fact some truth on both sides, but we do know that the Athenian judges decided in favour of Theopompus. Whether or not that was the right decision, Theopompus owed his acquittal in no small measure to the expertise of his logographer. Unlike Menexenus in Isaeus 5,[57] Theopompus did not enjoy the advantage of speaking first at the trial, and the prosecutor had clearly made some damaging allegations that would have left a strong impression in the minds of the judges. Isaeus's achievement was to negate that impression by launching an aggressive counter-attack, effectively reversing the positions of prosecutor and defendant and seizing the advantage for his client.

---

57 See p. 36.

## PEOPLE IN ISAEUS 11

Chaereleus, son of Apolexis of Prospalta and brother-in-law of Theopompus (§§48, 49); *PAA* 973955.

Eubulides I, son of Buselus of Oeum Ceramicum; *PAA* 427932.

Eubulides II, son of Philagrus of Oeum Ceramicum and grandson of Eubulides I (§§8, 9); *PAA* 427935.

Glaucon, son of Glaucetes of Oeum Ceramicum and matrilineal half-brother of Hagnias II, (§§11.8, 9, 30); *PAA* 277070.

Glaucus, son of Glaucetes of Oeum Ceramicum and matrilineal half-brother of Hagnias II; *PAA* 276400.

Hagnias I, son of Buselus of Oeum Ceramicum and father of Polemon and Phylomache I; *PAA* 106750.

Hagnias II, son of Polemon of Oeum Ceramicum, testator; *PAA* 106760.

Macartatus I, son of Apolexis of Prospalta and brother-in-law of Theopompus (§§11.48, 49); *PAA* 631490.

Macartatus II, natural son of Theopompus of Oeum Ceramicum and posthumously adopted son of Macartatus I of Prospalta; *PAA* 631485.

Phylomache I of Oeum Ceramicum, daughter of Hagnias I; *PAA* 966620.

Phylomache II, daughter of Eubulides II of Oeum Ceramicum (§§11.9, 16, 21) and wife of Sositheus of Oeum Ceramicum ([Dem.] 43.17); *PAA* 966625.

Stratius of Oeum Ceramicum, brother of Hagnias's mother (§§11.8, 10); *PAA* 836685.

Stratocles, son of Charidemus of Oeum Ceramicum and brother of Theopompus (§§11.8, 10, 20, 22, 26, 28, 40, 41, 44, 46); *PAA* 837785.

Theophon, brother of Stratocles's wife (§§41, 42, 45); *PAA* 512770.

Theopompus, son of Charidemus of Oeum Ceramicum ([Dem.] 43.24), speaker, married to a daughter of Apolexis of Prospalta ([Dem.] 43.48); *PAA* 509770.

# ISAEUS 11: ON THE ESTATE OF HAGNIAS

# ΠΕΡΙ ΤΟΥ ΑΓΝΙΟΥ ΚΛΗΡΟΥ

<ΝΌΜΟΙ>

Διὰ ταῦθ᾽ ὑμῖν ἀνέγνων τοὺς νόμους, ὅτι κατὰ τὸν πρῶτον αὐτῶν ἰσχυρίζεται τῷ παιδὶ τοῦ ἡμικληρίου προσήκειν, οὐκ ἀληθῆ λέγων. οὐ γὰρ ἦν ἡμῖν Ἁγνίας ἀδελφός, ὁ δὲ νόμος περὶ ἀδελφοῦ χρημάτων πρῶτον ἀδελφοῖς τε καὶ ἀδελφιδοῖς πεποίηκε τὴν κληρονομίαν, ἂν ὦσιν ὁμοπάτορες· τοῦτο γὰρ ἐγγυτάτω τοῦ τελευτήσαντος <τὸ> γένος ἐστίν. [2] ἐὰν δ᾽ οὗτοι μὴ ὦσι, δεύτερον ἀδελφὰς ὁμοπατρίας καλεῖ καὶ παῖδας τοὺς ἐκ τούτων. ἐὰν δὲ μὴ ὦσι, τρίτῳ γένει δίδωσι τὴν ἀγχιστείαν, ἀνεψιοῖς πρὸς πατρὸς μέχρι ἀνεψιῶν παίδων. ἐὰν δὲ καὶ τοῦτ᾽ ἐκλείπῃ, εἰς τὸ γένος πάλιν ἐπανέρχεται καὶ ποιεῖ τοὺς πρὸς μητρὸς τοῦ τελευτήσαντος κυρίους αὐτῶν, κατὰ ταὐτὰ καθάπερ τοῖς πρὸς πατρὸς ἐξ ἀρχῆς ἐδίδου τὴν κληρονομίαν. [3] ταύτας ποιεῖ τὰς ἀγχιστείας ὁ νομοθέτης μόνας, συντομωτέρως τοῖς ῥήμασιν ἢ ἐγὼ φράζω· τὴν μέντοι διάνοιαν ὧν βούλεται ταύτῃ δείκνυσιν. ὁ δὲ παῖς οὗτος οὐδὲ καθ᾽ ἓν τούτων τῶν ὀνομάτων Ἁγνίᾳ προσήκει τῇ ἀγχιστείᾳ, ἀλλ᾽ ἔξω τῆς συγγενείας ἐστίν. ἵνα δ᾽ ἀκριβῶς μάθητε περὶ ὧν ψηφιεῖσθε, τοὺς πολλοὺς λόγους ἐάσας οὗτος εἰπάτω ὅ τι ὁ παῖς προσήκει τουτωνὶ τῶν εἰρημένων τῷ τὸν κλῆρον καταλιπόντι· κἂν φανῇ κατά τι προσήκων, ἑκὼν ἐγὼ συγχωρῶ τὸ ἡμικλήριον εἶναι τοῦ παιδός. [4] εἰ δέ τοι μηδὲν τούτων ἕξει εἰπεῖν, πῶς οὐκ ἐλεγχθήσεται φανερῶς ἐμὲ μὲν συκοφαντῶν, ὑμᾶς δ᾽ ἐξαπατῆσαι παρὰ τοὺς νόμους ζητῶν; ἀναβιβασάμενος οὖν αὐτὸν ἐναντίον ὑμῶν ἐρωτήσω τὰ ἐν τοῖς νόμοις ὑπαναγιγνώσκων· οὕτω γὰρ εἴσεσθε εἰ προσήκει τῷ παιδὶ τῶν Ἁγνίου χρημάτων ἢ μή. λαβὲ οὖν αὐτοῖς τοὺς νόμους· σὺ δ᾽ ἀνάβηθι δεῦρο, ἐπειδὴ δεινὸς εἶ διαβάλλειν καὶ τοὺς νόμους διαστρέφειν. σὺ δ᾽ ἀναγίγνωσκε.

ΝΌΜΟΙ

[5] Ἐπίσχες. ἐρωτήσω σέ. ἀδελφός ἐσθ᾽ ὁ παῖς Ἁγνίου <ἢ> ἀδελφιδοῦς ἐξ ἀδελφοῦ ἢ ἐξ ἀδελφῆς γεγονώς, ἢ ἀνεψιός, ἢ ἐξ ἀνεψιοῦ πρὸς μητρὸς ἢ πρὸς πατρός; τί τούτων τῶν ὀνομάτων, οἷς ὁ νόμος τὴν ἀγχιστείαν δίδωσι; καὶ ὅπως μὴ ἐκεῖνο ἐρεῖς, ὅτι ἐμὸς ἀδελφιδοῦς. οὐ γὰρ περὶ τοῦ ἐμοῦ κλήρου νῦν ὁ λόγος ἐστί· ζῶ γάρ. εἰ δ᾽ ἦν ἄπαις ἐγὼ τετελευτηκὼς καὶ ἠμφισβήτει τῶν ἐμῶν, τοῦτο ἂν προσῆκεν ἀποκρίνασθαι ἐρωτωμένῳ. νῦν δὲ φῂς τῶν Ἁγνίου χρημάτων τὸ ἡμικλήριον εἶναι τοῦ παιδός· δεῖ δή σε τῆς ἀγχιστείας, ὅ τι ὁ παῖς Ἁγνίᾳ προσήκει, τὸ γένος εἰπεῖν. φράσον οὖν τουτοισί. [6] αἰσθάνεσθε ὅτι οὐκ ἔχει τὴν συγγένειαν εἰπεῖν, ἀλλ᾽ ἀποκρίνεται πάντα μᾶλλον ἢ ὃ δεῖ μαθεῖν ὑμᾶς. καίτοι τόν γε πράττοντά τι δίκαιον οὐ προσῆκεν ἀπορεῖν ἀλλ᾽ εὐθὺς λέγειν, καὶ μὴ μόνον τοῦτο ποιεῖν, ἀλλὰ καὶ διόμνυσθαι καὶ τοῦ γένους

LAWS

I have read the laws to you because my opponent says that, based on the first of them, the boy is entitled to half the estate. That is not true. For Hagnias was not our brother, and the law gives first claim to an inheritance to brothers and nephews on the father's side, since this is the closest relationship to the deceased. (2) Secondly, in default of these, the law names sisters by the same father and their children. In default of these also, it gives the right of succession in the third degree to cousins on the father's side up to the children of cousins. If these are also lacking, the law goes back into the family and gives control of the deceased's property to his relatives on his mother's side, just as it originally did to those on the father's side. (3) These are the only rights of succession recognized by the lawmaker; his wording is more succinct than my paraphrase, but he shows his intention clearly. And this boy is not related to Hagnias in any of the recognized ways, but is outside the kinship. So that you may understand exactly what you are going to vote about, let my opponent say as briefly as possible in which of the said degrees of relationship the boy stands to the man who left the estate. If he is shown to be related in some way, I willingly agree that half of the estate belongs to him. (4) But if he cannot specify the relationship, surely he will be clearly convicted of pursuing a malicious prosecution against me and trying to deceive you against the laws. I shall therefore have him stand in front of you and question him, reading out the text of the law. In that way you will know whether or not the boy is entitled to the estate of Hagnias. Please take the laws; and you, come forward, since you are so clever at slander and twisting the laws. And you, please read.

LAWS

(5) Stop. I will question you. Is the boy a brother of Hagnias, or a nephew (the son of his brother or sister), or a cousin, or the child of a cousin on his father's or mother's side? Which of these titles, on which the law confers the rights of succession? And don't say that he is my nephew; it's not a matter of my estate, since I am still alive. If I had died childless and my estate were in dispute, that would be an appropriate answer to the question. But now you're saying that half of Hagnias's estate belongs to the boy, so you must say what relationship gives the boy the right of succession to Hagnias. Tell them what it is.

(6) You see that he can't specify the relationship, but gives any answer rather than the information you need. Yet someone with a just cause should not be at a loss but speak directly, and not just that but he should also swear an

παρέχεσθαι μάρτυρας, ἵνα μᾶλλον [ἂν] ἐπιστεύετο ὑφ' ὑμῶν. νῦν δ' ἐφ' οἷς ἀπόκρισιν οὐ δέδωκεν, οὐ μάρτυρας παρέσχετο, οὐχ ὅρκον ὤμοσεν, οὐ νόμον ἀνέγνωκεν, οἴεται δεῖν ὑμᾶς, ὀμωμοκότας ψηφιεῖσθαι κατὰ τοὺς νόμους, αὐτῷ πειθομένους ἐμοῦ καταγνῶναι ταύτην τὴν εἰσαγγελίαν παρὰ τοὺς νόμους· οὕτω σχέτλιος καὶ ἀναιδὴς ἄνθρωπός ἐστιν. [7] ἀλλ' οὐκ ἐγὼ ποιήσω τούτων οὐδέν, ἀλλὰ καὶ τὸ γένος ἐρῶ τοὐμὸν καὶ ὅθεν μοι προσήκει τῆς κληρονομίας, καὶ τὸν παῖδα ἐπιδείξω καὶ τοὺς πρότερον ἀμφισβητήσαντας ἐμοὶ τοῦ κλήρου πάντας ἔξω τῆς ἀγχιστείας ὄντας, ὥσθ' ὑμᾶς ὁμολογεῖν. ἀνάγκη δ' ἐστὶν ἐξ ἀρχῆς τὰ συμβεβηκότα εἰπεῖν· ἐκ τούτων γὰρ γνώσεσθε τήν τε ἐμὴν ἀγχιστείαν καὶ ὅτι τούτοις οὐδὲν προσήκει τῆς κληρονομίας. [8] ἐγὼ γὰρ καὶ Ἁγνίας, ὦ ἄνδρες, καὶ Εὐβουλίδης καὶ Στρατοκλῆς καὶ Στρατίος ὁ τῆς Ἁγνίου μητρὸς ἀδελφὸς ἐξ ἀνεψιῶν ἐσμεν γεγονότες· καὶ γὰρ οἱ πατέρες ἡμῶν ἦσαν ἀνεψιοὶ ἐκ πατραδέλφων. Ἁγνίας οὖν, ὅτε ἐκπλεῖν παρεσκευάζετο πρεσβεύσων ἐπὶ ταύτας τὰς πράξεις αἳ τῇ πόλει συμφερόντως εἶχον, οὐκ ἐφ' ἡμῖν τοῖς ἐγγύτατα γένους, εἴ τι πάθοι, τὰ ὄντα κατέλιπεν, ἀλλ' ἐποιήσατο θυγατέρα αὑτοῦ ἀδελφιδῆν· εἰ δέ τι καὶ αὐτὴ πάθοι, Γλαύκωνι τὰ ὄντα ἐδίδου, ἀδελφῷ ὄντι ὁμομητρίῳ· καὶ ταῦτ' ἐν διαθήκαις ἐνέγραψε. [9] χρόνων δὲ διαγενομένων μετὰ ταῦτα τελευτᾷ μὲν Εὐβουλίδης, τελευτᾷ δ' ἡ θυγάτηρ ἣν ἐποιήσατο Ἁγνίας, λαμβάνει δὲ τὸν κλῆρον Γλαύκων κατὰ τὴν διαθήκην. ἡμεῖς δ' οὐ πώποτ' ἠξιώσαμεν ἀμφισβητῆσαι πρὸς τὰς ἐκείνου διαθήκας, ἀλλ' ᾠόμεθα δεῖν περὶ τῶν αὑτοῦ τὴν ἐκείνου γνώμην εἶναι κυρίαν, καὶ τούτοις ἐνεμένομεν. ἡ δ' Εὐβουλίδου θυγάτηρ μετὰ τῶν αὐτῇ συμπραττόντων λαγχάνει τοῦ κλήρου καὶ λαμβάνει νικήσασα τοὺς κατὰ τὴν διαθήκην ἀμφισβητήσαντας, ἔξω μὲν οὖσα τῆς ἀγχιστείας, ἐλπίσασα δ' (ὡς ἔοικεν) ἡμᾶς πρὸς αὐτὴν οὐκ ἀντιδικήσειν, ὅτι οὐδὲ πρὸς τὰς διαθήκας ἠμφισβητήσαμεν. [10] ἡμεῖς δέ, ἐγὼ καὶ Στρατίος καὶ Στρατοκλῆς, ἐπειδὴ τοῖς ἐγγύτατα γένους ἐγεγένητο ἐπίδικος ὁ κλῆρος, παρεσκευαζόμεθα ἅπαντες λαγχάνειν· πρὶν δὲ γενέσθαι τὰς λήξεις τῶν δικῶν ἡμῖν τελευτᾷ μὲν ὁ Στρατίος, τελευτᾷ δ' ὁ Στρατοκλῆς, λείπομαι δ' ἐγὼ μόνος τῶν πρὸς πατρὸς ὢν ἀνεψιοῦ παῖς, ᾧ μόνῳ κατὰ τοὺς νόμους ἐγίγνετο ἡ κληρονομία, πάντων ἤδη τῶν ἄλλων ἐκλελοιπότων, οἳ ταὐτὸν ἐμοὶ τῇ συγγενείᾳ προσήκοντες ἐτύγχανον. [11] τῷ δὲ γνώσεσθε τοῦθ', ὅτι ἐμοὶ μὲν ἀγχιστεύειν, τοῖς δ' ἐξ ἐκείνων γεγονόσιν οὐκ ἦν, ἐν οἷς οὗτος ὁ παῖς ἦν; αὐτὸς ὁ νόμος δηλώσει. τὸ μὲν γὰρ εἶναι τὴν ἀγχιστείαν ἀνεψιοῖς πρὸς πατρὸς μέχρι ἀνεψιῶν παίδων ὁμολογεῖται παρὰ πάντων. εἰ δὲ μεθ' ἡμᾶς δίδωσι τοῖς ἡμετέροις παισί, τοῦτ' ἤδη σκεπτέον ἐστί. λαβὲ οὖν αὐτοῖς τὸν νόμον καὶ ἀναγίγνωσκε.

oath and produce witnesses to the relationship, to enhance his credibility. Now, he thinks that you, having sworn to vote in accordance with the laws, should be persuaded by him about matters on which he has not given an answer, not produced witnesses, not sworn an oath, not cited a law, and convict me in this *eisangelia* contrary to the laws. That is the wicked and shameless person that he is. (7) But I will do none of those things; I will state my right of succession and the basis of my eligibility for the inheritance, and demonstrate to your satisfaction that the boy and all those who previously contested the estate with me are outside the order of succession. I need to explain from the beginning the facts from which you will know my relationship and understand that my opponent has no claim to the estate.

(8) Hagnias and I, gentlemen, and Eubulides and Stratocles and Stratius the brother of Hagnias's mother, were the children of cousins; our fathers were cousins, the sons of brothers by the same father. Well now, when Hagnias was preparing to embark on that embassy which turned out so well for the city, he did not leave his property to us as his next of kin, if anything should happen to him, but adopted his niece as his daughter. And if anything should happen to her, he gave his property to Glaucon, his half-brother by the same mother. And he wrote these dispositions in a will. (9) And after some time had passed, Eubulides died, and the daughter whom Hagnias had adopted also died, and Glaucon took the inheritance in accordance with the will. And we never thought of contesting his will, but thought it right that Hagnias's wishes about his own property should prevail, and we abided by those. And Eubulides's daughter, with her associates, claimed the inheritance and won the case against those who claimed on the basis of the will. Although she was outside the order of succession, she apparently hoped that we would not oppose her, because we had not contested the will either. (10) But we – Stratius, Stratocles, and I – when the estate became available for adjudication to the next of kin, all prepared to submit a claim. And before our claims came to court, both Stratius and Stratocles died, and I was left as the only surviving relative of Hagnias on his father's side, a cousin's son and the only person who, according to the law, had a claim to the estate, since all the others in the same relationship to him had already died. (11) But how are you to know that I have the right of succession, while the children of the others, including this boy, do not? The law itself will make this clear. It is agreed by everyone that the right of kinship belongs to cousins on the father's side, up to the children of cousins, but the point for consideration now is whether the law gives that right to our children after us. Take the law, then, and read it to them.

ΝΟΜΟΣ. Ἐὰν δὲ μηδεὶς ᾖ πρὸς πατρὸς μέχρι ἀνεψιῶν παίδων, τοὺς πρὸς μητρὸς κυρίους εἶναι κατὰ τὰ αὐτά.

[12] Ἀκούετε, ὦ ἄνδρες, ὅτι ὁ νομοθέτης οὐκ εἶπεν, ἐὰν μηδεὶς ᾖ πρὸς πατρὸς μέχρι ἀνεψιῶν παίδων, τοὺς τῶν ἀνεψιαδῶν εἶναι κυρίους, ἀλλὰ ἀπέδωκε τοῖς πρὸς μητρὸς τοῦ τελευτήσαντος, ἂν ἡμεῖς μὴ ὦμεν, τὴν κληρονομίαν ἤδη, ἀδελφοῖς καὶ ἀδελφαῖς καὶ παισὶ τοῖς τούτων καὶ τοῖς ἄλλοις, κατὰ ταὐτὰ καθάπερ καὶ ἐξ ἀρχῆς ἦν ὑπειρημένον· τοὺς δὲ ἡμετέρους παῖδας ἔξω τῆς ἀγχιστείας ἐποίησεν. οἷς δὲ μηδ' ἐὰν τετελευτηκὼς ἦν ἐγώ, δίδωσιν ὁ νόμος τὴν Ἁγνίου κληρονομίαν, πῶς ἐμοῦ τε ζῶντος καὶ κατὰ τοὺς νόμους ἔχοντος οἴονται αὑτοῖς εἶναι τὴν ἀγχιστείαν; οὐδαμῶς δήπουθεν. [13] ἀλλὰ μὴν εἰ τούτοις μὴ μέτεστιν, ὧν οἱ πατέρες ταὐτὸν ἐμοὶ προσῆκον, οὐδὲ τούτῳ τῷ παιδὶ γίγνεται· καὶ γὰρ ὁ τούτου πατὴρ ὁμοίως ἦν ἐκείνοις συγγενής. οὔκουν δεινὸν ἐμοὶ μὲν διαρρήδην οὕτω τῶν νόμων δεδωκότων τὴν κληρονομίαν, τούτους δ' ἔξω τῆς ἀγχιστείας πεποιηκότων, τολμᾶν τουτονὶ συκοφαντεῖν, καὶ διαγωνίσασθαι μέν, ἡνίκ' ἐγὼ τοῦ κλήρου τὴν δίκην ἐλάγχανον, μὴ οἴεσθαι δεῖν, μηδὲ παρακαταβάλλειν, οὗ περὶ τῶν τοιούτων εἴ τι δίκαιον εἶχεν εἰπεῖν διαγνωσθῆναι προσῆκεν, ἐπὶ δὲ <τῷ> τοῦ παιδὸς ὀνόματι πράγματ' ἐμοὶ παρέχειν καὶ περὶ τῶν μεγίστων εἰς κίνδυνον καθιστάναι; [14] καὶ περὶ μὲν τῶν ὁμολογουμένων εἶναι τοῦ παιδὸς χρημάτων μηδ' αἰτιᾶσθαί με, μηδ' ὥς τι εἴληφα ἔχειν εἰπεῖν (ἐφ' οἷς, εἴ τι αὐτῶν κακῶς διῴκουν ὥσπερ οὗτος, κρίνεσθαι μοι προσῆκεν), ἃ δ' ὑμεῖς ἐμὰ εἶναι ἐψηφίσασθε, τῷ βουλομένῳ δόντες ἐξουσίαν ἀμφισβητεῖν αὐτῶν, ἐπὶ τούτοις ἐμοὶ τοιούτους ἀγῶνας παρασκευάζειν καὶ εἰς τοῦτο ἀναισχυντίας ἥκειν; [15] οἴομαι μὲν οὖν καὶ ἐκ τῶν ἤδη εἰρημένων γιγνώσκεσθαι ὑμῖν ὅτι οὔτ' ἀδικῶ τὸν παῖδα οὐδὲν οὔτ' ἔνοχός εἰμι ταύταις ταῖς αἰτίαις οὐδὲ κατὰ μικρόν· ἔτι δὲ ἀκριβέστερον ἡγοῦμαι καὶ ἐκ τῶν ἄλλων ὑμᾶς μαθήσεσθαι, καὶ τὴν ἐμὴν ἐπιδικασίαν, ὡς γέγονεν, ἀκούσαντας περὶ αὐτῶν. ἐμοὶ γάρ, ὦ ἄνδρες, λαχόντι τοῦ κλήρου τὴν δίκην οὔτε οὗτος ὁ νῦν ἐμὲ εἰσαγγέλλων ᾠήθη δεῖν παρακαταβάλλειν ὑπὲρ τοῦ παιδός, οὔτε οἱ Στρατίου παῖδες οἱ ταὐτὸ τῷ παιδὶ προσήκοντες ... οὔτε δι' ἄλλο οὐδὲν αὑτοῖς ἐνόμιζον προσήκειν τούτων τῶν χρημάτων· [16] ἐπεὶ οὐδ' ἂν οὗτος νῦν ἐμοὶ πράγματα παρεῖχεν, εἰ τὰ τοῦ παιδὸς εἴων ἁρπάζειν καὶ μὴ ἠναντιούμην αὐτῷ. οὗτοι μὲν οὖν, ὥσπερ εἶπον, εἰδότες ὅτι ἔξω ἦσαν τῆς ἀγχιστείας, οὐκ ἠμφισβήτουν ἀλλ' ἡσυχίαν εἶχον· οἱ δ' ὑπὲρ τῆς

LAW. If there is no-one on the father's side up to children of cousins, those on the mother's side have the right of inheritance in the same order.

(12) As you hear, gentlemen, the legislator did not say that, if there is no-one on the father's side up to the children of cousins, their children have the right to inherit; on the contrary, if none of us are living, he has given the right to those who are related to the deceased on his mother's side: brothers and sisters, and their children, and the others, in the same order as was specified before. But he placed our children outside the order of succession. How, then, can those to whom the law gives no claim to the estate of Hagnias, even if I were dead, think that they have any right of succession while I am alive and legally in possession of the property? They have no such right. (13) Indeed, if the right does not belong to those whose fathers were related to him in the same way as I am, neither does it belong to this boy, for his father was related to him in the same way as they were. So isn't it outrageous, since the laws have explicitly given me the right of inheritance, while placing my opponents outside the order of succession, that this man should dare to bring a malicious prosecution against me and, just when I was claiming the estate, didn't see fit to contest it with me or pay a deposit – this being the right time to decide the issue, if he has a good claim – but to cause trouble for me in the name of the boy and subject me to the most serious risks? (14) And he is so shameless that he doesn't even accuse me about money that is agreed to belong to the boy, nor can he say I have received any such money (I would deserve to be prosecuted if I had administered property as badly as he has done) but he has concocted this kind of action against me, aimed at property that you adjudicated to me, after permitting anyone who so wished to dispute my claim to it.

(15) I think you realize from what I have already said that I am doing no wrong to the boy at all and I am not in the slightest degree guilty of these accusations. But I think you will understand even more clearly from the rest of my story, and in particular when you have heard how the estate came to be adjudicated to me. For when I claimed the estate, gentlemen, the man who is now denouncing me did not think it appropriate to pay a deposit on behalf of the boy, and neither did Stratius's sons, whose relationship is the same as the boy's, think [either because of this][1] or for any other reason that they were entitled to this money. (16) And he would not be causing trouble for me now, if I had allowed him to waste the boy's property and not opposed him. These people, as I have said, knew that they were outside the order of succession, so they did not contest the estate but kept quiet. But on the other hand, those who

1 There is a lacuna in the text at this point.

Εὐβουλίδου θυγατρὸς πράττοντες, τῆς τὸ αὐτὸ τῷ παιδὶ καὶ τοῖς Στρατίου παισὶ προσηκούσης, καὶ οἱ κύριοι τῆς Ἁγνίου μητρὸς ἦσαν οἷοί [τε] πρὸς ἐμὲ ἀντιδικεῖν. [17] εἰς τοσαύτας δ᾽ ἀπορίας κατέστησαν ὅ τι ἀντιγράψωνται περὶ τῆς ἀγχιστείας, ὥστε ἡ μὲν τὸν κλῆρον ἔχουσα καὶ οἱ λέγοντες τὸ περὶ αὐτῆς γένος, ἐπειδὴ κατεψεύσαντο, ῥᾳδίως ὑπ᾽ ἐμοῦ τότε ἐξηλέγχθησαν οὐκ ἀληθές τι γράψαι τολμήσαντες, οἱ δ᾽ ὑπὲρ τῆς Ἁγνίου μητρὸς γένει μὲν ἐμοὶ ταὐτὸ προσηκούσης (ἀδελφὴ γὰρ ἦν τοῦ Στρατίου) νόμῳ δὲ ἀποκλειομένης, ὃς κελεύει κρατεῖν τοὺς ἄρρενας, τοῦτο μὲν εἴασαν, οἰόμενοι δ᾽ ἐμοῦ πλεονεκτήσειν μητέρα εἶναι τοῦ τελευτήσαντος ἔγραψαν· ὃ συγγενέστατον μὲν ἦν τῇ φύσει πάντων, ἐν δὲ ταῖς ἀγχιστείαις ὁμολογουμένως οὐκ ἔστιν. [18] εἶτα γράψας ἀνεψιοῦ παῖς εἶναι κἀκείνας ἐξελέγξας οὐκ οὔσας ἐν ταῖς ἀγχιστείαις, οὕτως ἐπεδικασάμην παρ᾽ ὑμῖν, καὶ αὐτῶν οὐκ ἴσχυσέ τι οὔτε τῇ τὸν κλῆρον ἐχούσῃ τὸ προνενικηκέναι τοὺς κατὰ διαθήκην ἀμφισβητήσαντας, οὔτε τῇ ἑτέρᾳ τὸ μητέρα εἶναι τοῦ τὸν κλῆρον καταλιπόντος, ἀλλ᾽ οὕτως οἱ τότε δικάζοντες καὶ τὸ δίκαιον καὶ τοὺς ὅρκους περὶ πολλοῦ ἐποιήσαντο, ὥστ᾽ ἐμοὶ τῷ κατὰ τοὺς νόμους ἀμφισβητοῦντι τὴν ψῆφον ἤνεγκαν. [19] καίτοι εἰ τὰς μὲν νενίκηκα τοῦτον τὸν τρόπον, ἐπιδείξας μηδὲν Ἁγνίᾳ κατ᾽ ἀγχιστείαν προσηκούσας, οὗτος δὲ μὴ ἐτόλμησεν ἀντιδικῆσαι τῷ παιδὶ τοῦ ἡμικληρίου πρὸς ἡμᾶς, οἱ δὲ Στρατίου παῖδες οἱ ταὐτὸν τούτῳ προσήκοντες μηδὲ νῦν ἀξιοῦσιν ἀντιδικῆσαι πρὸς ἐμὲ περὶ αὐτῶν, ἔχω δ᾽ ἐγὼ τὸν κλῆρον ἐπιδικασάμενος παρ᾽ ὑμῖν, ἐξελέγχω δὲ τοῦτον μηδέπω καὶ τήμερον ἔχοντ᾽ εἰπεῖν ὅ τι ὁ παῖς Ἁγνίᾳ προσήκει κατ᾽ ἀγχιστείαν, τί ἔτι δεῖ μαθεῖν ὑμᾶς ἢ <τί> ποθεῖτε ἀκοῦσαι περὶ τούτων; ἐγὼ μὲν γὰρ ὡς εὖ φρονοῦσιν ὑμῖν ἱκανὰ τὰ εἰρημένα νομίζω. [20] οὗτος τοίνυν ῥᾳδίως ὅ τι ἂν τύχῃ ψευδόμενος, καὶ τὴν αὑτοῦ πονηρίαν οὐδεμίαν ζημίαν εἶναι νομίζων, τολμᾷ με διαβάλλειν ἄλλα τε πολλά, περὶ ὧν ποιήσομαι τοὺς λόγους τάχα, καὶ νυνὶ λέγει ὡς ἐκοινωσάμεθα ἐγώ τε καὶ Στρατοκλῆς, τὸν ἀγῶνα εἰσιέναι περὶ τοῦ κλήρου μέλλοντες. ὃ μόνοις ἡμῖν τῶν ἀμφισβητεῖν παρεσκευασμένων οὐκ ἐνῆν, διομολογήσασθαι πρὸς ἀλλήλους. [21] τῇ μὲν γὰρ Εὐβουλίδου θυγατρὶ καὶ τῇ Ἁγνίου μητρὶ πρὸς ἡμᾶς ἀγωνιζομέναις, μὴ κατὰ ταὐτὸ ἀμφισβητούσαις, ἐνῆν ποιήσασθαι συνθήκας, ἂν ἡ ἑτέρα νικᾷ, μετεῖναί τι καὶ τῇ ἡττηθείσῃ· καδίσκος γὰρ ἔμελλεν ἑκατέρᾳ τεθήσεσθαι. τὸ δ᾽ ἡμέτερον οὐ τοιοῦτον ἦν, ἀλλ᾽ ἓν τὸ γένος, δύο δὲ λήξεις, ἡμικληρίου ἑκατέρῳ· τοῖς δὲ κατὰ ταὐτὰ ἀμφισβητοῦσιν εἷς τίθεται καδίσκος, οὗ οὐκ ἂν ἦν τὸν μὲν ἡττᾶσθαι τὸν δὲ νικᾶν, ἀλλ᾽ ὁμοίως ἀμφοτέροις ἦν ὁ αὐτὸς κίνδυνος, ὥστ᾽ οὐκ ἐνῆν κοινωνίαν οὐδὲ διομολογίαν ποιήσασθαι περὶ αὐτῶν. [22] ἀλλ᾽ οὗτος, ἐπειδὴ Στρατοκλῆς ἐτελεύτησε πρὶν γενέσθαι τοῦ ἡμικληρίου τὰς λήξεις ἡμῶν ἑκατέρῳ, καὶ οὐκέτ᾽ ἦν μετουσία τῷ Στρατοκλεῖ τούτων οὐδὲ τῷ παιδὶ τῷδε διὰ τὸν νόμον, ἀλλ᾽ ἐγίγνετο εἰς ἐμὲ ἡ κληρονομία κατ᾽ ἀγχιστείαν πάντων, εἰ νικήσαιμι τοὺς ἔχοντας, τότ᾽ ἤδη

were acting on behalf of Eubulides's daughter, whose relationship is the same as that of the boy and Stratius's sons, were inclined to oppose me, and so were the legal representatives of Hagnias's mother. (17) But they were at such a loss about what to write in their claim about her right of succession that the woman who was in possession of the estate, and those who were lying when they tried to explain her kinship, were easily convicted by me of having the audacity to write what was not true. And those acting on behalf of Hagnias's mother, who stands in the same relationship as I do (for she was a sister of Stratius) but who is excluded by the law, which prescribes that males have precedence, did not mention that but thought they could get the better of me by describing her as the mother of the deceased – the closest of all ties by nature, but agreed to be outside the order of succession. (18) Thus, when I wrote that I was a cousin's son, and proved that these women were not within the order of succession, you adjudicated in my favour. The woman who was in possession of the estate gained no benefit from her former victory over those who claimed on the basis of a will, and neither did the other woman get any advantage from being the mother of the man who left the estate, but those who were then acting as judges valued justice and their oaths so highly that they gave their vote to me because I was contesting the estate in accordance with the law. (19) And yet if I defeated the women in this way, proving that they had no right to Hagnias's estate according to the order of succession, and if my present opponent did not dare to take me to court and demand half the estate for the boy, and if the sons of Stratius – who were in the same relationship [to Hagnias] – do not even think of bringing a claim for the estate against me, and if I hold the estate by your adjudication and can prove that my opponent cannot even now say how the boy is related to Hagnias according to the order of succession – what further information do you need, and what more do you want to hear about these matters? I think that what I have said is enough for you, as men of good sense.

(20) Well now, my opponent, thinking he can tell any lie he pleases with impunity, has the audacity to slander me frequently, and I'll speak about that shortly. Now he is saying that Stratocles and I made an agreement when we were about to contest the estate, but we were the only ones preparing to make a claim for whom it was impossible to reach a mutual agreement. (21) Eubulides's daughter and Hagnias's mother, our opponents, could have made an agreement to share the estate if one of them won and the other was defeated, because they were not contesting the estate on the same grounds, and there would be a separate voting urn for each of them. But it was not the same with us; we had the same relationship [to Hagnias] and we submitted two claims, each to half of the estate. And for two people claiming on the same grounds there is a single

πλάττει ταῦτα καὶ μηχανᾶται, προσδοκῶν τούτοις τοῖς λόγοις ῥᾳδίως ὑμᾶς ἐξαπατῆσαι. ὅτι δ᾽ οὐχ οἷόν τ᾽ ἦν τούτων γίγνεσθαι οὐδέν, ἀλλὰ διείρηται καθ᾽ ἕκαστον περὶ αὐτῶν, ἐκ τοῦ νόμου γνῶναι ῥᾴδιον. λαβὲ δ᾽ αὐτοῖς καὶ ἀναγίγνωσκε.

ΝΟΜΟΣ

[23] Ἆρ᾽ ὑμῖν ὁ νόμος δοκεῖ ποιεῖν ἐξουσίαν κοινωνίας, ἀλλ᾽ οὐκ ἄντικρυς οὑτωσὶ πᾶν τοὐναντίον, εἰ καὶ τὸ πρότερον ὑπῆρχε κοινωνία, προστάττει, διαρρήδην κελεύων τοῦ μέρους ἕκαστον λαγχάνειν καὶ τοῖς κατὰ ταὐτὸ ἀμφισβητοῦσι τιθεὶς ἕνα καδίσκον καὶ τὰς ἐπιδικασίας τοῦτον τὸν τρόπον ποιῶν; ὁ δέ, ταῦτα τῶν νόμων λεγόντων καὶ οὐκ ἐνούσης γενέσθαι διομολογίας, οὕτως ἀλόγως πρᾶγμα τηλικοῦτον ψεύσασθαι τετόλμηκεν. [24] οὐ μόνον δὲ τοῦτο πεποίηκεν, ἀλλὰ καὶ τὸ πάντων ἐναντιώτατον πρᾶγμα εἴρηκεν, ᾧ προσέχετε τὸν νοῦν, ὦ ἄνδρες. φησὶ γὰρ ὁμολογῆσαί με τοῦ κλήρου τῷ παιδὶ τὸ ἡμικλήριον μεταδώσειν, εἰ νικήσαιμι τοὺς ἔχοντας αὐτόν. καίτοι εἰ μέν τι καὶ αὐτῷ μετῆν κατὰ τὸ γένος, ὡς οὗτος λέγει, τί ἔδει γενέσθαι ταύτην αὐτοῖς παρ᾽ ἐμοῦ τὴν ὁμολογίαν; ἦν γὰρ ὁμοίως καὶ τούτοις ἐπίδικον τὸ ἡμικλήριον, εἴ περ ἀληθῆ λέγουσιν. [25] εἰ δὲ μὴ προσῆκεν αὐτοῖς τῆς ἀγχιστείας μηδέν, διὰ τί ἂν μεταδώσειν ὡμολόγουν, τῶν νόμων ἐμοὶ πάντων αὐτῶν δεδωκότων τὴν κληρονομίαν; πότερα δ᾽ οὐκ ἦν μοι λαχεῖν, εἰ μὴ πείσαιμι τούτους; ἀλλ᾽ ὁ νόμος τῷ βουλομένῳ δίδωσι τὴν ἐξουσίαν, ὥστε τοῦτο οὐκ ἦν αὐτοῖς εἰπεῖν. ἀλλ᾽ εἶχόν τινά μοι μαρτυρίαν τοῦ πράγματος, ἣν εἰ μὴ ἐμαρτύρουν, οὐκ ἔμελλον ἐπιδικάσασθαι τούτων; ἀλλὰ κατὰ γένος ἠμφισβήτουν, οὐ κατὰ δόσιν, ὥστ᾽ οὐδὲν ἔδει μαρτύρων. [26] ἀλλὰ μὴν εἰ μήτε κοινώσασθαι τὸ πρᾶγμα ἐνῆν, ὅτ᾽ ἔζη Στρατοκλῆς, μήτε ὁ πατὴρ αὐτῷ κατέλιπεν ἐπιδικασάμενος τούτων μηδέν, μήτε εἰκὸς ἦν μεταδώσειν ἐμὲ τὸ ἡμικλήριον ὁμολογῆσαι αὐτῷ, ἀπέδοτε <δ᾽> ὑμεῖς ἐπιδικάσαντές μοι τοῦτον τὸν κλῆρον, οἱ δὲ μήτε ἔλαχον τότε αὐτῶν μήτ᾽ ἀμφισβητῆσαι πώποτ᾽ ἠξίωσαν, πῶς χρὴ πιστοὺς εἶναι νομίζειν τοὺς τούτων λόγους; ἐγὼ μὲν οἴομαι οὐδαμῶς. [27] προσποιεῖται τοίνυν οὗτος (ἐπειδὴ τοῦτ᾽ εἰκότως ἂν θαυμάζοιτε, ὅτι τοῦ ἡμικληρίου τότε

voting urn, so it is impossible for one to win and the other to lose; we both ran the same risk, and there was no way in which we could have made a common arrangement or agreement about the estate. (22) But when Stratocles died before our claims to half the estate could be heard, and by law neither Stratocles nor the boy had any share in the estate but the entire inheritance came to me according to the order of succession if I could defeat those in possession of the estate – only then does my opponent start to devise and fabricate these tales, with the expectation of easily deceiving you with such stories. It can be easily seen from the law that no such arrangement was possible, but the procedure is laid down in detail. Please take the law and read it to them.

LAW

(23) Do you think that the law makes a private agreement possible, or does it not do exactly the opposite, even if there was a previous arrangement, by explicitly prescribing that each claimant must claim his own share, and providing one voting urn for those who claim on the same grounds, making this the system of adjudication? But he, despite these provisions of the law making an agreement impossible, has dared to fabricate such an irrational lie. (24) And that's not all he's done; he has also produced the most contradictory story of all, to which, gentlemen, please give your attention. For he says that I agreed to give half of the estate to the boy, if I defeated those who were in possession of it. Yet if, as he says, the boy was entitled to a share on the basis of kinship, why would I need to make an agreement with them? For if what they say is true, half of the estate was adjudicable to them just as it was to me. (25) But if they had no place in the order of succession, why should I have agreed to share the inheritance with them when the laws have given me the right to inherit the whole estate? Or was it impossible for me to make a claim unless they agreed? They could not possibly say that, since the law gives the right to claim to anyone who wishes. So did they have some testimony about the matter, without which I was unlikely to win the case? But I was claiming on the basis of kinship, not a will, so there was no need for witnesses. (26) Indeed, if it was impossible to come to an agreement with Stratocles while he was alive; if the boy's father didn't leave him the property because it was never adjudicated to him; if it was unlikely that I would have agreed to give him half the inheritance; and since you adjudicated this inheritance to me, and my opponents made no claim at that time and never thought of disputing it with me, how can you believe what they say? Not at all, in my view.

(27) Since you might reasonably be surprised that at the time they made no claim to half the estate, my opponent pretends that their failure to submit

τὴν δίκην οὐκ ἐλάγχανον) τοῦ μὲν μὴ λαχεῖν πρὸς ἐκείνους ἐμὲ εἶναι αἴτιον ὡς ὁμολογήσαντα μεταδώσειν, ὥστε διὰ τοῦτ᾽ οὐ παρακαταβάλλειν αὐτοῖς, τῆς δὲ πρὸς ἐμὲ λήξεως ἐμποδὼν εἶναι τοὺς νόμους (οὐ γὰρ εἶναι τοῖς ὀρφανοῖς κατὰ τῶν ἐπιτρόπων), οὐδέτερ᾽ ἀληθῆ λέγων. [28] οὔτε γὰρ ἂν νόμον δείξειεν ὃς κωλύει τοῦτον ὑπὲρ τοῦ παιδὸς δίκην παρ᾽ ἐμοῦ λαμβάνειν· οὐ γάρ ἐστιν ἐναντιούμενος οὐδείς, ἀλλ᾽ ὥσπερ καὶ γραφὰς κατ᾽ ἐμοῦ δέδωκεν, οὕτω καὶ δίκας ἐμοὶ εἶναι καὶ τῷ παιδὶ πεποίηκεν· οὔτ᾽ αὖ διὰ ταῦτα ἐκείνοις τοῖς ἔχουσι τοῦ κλήρου οὐκ ἐλάγχανον, ὡς ἐμοῦ μεταδώσειν ὁμολογήσαντος, ἀλλ᾽ ὅτι οὐδ᾽ ὁτιοῦν αὐτοῖς τούτων τῶν χρημάτων προσῆκεν. [29] εὖ δ᾽ οἶδ᾽ ὅτι <οὐδ᾽> εἰ συνεχώρουν τῷ παιδὶ λαβεῖν ἐπιδικασαμένῳ παρ᾽ ἐμοῦ τὸ ἡμικλήριον, οὐκ ἄν ποτε ταῦτ᾽ ἐποίησαν οὐδ᾽ ἐπεχείρησαν, εἰδότες <ὅτι>, ὁπότ᾽ ἐν τῇ ἀγχιστείᾳ μὴ ὄντες εἶχόν τι τῶν μὴ προσηκόντων, τοῦτ᾽ ἂν ὑπὸ τῶν ἐγγύτατα γένους ῥᾳδίως ἀφῃρέθησαν. ὅπερ γὰρ καὶ πρότερον εἶπον, οὐ δίδωσι μεθ᾽ ἡμᾶς τοῖς ἡμετέροις παισὶ τὸ παράπαν τὴν ἀγχιστείαν ὁ νόμος, ἀλλὰ τοῖς πρὸς μητρὸς τοῦ τελευτήσαντος. [30] ἧκεν ἂν οὖν ἐπ᾽ αὐτὰ τοῦτο μὲν ὁ Γλαύκων ὁ τοῦ Ἁγνίου ἀδελφός, πρὸς ὃν μὴ ὅτι γένος εἶχον ἄμεινον εἰπεῖν, ἀλλὰ καὶ ἔξω τῆς ἀγχιστείας ἐφαίνοντ᾽ ἂν ὄντες, τοῦτο δ᾽, εἰ μὴ ἐβούλετο οὗτος, ἡ Ἁγνίου κἀκείνου μήτηρ, προσῆκον καὶ αὐτῇ τῆς ἀγχιστείας τοῦ αὐτῆς ὑέος, ὥσθ᾽ ὁπότ᾽ ἠγωνίζετο πρὸς τοὺς μηδὲν γένει προσήκοντας, φανερῶς ἂν ἔλαβε τὸ ἡμικλήριον παρ᾽ ὑμῶν, τοῦτο τοῦ δικαίου καὶ τῶν νόμων αὐτῇ δεδωκότων. [31] οὐκοῦν διὰ ταῦτ᾽ οὐκ ἐλάγχανεν, οὐχ ὡς δι᾽ ἐμὲ ἢ τοὺς νόμους κωλυόμενος, ἀλλὰ ταύτας [τὰς] προφάσεις ποιούμενος ἐπὶ ταύτας τὰς συκοφαντίας ἐλήλυθεν, ἐξ ὧν γραφὴν γραψάμενος καὶ ἐμὲ διαβάλλων ἐλπίζει χρήματα λήψεσθαι καὶ ἐμὲ τῆς ἐπιτροπῆς ἀπαλλάξειν. καὶ οἴεται δεινοῦ τινος ἀνδρὸς ἔργον διαπράττεσθαι ταύταις ταῖς παρασκευαῖς, ὅτι μὴ κατορθώσας μὲν οὐδὲν ἀπολεῖ τῶν αὑτοῦ, διαπραξάμενος δ᾽ ἃ βούλεται καὶ τὰ τοῦ παιδὸς ἀδεῶς ἤδη διαφορήσει. [32] οὐκοῦν οὐ δεῖ προσέχειν ὑμᾶς τοῖς τούτου λόγοις τὸν νοῦν, οὐδ᾽ ἐπιτρέπειν, οὐδ᾽ ἐθίζειν εἶναι γραφὰς περὶ ὧν ἰδίας δίκας οἱ νόμοι πεποιήκασιν. ἁπλᾶ γὰρ τὰ δίκαια παντάπασίν ἐστι καὶ γνώριμα μαθεῖν· ἃ ἐγὼ διὰ βραχέων εἰπὼν καὶ παρακαταθέμενος ὑμῖν μνημονεύειν, ἐπὶ τὴν ἄλλην ἀπολογίαν ἤδη τρέψομαι τῶν κατηγορηθέντων. [33] τί οὖν ἔστι ταῦτα, καὶ τί διορίζομαι; εἰ μὲν κατ᾽ ἀγχιστείαν τῶν Ἁγνίου μετεῖναί φησι τῷ παιδί, τοῦ ἡμικληρίου λαχέτω πρὸς τὸν ἄρχοντα, κἂν ὑμεῖς ψηφίσησθε, λαβέτω· ταῦτα

a claim against the others was my fault, because I had agreed to give them a share, and that was why they did not pay a deposit on their own behalf. He also says it would have been illegal for them to submit a claim against me because orphans are not allowed to claim against their guardians, but neither of those statements is true. (28) For he could not produce a law that forbids him to bring a private action against me on behalf of the boy, since there is no law that prevents it; but, just as the law allows a public action against me, so it permits either me or the boy to bring a private action. Again, it was not because I agreed to give them a share that they refrained from claiming against those in possession of the estate, but because they had no claim at all to the money. (29) And even if I had conceded that the boy should be awarded half of the estate by the court at my expense, I am sure they would never have carried out such an agreement or even attempted to do so, because they knew that if they had held any property to which they were not entitled, since they were not within the order of succession, they would easily have been deprived of it by the next of kin. For, as I have already said, the law gives no right of succession after us to our children, but to the relatives of the deceased on his mother's side. (30) So Glaucon, Hagnias's brother, was the first in line, and they could not say that they were more closely related but would obviously have been outside the order of succession; then, if he had not wanted to come forward, the mother of Hagnias and Glaucon could have done so, since she was also within the order of succession to her son, so if she had contested the inheritance against those who had no right of kinship, she would obviously have received half the estate from you, as justice and the laws have entitled her. (31) These, then, are the reasons why he did not submit a claim, not because he was prevented by me or by the laws, but he has made these excuses for engaging in sykophantic proceedings; on these pretexts he has started a public action, and by slandering me he hopes to get money and remove me from the guardianship. And he thinks he's being clever in using these devices, because he won't lose anything of his own if he is not successful, while if he gets the result he wants, he will in future be able to squander the boy's property as well with impunity.

(32) You must not, therefore, pay attention to his arguments, or yield to them, or encourage the bringing of public actions about matters for which the laws have created private actions. For the rights of the case are perfectly simple and easy to understand; I'll deal with them briefly and leave them in your memory, then turn to the rest of my defence against the accusations. (33) So what are the rights of the case, and how would I define them? If, on the one hand, he says that the boy is entitled to a share in the property of Hagnias according to the order of succession, let him submit a claim for half the estate to the archon,

γὰρ οἱ νόμοι κελεύουσιν. εἰ δὲ μὴ κατὰ τοῦτο ἀμφισβητεῖ, φησὶ δὲ ὁμολογῆσαί με τῷ παιδὶ μεταδώσειν, φάσκοντος ἐμοῦ τούτων εἶναι μηδέν, δικασάσθω, κἂν ἐξελέγξῃ με ὡς ὡμολόγησα, τότ' ἤδη πραξάσθω· δίκαιον γὰρ οὕτως ἐστίν. [34] εἰ δὲ μήτε πρὸς ἐμὲ μήτε κατ' ἐμοῦ δίκην εἶναί φησι τῷ παιδί, τὸν κωλύοντα νόμον εἰπάτω, κἂν ἔχῃ δεῖξαι, λαβέτω καὶ οὕτω τὸ μέρος τῶν χρημάτων. εἰ δ' αὖ μήτ' ἐπιδικάσασθαί φησι δεῖν τοῦ ἡμικληρίου μήτ' ἐμοὶ δικάσασθαι, ἀλλ' ἤδη εἶναι ταῦτα τοῦ παιδός, ἀπογραψάσθω πρὸς τὸν ἄρχοντα εἰς τὴν μίσθωσιν τῶν ἐκείνου χρημάτων, ἣν ὁ μισθωσάμενος εἰσπράξει με ταῦτα ὡς ὄντα τοῦ παιδός. [35] ταῦτα μεγάλα δίκαιά ἐστι. ταῦτα καὶ οἱ νόμοι κελεύουσιν, οὐ μὰ Δία οὐ γραφὰς ἐμὲ φεύγειν περὶ ὧν δίκας ἰδίας εἶναι πεποιήκασιν, οὐδὲ κινδυνεύειν περὶ τοῦ σώματος, ὅτι οὐ μεταδίδωμι τῷ παιδὶ τούτων, ἃ ψήφῳ κρατήσας ἐγὼ τοὺς ἔχοντας οὕτω παρ' ὑμῶν ἔλαβον· ἀλλ' εἴ τι τῶν ὁμολογουμένων εἶναι τοῦ παιδὸς εἶχον καὶ κακῶς διέθηκα ὥστ' ἐκεῖνον κακοῦσθαι, τότε ἄν μοι κατὰ ταύτην προσῆκε κρίνεσθαι τὴν γραφήν, οὐ μὰ Δί' οὐκ ἐπὶ τοῖς ἐμοῖς. [36] ὅτι μὲν οὖν οὔτε περὶ τούτων οὐδὲν δίκαιον πεποίηκεν οὔτε περὶ τῶν ἄλλων ἀληθὲς οὐδὲν εἴρηκεν, ἅπαντα δὲ δεινῶς πλεονεξίᾳ μεμηχάνηται διαβάλλων καὶ τοὺς νόμους παράγων καὶ ὑμῶν καὶ ἐμοῦ παρὰ τὸ δίκαιον περιγενέσθαι ζητῶν, οἶμαι μὰ τοὺς θεοὺς οὐδ' ὑμᾶς ἀγνοεῖν ἀλλ' ὁμοίως εἰδέναι πάντας, ὥστ' οὐκ οἶδ' ὅ τι δεῖ πλείω περὶ τούτων λέγειν. [37] ὁρῶ δέ, ὦ ἄνδρες, τὴν πλείστην διατριβὴν τῶν λόγων ποιούμενον περὶ τὴν τοῦ παιδὸς οὐσίαν καὶ περὶ τὴν ἐμήν, καὶ τὰ μὲν ἐκείνου παντάπασιν ὡς ἄπορα διεξιόντα, περὶ δ' ἐμὲ πλοῦτόν τινα τῷ λόγῳ κατασκευάσαντα, καί τινα κακίαν κατηγοροῦντα ὡς ἐγὼ τεττάρων οὐσῶν Στρατοκλέους θυγατέρων οὐδεμιᾷ τολμῶ συνευπορῆσαι προικός, καὶ ταῦτ' ἔχων (ὡς οὗτός φησι) τὰ τοῦ παιδίου. [38] βούλομαι δὴ καὶ περὶ τούτων εἰπεῖν· ἐλπίζει γὰρ διὰ τῶν λόγων ἐμοὶ μὲν τινα φθόνον γενήσεσθαι παρ' ὑμῶν περὶ τῶν προσγεγενημένων χρημάτων, τοῖς δὲ παισὶν ἔλεον, ἂν ἄποροι παρ' ὑμῖν εἶναι δόξωσιν. οὔκουν ἀγνοῆσαι δεῖ περὶ αὐτῶν ὑμᾶς οὐδέν, ἀλλ' ἀκριβῶς καὶ ταῦτα μαθεῖν, ἵν' εἰδῆθ' ὅτι ψεύδεται, ὥσπερ καὶ περὶ τῶν ἄλλων ἁπάντων. ἐγὼ γάρ, ὦ ἄνδρες, πάντων <ἂν> ὁμολογήσαιμι εἶναι κάκιστος, εἰ Στρατοκλέους ἄπορα τὰ πράγματα καταλιπόντος αὐτὸς εὔπορος ὢν [καὶ] μηδεμίαν ἐπιμέλειαν ποιούμενος φαινοίμην τῶν ἐκείνου παίδων. [39] εἰ δὲ πλείονα κατέλιπεν αὐτοῖς τὰ ὄντα τῶν ἐμῶν καὶ βεβαιότερα, καὶ ταῦτα τοσαῦτ' ἐστὶν ὥστε καὶ τὰς θυγατέρας ἐξ αὐτῶν διαθεῖναι καλῶς καὶ τὸν παῖδα ἐκ τῶν λοιπῶν μηδὲν ἧττον εἶναι

and if you vote in his favour, let him take it, for that is what the laws prescribe. If, on the other hand, he doesn't contest the case on those grounds, but says that I agreed to give the boy a share – although I deny that there is any truth in that – let him bring a private action, and if he can prove that I made such an agreement, then let him enforce it, for that is only right. (34) But if he asserts that the boy can neither claim a share from me nor sue me in a private action, let him say what law forbids this, and if he can produce it, let him receive his share of the estate in this way too. Again, if he says there is no need for the half share to be adjudicated, or for any litigation against me, but that the property already belongs to the boy, let him register it with the archon to be included in the lease of the orphan's estate, for the lessee to collect from me as belonging to the boy. (35) Those are the essential rights of the case, and also what the laws prescribe – not, by Zeus, to prosecute me in a public action about a matter on which the laws have created a private action, or to put me at personal risk because I won't share with the boy an estate which I received by your vote when I defeated those who were in possession. If I were holding property that was agreed to belong to the boy, and had harmed him by maladministering any of it, then it would be appropriate for him to bring a public action against me – not, by Zeus, about my own property.

(36) He has done nothing right or said anything true about these matters, but has cleverly devised everything from greed, slandering, distorting the laws, and seeking unlawfully to get the better of both you and me. I think, by the gods, that you are well aware of this and that you all understand, so I don't know what more I need to say.

(37) I see, gentlemen, that he has devoted most of his speech to an account of the boy's fortune and mine, describing the former as wholly impoverished while for me he constructs a verbal picture of wealth. And he accuses me of dishonourable behaviour in that I don't offer to contribute to the dowries of any of Stratocles's four daughters, even though (as he says) I hold the boy's property. (38) I want to speak about these matters, too. For he hopes that his speech will arouse your envy against me, on the one hand, because of the wealth that has come to me, and pity for the children, on the other hand, if you think they are poor. Therefore, you need to know everything about these matters, and understand the details, so that you know he is lying, just as he has lied about everything else. For I would admit, gentlemen, that I was the most wicked of men if it were shown that Stratocles had left his affairs in disorder, while I was wealthy but failed to take care of his children. (39) But if he left them a larger and more secure fortune than mine, enough to provide handsomely for his daughters without leaving the boy significantly worse off, and if I am managing

πλούσιον, ἐπιμελοῦμαί τε τοῦτον τὸν τρόπον αὐτῶν ὥστε καὶ πολλῷ πλείω γενέσθαι τὴν οὐσίαν, εἰκότως μὲν οὐκ ἂν ἔχοιμι μέμψιν, εἰ μὴ τἀμαυτοῦ προστίθημι τούτοις, σώζων δὲ τὰ τούτων καὶ πλείω ποιῶν δικαίως ἂν ἐπαινοίμην. ὅτι δὲ ταῦτα οὕτως ἔχει, ῥᾳδίως ἐπιδείξω. [40] πρῶτον μὲν οὖν τὰ τῆς οὐσίας διέξειμι, μετὰ δὲ ταῦτα ὡς καὶ διοικεῖν ἀξιῶ τὰ τοῦ παιδός. Στρατοκλεῖ γὰρ κἀμοὶ τὰ μὲν ὑπάρξαντα πατρῷα τοσαῦτα ἦν, ὥστε εἶναι μὲν [οὐχ] ἱκανά, λῃτουργεῖν δὲ μὴ ἄξια. τεκμήριον δέ· εἴκοσι μνᾶς ἑκάτερος ἡμῶν ἐπὶ τῇ γυναικὶ προῖκα ἔλαβε, τοσαύτη δὲ προὶξ οὐκ ἂν εἰς πολλήν τινα οὐσίαν δοθείη. [41] συνέβη δὲ Στρατοκλεῖ πρὸς τοῖς ὑπάρχουσι πλέον ἢ πένθ᾽ ἡμιταλάντων οὐσίαν λαβεῖν· Θεοφῶν γὰρ ὁ τῆς γυναικὸς αὐτοῦ ἀδελφὸς ἀποθνῄσκων ἐποιήσατο τῶν θυγατέρων αὐτοῦ μίαν, καὶ τὰ ὄνθ᾽ αὑτοῦ ἔδωκεν, ἀγρὸν τὸν Ἐλευσῖνι δυοῖν ταλάντοιν, πρόβατα ἑξήκοντα, αἶγας ἑκατόν, ἔπιπλα, ἵππον λαμπρὸν ἐφ᾽ οὗ ἐφυλάρχησε, καὶ τὴν ἄλλην κατασκευὴν ἅπασαν, [42] ἧς κύριος ἐκεῖνος γενόμενος ἐννέα ἔτη ὅλα κατέλιπε πέντε ταλάντων οὐσίαν καὶ τρισχιλίων δραχμῶν σὺν τοῖς ἑαυτοῦ πατρῴοις, χωρὶς ἐκείνης ἧς Θεοφῶν τῇ θυγατρὶ αὐτοῦ ἔδωκεν, ἀγρὸν μὲν Θριᾶσι πένθ᾽ ἡμιτάλαντα εὑρίσκοντα, οἰκίαν δὲ Μελίτῃ τρισχιλίων ἐωνημένην, ἄλλην δὲ Ἐλευσῖνι πεντακοσίων. ἐδάφη μὲν ταῦτα, ἀφ᾽ ὧν ἡ μίσθωσις τοῦ μὲν ἀγροῦ δώδεκα μναῖ, τῶν δὲ οἰκιῶν τρεῖς, αἳ πεντεκαίδεκα μναῖ συναμφότερα γίγνονται· χρέα δ᾽ ἐπὶ τόκοις ὀφειλόμενα περὶ τετρακισχιλίας, ὧν τὸ ἔργον ἐπ᾽ ἐννέα ὀβολοῖς ἑπτακόσιαι καὶ εἴκοσι δραχμαὶ γίγνονται τοῦ ἐνιαυτοῦ ἑκάστου. [43] πρόσοδος μὲν αὕτη δύο καὶ εἴκοσι μναῖ καὶ πρός· χωρὶς δὲ τούτων κατέλιπεν ἔπιπλα, πρόβατα, κριθάς, οἶνον, ὀπώρας, ἐξ ὧν ἐνεπόλησαν τετρακισχιλίας ἐννακοσίας· ἔτι δὲ ἔνδον ἐννακοσίας δραχμάς. πρὸς δὲ τούτοις ἐξ ἐράνων ὀφλήματα εἰσπεπραγμένα, μικροῦ δεούσας χιλίας δραχμάς, μαρτύρων ἐναντίον ἡ μήτηρ αὐτοῦ, τοῦ παιδός, ἀπεγράψατο. καὶ οὔπω λέγω περὶ τῶν ἄλλων, ἃ κατελείφθη μὲν οὗτοι δ᾽ οὐκ ἀποφαίνουσιν, ἀλλὰ τὰ φανερὰ καὶ τὰ ὑπὸ τούτων ὁμολογούμενα. κάλει δέ μοι τῶν εἰρημένων τοὺς μάρτυρας.

ΜΑΡΤΥΡΕΣ

[44] Ἡ μὲν τοίνυν Στρατοκλέους οὐσία καὶ πλείων ταύτης ἐστίν· ἀλλ᾽ ὕστερον περὶ τῶν παρακλεπτομένων ὑπὸ τούτων ποιήσομαι τοὺς λόγους· ἡ δ᾽ ἐμὴ πόση τις; χωρίον ἐν Οἰνόῃ πεντακισχιλίων καὶ Προσπαλτοῖ τρισχιλίων, καὶ οἰκία ἐν ἄστει δισχιλίων, πρὸς δὲ τούτοις <ὁ> κλῆρος ὃν Ἁγνίας κατέλιπε, περὶ δύο τάλαντα· οὐ γὰρ ἂν οἶδ᾽ ὅτι πλέον εὕροι τούτου. ταῦτ᾽ ἐστὶ τρία τάλαντα καὶ τετρακισχίλιαι μόνον, δέκα καὶ ἑκατὸν μναῖς ἐλάττω τῶν τοῦ παιδός. [45] κἀγὼ μὲν ἐγκαταλογίζομαι καὶ τὰ τοῦ ὑέος τοῦ ἐκποιηθέντος εἰς ταῦτα, τοῖς τοῦ παιδὸς δὲ οὐ προσέθηκα τὴν Θεοφῶντος οὐσίαν, πένθ᾽ ἡμιταλάντων οὖσαν, ἐφ᾽ ᾗ ἐποιήσατο τὴν ἀδελφὴν αὐτοῦ· ῥᾳδίως γὰρ ἂν εὑρεθείη καὶ ὀκτὼ

the property in such a way as to greatly enlarge it, I cannot reasonably be blamed for not adding my own resources to theirs; rather, I deserve praise for conserving and increasing their estate. I will easily prove to you that this is in fact the case. (40) First of all, I will go through the details of the boy's property, and then tell you how I see fit to administer it.

The estate that Stratocles and I inherited from our father was sufficient for our needs, but not large enough to support liturgies. As an indication of this, we each received 20 minas with our wives, and such a small dowry would not have been given to a husband of substantial means. (41) But Stratocles received an additional fortune of more than two and a half talents, for when his wife's brother Theophon died, he adopted one of Stratocles's daughters and gave her his fortune: land at Eleusis worth two talents, 60 sheep, 100 goats, furniture, a fine horse which he rode as phylarch, and all the rest of his possessions. (42) After having control of this property for nine whole years, Stratocles left a fortune of five talents and 3,000 drachmas (including his own patrimony but excluding what Theophon had left to his daughter): land at Thria worth two and a half talents, a house at Melite bought for 3,000 drachmas, and another at Eleusis for 500. That was his real estate, of which the land was rented at 12 minas and the houses at three, making a total of 15 minas. He also had about 4,000 drachmas lent out at interest, a monthly rate of nine obols making an annual income of 720 drachmas. (43) So his total income was more than 22 minas, and apart from this he left furniture, sheep, barley, wine, and fruits, which were sold for 4,900 drachmas, and there were also 900 drachmas in the house. In addition to this, the boy's mother, in the presence of witnesses, listed the debts collected from interest-free loans, amounting to almost 1,000 drachmas. And I'm not yet talking about the other property left, which my opponents won't disclose, but only the real estate and what was agreed by them. Please call the witnesses to what I have said.

WITNESSES

(44) Well, Stratocles's fortune is even larger than this, but I'll speak later about what my opponents have pilfered. And how much is my property worth? An estate at Oenoë worth 5,000 drachmas, another at Prospalta, 3,000, and a house in the city, 2,000, and in addition to this the estate that Hagnias left, worth about two talents – I know it would not fetch more. That makes just three talents and 4,000 drachmas, 110 minas less than the boy's property. (45) And I have also included in my own calculations the property of my son who was adopted out of the family, but not added to the boy's property the fortune of two and a half talents with which Theophon adopted his sister. Their family's estate

ταλάντων ὁ τούτων οἶκος· ἀλλ' ἐκεῖνα ἀφῄρηται χωρίς. κἀμοὶ μὲν ὁ κλῆρος ὃν Ἁγνίας κατέλιπεν, οὗτος οὔπω βέβαιός ἐστι· [46] δίκαι γὰρ ἐνεστήκασι ψευδομαρτυρίων, κελεύει δ' ὁ νόμος, ἐὰν ἁλῷ τις τῶν ψευδομαρτυρίων, πάλιν ἐξ ἀρχῆς εἶναι περὶ αὐτῶν τὰς λήξεις· τὰ δὲ τοῦ παιδὸς ὡμολογημένα καὶ ἀναμφισβήτητα καταλέλοιπε Στρατοκλῆς. ὅτι δὲ τοσαῦτά ἐστι τἀμὰ σὺν τοῖς τοῦ ἐκποιήτου ὑέος, καὶ ψευδομαρτυριῶν ἐνεστᾶσι δίκαι περὶ τῶν Ἁγνίου, λαβὲ τὰς μαρτυρίας καὶ ἀνάγνωθι.

ΜΑΡΤΥΡΙΑΙ

[47] Ἆρα μικρὰ τὰ διάφορα ἑκατέροις τῆς οὐσίας ἡμῶν ἐστιν, ἀλλ' οὐ τηλικαῦτα ὥστε <ἐμοὶ> μηδεμίαν γενέσθαι παρὰ τοὺς Στρατοκλέους παῖδας; <οὐκοῦν> οὐκ ἄξιον τοῖς τούτου λόγοις πιστεύειν, ὃς τοσαύτης οὐσίας καταλελειμμένης ἐτόλμησεν ἐπὶ διαβολῇ ψεύσασθαι κατ' ἐμοῦ τηλικαῦτα τὸ μέγεθος. καταλογίζεται τοίνυν ὡς ἐγὼ τρεῖς κλήρους εἰληφὼς καὶ πολλῶν χρημάτων εὐπορῶν ἀφανίζω τὴν οὐσίαν, ἵν' ὡς ἐλάχισθ' ὑμεῖς αὐτῶν ἀπολαύητε. τοῖς γὰρ μηδὲν δίκαιον ἔχουσι περὶ τῶν πραγμάτων λέγειν ἀνάγκη πορίζεσθαι τοιούτους λόγους, ἐξ ὧν [ἂν] διαβάλλοντες πλέον ἔχειν δυνήσονται τῶν ἀντιδίκων. [48] ἐμοὶ δὲ μάρτυρές ἐστε πάντες ὅτι οἱ τῆς ἐμῆς γυναικὸς ἀδελφοί, Χαιρέλεως καὶ Μακάρτατος, οὐ τῶν λῃτουργούντων ἦσαν ἀλλὰ τῶν βραχεῖαν κεκτημένων οὐσίαν. Μακάρτατον γὰρ ἴστε ὅτι τὸ χωρίον ἀποδόμενος καὶ τριήρη πριάμενος καὶ ταύτην πληρωσάμενος εἰς Κρήτην ἐξέπλευσεν· οὐ γὰρ τὸ ἔργον ἀφανὲς ἐγένετο, ἀλλὰ καὶ λόγον ἐν τῷ δήμῳ παρέσχε, μὴ πόλεμον ἡμῖν ἀντ' εἰρήνης ἐκεῖνος πρὸς Λακεδαιμονίους ποιήσειε. [49] Χαιρέλεως δὲ τὸ Προσπαλτοῖ χωρίον κατέλιπεν, ὃ πλέον οὐκ ἂν εὕροι τριάκοντα μνῶν. συνέβη δὲ τὸν μὲν ταῦτα καταλιπόντα τελευτῆσαι πρότερον ἢ Μακάρτατον, ἐκεῖνον δὲ μετὰ ταύτης τῆς οὐσίας, ἣν ἔχων ἐξέπλευσεν· ἅπαντα γὰρ καὶ τὴν τριήρη καὶ αὐτὸν κατὰ τὸν πόλεμον ἀπώλεσε. καταλειφθέντος δὲ τοῦ Προσπαλτοῖ χωρίου καὶ γιγνομένου τῆς ἐκείνων ἀδελφῆς, ἐμῆς δὲ γυναικός, ἐπείσθην ὑπ' ἐκείνης εἰσποιῆσαι Μακαρτάτῳ τὸν ἕτερον τῶν παίδων· οὐχ ἵνα <μὴ> λῃτουργοίην, εἰ προσγένοιτό μοι τοῦτο τὸ χωρίον. [50] ὁμοίως γὰρ καὶ [μὴ] εἰσποιήσαντος τοῦτό γ' ὑπῆρχεν· οὐδὲ γὰρ ἐλῃτούργουν διὰ τοῦτό γ' ἧττον οὐδέν, ἀλλὰ καὶ τῶν εἰσφερόντων ἦν καὶ τῶν τὰ προσταττόμενα ὑμῖν ἅπαντα ποιούντων. ὁ δὲ ὡς περὶ ἀχρήστου μὲν πλουσίου δὲ ἐπὶ διαβολῇ ποιεῖται τούτους τοὺς λόγους.

Ἐγὼ δ' ἓν κεφάλαιον ἐρῶ πάντων μέγιστον, ὃ καὶ ὑμῖν οἶδ' ὅτι δόξει δίκαιον. κοινώσασθαι γὰρ ἐθέλω τὴν οὐσίαν τὴν ἐμὴν τῇ τοῦ παιδός, καὶ εἴτε

could easily be reckoned at eight talents, but what came from Theophon has been counted separately. As for the estate that Hagnias left, it's not yet securely mine, because prosecutions for false testimony are under way, (46) and the law prescribes that if anyone is convicted of false testimony, the claims for an estate must start again from the beginning. On the other hand, the boy's property, left to him by Stratocles, is agreed and uncontested. Please take and read the witness statements confirming that this is the amount of my property, including that of my son who was adopted out of the family, and that prosecutions for false testimony concerning Hagnias's estate are pending.

WITNESS STATEMENTS

(47) Is there only a small difference between the size of our respective fortunes, or is it not rather so great that mine is nothing compared with that of Stratocles's children? So it's not right to believe what my opponent says; although such a large fortune has been left to them, he has had the audacity to slander me by lying about the size of mine. He reckons that I've received three inheritances and have plenty of money, but that I'm concealing my wealth so that you get as little benefit from it as possible. Those who have nothing just to say about the issues at stake have to devise such arguments to get the better of their opponents by slandering them. (48) But you are all my witnesses that my wife's brothers, Chaereleus and Macartatus, were not liturgists but possessed only small fortunes. You know that Macartatus sold his land and bought a trireme, manned it, and sailed away in it to Crete, for this was no secret deed but even caused a debate in the Assembly, since it was feared that he might provoke a war instead of peace between us and Sparta. (49) And Chaereleus left the estate at Prospalta, which would not raise more than 30 minas. As it happened, the brother who left this estate died before Macartatus, and the latter died with all the possessions he took with him when he sailed away, for he lost everything, including the trireme, and perished himself in the war. The estate at Prospalta was left and became the property of their sister, my wife, and I was persuaded by her to have our second son adopted into the family of Macartatus – not to avoid performing liturgies, if this land was added to my property, (50) since the adoption made no difference. In fact, I did not perform fewer liturgies than before because of it; indeed, I was among those who both paid war taxes and carried out all the public duties you prescribed, but my opponent is slandering me by portraying me as a wealthy but useless citizen.

To sum up I will make a single proposal, the strongest of all my arguments, which I know you will consider to be just. I am willing to combine my estate πολλὰ εἴτ᾽ ὀλίγα ἐστίν, ἐν κοινῷ γενομένης λάβωμεν τὰ ἡμίσεα ἑκάτερος, ἵνα μηδὲν πλέον ἔχῃ ἅτερος τοῦ ἑτέρου τοῦ προσήκοντος· ἀλλ᾽ οὐκ ἐθελήσει …

with that of the boy, and let each of us take half the total, whether large or small, so that neither of us has more than is appropriate. But he will not accept that.

[The rest of the speech is missing.]

# COMMENTARY

*1–7: Introduction (discussion of Athenian inheritance law)*

The opening of the speech, with no formal proem (introduction), is highly unconventional. Dispensing with such customary features as an address to the judges (see on 'gentlemen', §8) or an appeal for their goodwill, it begins instead with a reading and discussion of the laws upon which (according to Theopompus) the prosecutor has based his claim that Theopompus's nephew and ward is entitled to half of the estate of Hagnias. This is followed by a brief interrogation of the prosecutor, designed to expose the inadequacy of his case and pave the way for Theopompus's later denunciation of his motives for bringing the litigation.

The strikingly abrupt opening, although it might arouse suspicion that the manuscript text is defective, is entirely in keeping with the overall tone of the speech. As Thompson (1976, 4) explains: 'Since on legal grounds he had every right to possess Hagnias's estate, and his opponent had no standing at all, Theopompos wanted to present that legal position as simply and lucidly as possible, and he had no need to prevaricate or engage in rhetorical flourishes. Since his case is based on the law, he begins with the law'.

**1 I have read the laws to you:** Any laws adduced by an Athenian litigant would normally have been read out by the court clerk, as would other documentary evidence such as witness testimony or wills, and any such readings would not count towards the time allocated for the speech. In this case the wording, if taken literally, indicates that Isaeus took the unusual step of having his client begin his speech by reading from the laws himself. It remains possible, however, that it was in fact the clerk who read the laws (as Thompson, 1976, 4, assumes). Cf. Dem. 21.10 (trans. MacDowell, 1990), where Demosthenes says 'Now, I want to read you also the next law to this one', but then makes it clear, with the instruction 'Read the law', that it was the clerk who actually did so.

**because my opponent says that … the boy is entitled to half the estate:** Theopompus's reason for reading the laws was not to defend his own entitlement to Hagnias's estate, which was awarded to him in an earlier trial (§§15–19) but to refute his opponent's interpretation, according to which Stratocles's son was entitled to share it with him. Cf. Rubinstein (2018, 174): 'While the prosecutor had brought his action as a case of *kakōsis orphanou*, it is clear from Isa. 11.1 that he had deployed the inheritance law in order to substantiate his claim that the orphan's interests had indeed been harmed, and it is the prosecutor's interpretation and application of this law that is challenged directly by the defendant'.

**the boy:** Throughout the speech, Theopompus refers to his nephew and ward (Stratocles's son) as 'the boy' or 'this boy'; his name is never mentioned, and he is not even explicitly identified as Stratocles's son or Theopompus's nephew. This does not, of course, mean that the boy's identity was not made known to the court; he was almost certainly named in the documentation submitted by the prosecutor, and probably also mentioned by name in the prosecution speech. Isaeus, then, presumably chose to maintain the anonymity of 'the boy' as a deliberate tactic to depersonalize him and minimize any sympathy that the judges might have felt for him (cf. Griffith-Williams, 2013, 63). For similar reasons, no doubt, Isaeus also generally avoids using the emotive word 'orphan' (Gk. *orphanos*) to designate the boy (see on 'orphans, alone and destitute', 5.10), but cf. on 'because orphans are not allowed to claim against their guardians', §27, and 'the orphan's estate', §34.

**Hagnias was not our brother:** 'Our' refers to Theopompus and his brother Stratocles. As Theopompus will explain (see following notes), his opponent has interpreted the law as if Hagnias had been their brother, not their cousin.

**brothers and nephews on the father's side:** If an Athenian died leaving no legitimate direct descendants, his brother or brothers by the same father, if any, had the first claim on his estate as next of kin. If he left more than one brother, each of them was entitled to an equal share. If a brother had already died leaving a son, that son would inherit his father's share, in accordance with what is known in modern legal terminology as the 'principle of representation': the child of the relative who has died takes a share of the estate as a 'representative' of his or her deceased parent.

The operation of this law is illustrated by part of the narrative in Isaeus 7. Two brothers, Mneson and Thrasyllus, died around the same time. Mneson was unmarried and left no children, so his estate should have been divided between his surviving brother (Eupolis) and his nephew, Apollodorus, the son of his deceased brother Thrasyllus (7.5–6). But Eupolis fraudulently took the whole estate for himself, until Apollodorus reached adulthood and recovered his share through legal action (7.7).

**the closest relationship to the deceased:** Literally 'closest to the deceased in respect of kinship (*genos*)'. Noting that *genos* is 'a difficult term to translate', Edwards (2007, 179) renders the phrase as 'the nearest degree of relationship to the deceased'. For discussion of the Greek kinship terminology used in Isaeus 11, and the difficulties it presents to translators, see the introduction to this speech, pp. 132–33.

**2 sisters by the same father and their children:** In accordance with the principle of male precedence, a sister could not inherit from her deceased brother unless she had no surviving brothers. The same principle applied to all degrees of kinship: a woman could not inherit property unless she was more closely related to the deceased than any of his surviving male relatives. Cf. on 'excluded by the law, which prescribes that males have precedence', §17.

As was the case when a brother had died leaving offspring (see on 'brothers and nephews on the father's side', §1), the principle of representation also applied to the children of a sister who would have inherited her brother's estate (or a share of it) had she not predeceased him.

**the right of succession:** Translated here as 'right of succession', the Greek word *anchisteia* has a more precise legal meaning than other kinship terminology. In the context of Athenian inheritance law, a man's *anchisteia* comprised those members of his family who were considered to be the most closely related to him, and who were entitled to inherit his property, in the order prescribed by the law, if he left no direct descendants. Membership of Hagnias's *anchisteia* is thus a key issue in the dispute between Theopompus and his opponent. Since there is no direct English equivalent of the Greek term, it is translated, according to context, as either 'right(s) of succession' (§§2, 3, 5, 7, 11, 12, 17, 29) or 'order of succession' (§§7, 9, 12, 13, 17, 18, 19, 22, 25, 29, 30, 33).

**up to the children of cousins:** The phrase 'children of cousins' (Gk. *anepsiōn paides*) is repeated at §§8, 11, 12, and in the text of the law cited at §11. Its meaning, and the scholarly misunderstandings about its significance in the dispute between Theopompus and his opponent, are discussed in the introduction to this speech, pp. 120–22.

**the law goes back into the family:** Theopompus himself claimed the estate of Hagnias as a 'cousin's son' (§10), and his claim was upheld by the court in the second *diadikasia*. Crucially for his case in the present trial, the principle of representation (as Isaeus interprets the law) no longer applies at this stage: if the deceased has left no surviving 'children of cousins' on his father's side, the right to inherit does not pass to *their* children but to his closest relatives on his mother's side. It follows from this that Stratocles's son has no legal claim to the estate (see on 'whether the law gives that right to our children after us', §11, and 'But he placed our children outside the order of succession', §12).

I follow Thompson (1982) in rejecting earlier editorial emendations and restoring the manuscript text of this sentence. Whatever text is adopted, the sentence is not easy to translate, but the general sense is clear: if someone dies leaving no eligible relatives on his father's side, the order of succession starts again with those on the mother's side.

**3 the only rights of succession recognized by the lawmaker:** See on 'the right of succession', §2.

**outside the kinship:** The Greek word translated here as 'kinship' (*syngeneia*) implies blood relationship or common descent; its meaning is more general than that of *anchisteia*, and it has no precise legal significance. Its use at this point is surprising; Isaeus cannot have meant that Stratocles's son was completely unrelated to Hagnias, so he was probably trying to avoid repeating *anchisteia* from earlier in the same sentence (cf. Thompson, 1976, 7–8). *Syngeneia* occurs only once again in this speech, at §10.

**If he is shown to be related in some way ...:** A distinctive stylistic feature of this speech is the frequent use of conditional clauses. At this early stage, Isaeus first uses 'logical conditions' to present alternatives in the form 'If (on the one hand) ... but if (on the other hand)', neither confirming nor denying the hypothesis. (Cf. Pritchett, 1955, 5, cited by Thompson, 1976, 36.) This technique, which is developed more fully at §§33–34, enables him to characterize Theopompus as a fair and reasonable man because he is (ostensibly) prepared to admit the possibility that his opponent is right. Logical conditions, according to Pritchett (1955, 6) are frequently used in argumentation: 'For the argument of a practical lawyer, the logical condition is indispensable'.

**4 if he cannot specify the relationship:** In the first 19 sections of the speech, Isaeus treats the boy's legal entitlement to a share in the estate as if it were the only issue, ignoring the question of a private agreement between Theopompus and Stratocles (cf. on 'Now he is saying', §20).

**surely he will be clearly convicted:** This language implies that Theopompus is the prosecutor and his opponent the defendant. This sets the tone for an attack on the prosecutor's integrity that continues throughout the speech.

**pursuing a malicious prosecution:** The Greek verb rendered here as 'pursuing a malicious prosecution', is *sykophantein*, implying that the prosecutor is not interested in justice but is exploiting the legal system for his own benefit. (On the meaning of 'sykophancy', as distinct from modern English 'sycophancy', cf. Griffith-Williams, 2022, 60.) Isaeus does not use the personal noun 'sykophant' (Gk. *sykophantēs*), but the verb recurs at §13, and the abstract noun 'sykophancy' (Gk. *sykophantia*) appears at §31. The use of this vocabulary contributes to Isaeus's wider strategy of undermining the prosecutor's credibility: he has 'twisted' or 'distorted' the laws (§§4, 36), lied about the facts of the case (§§20, 38, 47), slandered (*diaballein*, §§4, 20, 31, 36, 47, 50) Theopompus with his false accusations, and tried to deceive the judges (§§4, 22). He is 'causing trouble' for Theopompus (§16), pursuing the case from motives of personal malice arising from a quarrel with Theopompus about the management of the orphan's estate (§§14, 16), and his inappropriate choice of a public action, the *eisangelia*, has exposed Theopompus to personal risk (§35) while ensuring that the prosecutor himself will incur no penalty in the event of failure (§31). The significance of this strategy for Theopompus's defence is discussed in the introduction to this chapter, pp. 126–30.

The language of sykophancy is used in only one of Isaeus's other speeches, Isaeus 1; see Griffith-Williams (2022, 22–23 and 60).

**trying to deceive you:** On the tendency of Athenian litigants to accuse their opponents of deceiving (or trying to deceive) the judges, see on 'so that you are not deceived', 5.5. Compared with the speaker of Isaeus 5, Theopompus is relatively restrained, accusing his opponent of deception only twice (cf. on 'easily deceive you', §22).

**I shall ... question him:** Examples of litigants who exercise the right to ask questions of their opponents are comparatively rare in the extant speeches of the Attic orators (cf., e.g., Lys. 12.25, 13.30–33, 22.5, cited by Thompson, 1976, 8). A logographer who composed speeches for delivery by his clients might have been reluctant to allow the speaker to ask questions if the answers were unpredictable. In this case, however, it appears that there was little need for Theopompus to extemporize.

**Please take the laws:** This instruction makes it clear that the laws are now to be read by the court clerk (cf. on 'I have read the laws to you', §1).

**you, come forward:** Theopompus now turns away from the clerk to address his opponent, but (unlike Menexenus in Isaeus 5) without using his name, which is never revealed in the speech. The personal pronoun 'you' (Gk. *su*) suggests a tone of contempt (cf. Denommé, 1974, 138). For Isaeus's use of apostrophe (direct address to a speaker's opponent), see on 'But you, Dicaeogenes', 5.43.

**so clever at slander and twisting the laws:** Athenian litigants often describe their opponents as 'clever' (Gk. *deinos*) in a pejorative sense, implying devious or deceptive argumentation. On Theopompus's accusations of 'slander' against his opponent, see on 'pursuing a malicious prosecution', §4. The opponent has 'twisted' the laws by claiming that Stratocles's son is entitled to a share of the estate, as if he had been a nephew of Hagnias rather than the son of a second cousin. (See on 'Hagnias was not our brother', §1.) As noted by Arnaoutoglou (2018, 182), the Greek verb *diastrephein* ('to twist'), 'although not often attested in Athenian lawcourt speeches, can be associated with the archaic opposition between straight (*eutheia*) and crooked (*skolia*) judgment (*dikē*)'.

**5 Stop. I will question you:** In another abrupt change of addressees, Theopompus first instructs the court clerk to stop reading the law, then turns back to his opponent. Denommé (1974, 142) points out that Isaeus sometimes uses a string of questions after the reading of a law, in order to demonstrate the contrast between the requirements of the law and the behaviour of the speaker's opponent (cf. Isae. 3.39).

**6 You see:** The speaker has now turned away from his opponent to address the judges, and 'you' is once again in the plural.

**produce witnesses to the relationship:** In suggesting that his opponent should produce witnesses to the child's relationship to Hagnias, Theopompus sets a higher standard of proof for his opponent than for himself; cf. §25, where he says that he had no need of witnesses to support his own claim to Hagnias's estate, because he was claiming on the basis of kinship rather than a will.

**having sworn to vote in accordance with the laws:** This refers to the oath sworn by Athenian judges (the 'dicastic oath') which required them to vote 'in accordance with the laws'. For an analysis and reconstruction of the dicastic oath, with references to earlier discussion, see Sommerstein (2013).

**persuaded by him:** On the pejorative connotations of 'persuasion' by an opponent, see on 'Dicaeogenes persuaded the judges', 5.15.

**not given an answer, not produced witnesses, not sworn an oath, not cited a law:** An example of the stylistic device known as asyndeton – a string of clauses not linked by the conjunctions normally expected in classical Greek prose – impresses the judges with a sense of rapidity and liveliness (Denommé, 1974, 166). Here, the accumulation of negatives adds weight to Theopompus's allegation that his opponent is acting deviously and trying to deceive the judges.

Denommé (1974, 65) suggests that this construction might sound strange in the mouth of an inexperienced litigant. If so, it would be entirely appropriate for Theopompus, who does have previous experience of litigation (as he explains at §§15–19) and is presented throughout as a confident and businesslike speaker.

***eisangelia*:** Theopompus's opponent has prosecuted him in a public action, an *eisangelia kakōseōs orphanou* (denunciation for mistreatment of an orphan). The *eisangelia* (lit. 'denunciation' or 'impeachment') was a special type of public action available for serious offences against the state and also for allegations of mistreatment of certain vulnerable individuals (elderly parents and *epiklēroi* or 'heiresses', as well as orphans). This early reference to the procedure foreshadows Theopompus's allegations that the prosecutor's choice of procedure was inappropriate (§§27–31).

On the scope of the *eisangelia*, see the introduction to this speech, pp. 127–28, and for the Athenian distinction between public and private actions, see the General Introduction, pp. 6–7.

**contrary to the laws:** If the judges convict Theopompus, he says, they will be dishonouring their oath to vote 'in accordance with the laws'.

**7 outside the order of succession:** On the significance of the 'order of succession' (Gk. *anchisteia*), see on 'the right of succession', §2. Theopompus claims to be the only surviving relative of Hagnias who is entitled to inherit the estate; neither Stratocles's son nor his opponents in the previous litigation are within the relationships recognized by the law. The repetition of the phrase 'outside the order of succession' (Gk. *exō tēs anchisteias*) at §§9, 12, 13, 16, and 30 helps to reinforce the message that neither Stratocles's son nor any of Theopompus's earlier opponents are entitled to a share of the estate.

**from the beginning:** Athenian litigants frequently promise to tell their story 'from the beginning', perhaps intending to imply that they will tell the 'whole truth'. For parallels, see Griffith-Williams (2022, 93).

Usher (1999, 155) points out that the presence in §7 of 'the conventional topoi for ending a proemium' (i.e. a summary of the facts to be proved and a promise to tell the story from the beginning) confirms that the opening sections of the speech are 'technically introductory' and 'removes any doubts about a possible missing opening'. (Cf. the introductory note to §§1–7.)

*8–10: The previous litigation over Hagnias's estate (narrative)*
A brief passage of narrative, introduced with a statement of Theopompus's relationship to Hagnias, covers the making of Hagnias's will, the death of his adopted daughter, the first *diadikasia*, at which Phylomache successfully challenged the will and reclaimed the estate from Glaucon, and the second *diadikasia*, at which she was defeated by Theopompus. At this early stage of the speech, Isaeus's aim is not to give a full account of previous events, but to leave the judges with a clear impression that Theopompus always behaved in conformity with the law and that he was the only surviving relative of Hagnias with a legitimate claim to the estate. So the narrative is, inevitably, selective and subjective; some details are omitted, either because they are not relevant to the present case or because their inclusion would risk confusing the judges or distracting them from the real issues. A more detailed (but still highly selective) account of the trial won by Theopompus is given at §§15–18.

**8 gentlemen:** See on 'We thought, gentlemen', 5.1. Here, Isaeus marks the beginning of the narrative with a direct address to the judges in the vocative, after dispensing with that formality at the opening of the speech. The judges are addressed only six times in the 50 extant paragraphs of this speech (cf. §§12, 15, 24, 37, and 38), compared with 21 addresses in the 47 paragraphs of Isaeus 5, a more typical frequency. In this speech, as in Isaeus 5, Isaeus uses only his preferred form of address, 'gentlemen' (Gk. *ō andres*).

Only nine of the 99 forensic speeches in the entire corpus of the Attic orators have no address to the judges in the opening sentence: Dem. 28, Din. 3, Isae. 11, Isoc. 16, 18, 20, 21, Lys. 9, 20 (cited by Todd, 2007, 604, n.1).

**Eubulides:** Isaeus introduces Eubulides as one of Hagnias's second cousins, along with Stratius, Stratocles, and Theopompus, all of whom were descended through their fathers from their common great-grandfather, Buselus. He does not mention, here or elsewhere in the speech, that Eubulides, through his mother (Phylomache I) was (or claimed to be) also a first cousin of Hagnias, and thus more closely related to him than the others. For the significance of this in the context of the inheritance dispute, see on 'those who were lying … what was not true', §17.

According to three of the witnesses who testified for Sositheus against Macartatus ([Dem.] 43.43, 44, 45), Eubulides submitted a claim to the estate as Hagnias's next of kin, and no-one else claimed the estate on the basis of kinship at that time. It is not clear whether Eubulides submitted his claim immediately after Hagnias's death or at some later date; cf. on 'Eubulides died', §9, and for the text of the depositions in [Dem.] 43, see Scafuro (2011, 157, n.77). In any event, Eubulides's claim is not mentioned by Isaeus.

**the children of cousins:** Theopompus now explains that he, and those who originally claimed the estate with him (as well as Hagnias himself), were 'children of cousins' in the sense that their fathers were all first cousins of one another (cf. on 'our fathers were cousins', below). For the scholarly debate on the meaning of 'children of cousins', see the introduction to this speech, pp. 120–22.

**Hagnias's mother:** The name of Hagnias's mother is not known; she is identified only by her relationship to her sons (cf. §§17, 21, 30) and to her brother Stratius (§§8, 17). She is not mentioned by Sositheus in [Dem.] 43. On the naming of women in the case, see on 'Eubulides's daughter', §9.

The mother of a deceased Athenian was not *ipso facto* entitled to inherit his estate, but in this case Hagnias's mother was also her son's second cousin and therefore a member of his *anchisteia* (at least in accordance with Theopompus's interpretation of 'children of cousins'; cf. on 'It is agreed by everyone', §11). As Theopompus later explains, however, she had no prospect of success because of the principle of male precedence (see on 'excluded by the law, which prescribes that males have precedence', §17).

**our fathers were cousins:** The father of Theopompus and Stratocles is identified at [Dem.] 43.24 as Charidemus, the son of Hagnias's brother Stratius. Neither Charidemus nor the fathers of Hagnias, Eubulides, and Stratius, are named in this speech, presumably because they are not active participants in the narrative and Isaeus wanted to avoid confusing the judges with inessential details. As discussed in the introduction to this speech, pp. 115–16. the writer of [Dem.] 43, perhaps Sositheus himself, goes to the opposite extreme, so we know that Hagnias's father was Polemon ([Dem.] 43.23), and the father of Eubulides was Philagrus ([Dem.] 43.24). Owing to corruption in the manuscript tradition of [Dem.] 43, there has been some confusion over the parentage of Stratius and his sister (Hagnias's mother), but it is most likely that their father was Phanostratus. (For discussion, see Scafuro, 2011, 139, n.29.)

**preparing to embark:** Hagnias made the will in which he adopted his niece as a precautionary measure before setting out on a risky mission. As Humphreys (1983, 225) points out, it is implicit in the narrative that Hagnias died while serving as an ambassador, or shortly afterwards, but Isaeus does not explicitly say that he died while on the embassy. Here, and at §10, the Greek verb *paraskeuazein* is used with its literal meaning 'to prepare'. On the pejorative usage in the context of litigation, see on 'concocted', §14.

**that embassy which turned out so well for the city:** As discussed by Humphreys (1983, 224–25), these words cast doubt on the traditional identification of Hagnias with the ambassador of that name who was killed on an embassy to Persia in 396 BC: it would be odd to describe a mission on which all the ambassadors died (and may not even have reached their destination) as one that 'turned out well' for the city. Moreover, the judges at a trial nearly 40 years later would not have been likely to recognize such a casual allusion to that event. Observing that the name Hagnias was 'common enough in Attica', and that 'plenty of embassies left Athens between 400 and 360', Humphreys (1983, 225) suggests that the Hagnias of Isaeus 11 may have been one of the five or seven ambassadors sent from Athens to Macedon in 375 or 373. For further discussion of dating and chronology, see the introduction to this speech, pp. 112–13.

**did not leave his property to us as his next of kin:** Theopompus, Eubulides, Stratocles, and Stratius were second cousins of Hagnias on his father's side. In terms of Athenian inheritance law this made them more closely related to him than his half-brothers by the same mother (see on 'Glaucon …', below).

**if anything should happen to him:** The Greek expression, literally meaning 'if he should suffer anything', is, like the English equivalent, a euphemism. It was frequently used by Athenian litigants, especially in inheritance cases, with reference to the disposition of property in the event of the owner's death. Cf. Isae. 1.4, 6.5, 7.1, 9, 27, Isoc. 17.6, Lys. 32.6, Dem. 23.7, [Dem.] 52.24, [Dem.] 59.58 (all cited by Griffith-Williams, 2013, 44).

**adopted his niece as his daughter:** Kinship terminology in Greek, as in English and other European languages, makes no distinction between a sister's son and a brother's son, and Hagnias's precise relationship to his niece (Gk. *adelphidēs*) is not mentioned in the speech. So she could have been his sister's daughter, as most scholars have assumed, but in that case (as pointed out by Wyse, 1904, *ad loc.*) she – not Theopompus and his cousins – would have been his next of kin, unless her mother was only a half-sister of Hagnias. It is perhaps more likely that she was the daughter of one of Hagnias's half-brothers (see on 'Glaucon …', below).

Hagnias is one of only two Athenians known to have adopted a daughter; the other is Theophon, Stratocles's brother-in-law (§41). Rubinstein (1993, 20) mentions a third case, where Apollodorus, before setting off on military service to Corinth, made a will in which he gave his property to his half-sister and arranged her marriage (Isae. 7.9). But Isaeus does not specify that Apollodorus's will involved adoption, and in any event it never came into effect because he returned alive from the war and later adopted a son *inter vivos*.

Adopting a daughter, rather than a son, would not have been the optimal strategy for a childless Athenian, because her children would be members of her husband's *oikos*, not her (adoptive) father's, so it was probably seen as a last resort in cases where there was no male candidate for adoption within the family circle. (Cf. on 'adopted one of Stratocles's daughters', §41.) As Rubinstein (1993, 89–90) explains: 'adopting a woman would only make sense if the adopter could have some confidence that a son born from his adopted daughter would later be transferred to his *oikos* by means of adoption. [Hagnias] may have stipulated in his will that a posthumous adoption was later to be carried out …'. (On posthumous adoption, see on 'adopted into the family of Macartatus', §49.)

**Glaucon, his half-brother by the same mother:** Glaucon and his full brother Glaucus (who is not mentioned in this speech) were sons of Glaucetes of Oeum Ceramicum, one of the husbands of Hagnias's mother. She was thus married twice within the deme, although the relationship of Glaucetes to the Buselidae is uncertain (cf. Cox, 1998, 6). According to Cudjoe (2000, 463), Hagnias's choice of Glaucon as his contingent heir implies that Hagnias had been brought up as a stepson by his mother's second husband, Glaucetes.

**wrote these dispositions in a will:** Hagnias could have adopted his niece *inter vivos*, but he chose to do so by will, presumably thinking that if he returned alive from the embassy he might yet father a natural son. (Cf. Rubinstein, 1993, 23, on the advantages of testamentary adoption for a man facing imminent danger.)

**9 after some time had passed:** Isaeus's treatment of chronology is typically imprecise, giving no indication of the length of time between Hagnias's making his will and the death of Eubulides. He does not even say explicitly that Hagnias died, and that the will adopting his niece was ratified by the court, but that is implicit in the subsequent narrative.

**Eubulides died:** The sequence of events as recorded by Isaeus, whose account is somewhat perfunctory, implies that Eubulides died before Hagnias's adopted daughter. If so, and if he did submit a claim to Hagnias's estate (see on 'Eubulides', §8), he must have intended to challenge her claim under the will. Presumably, then, he died before his claim came to court.

**Glaucon took the inheritance in accordance with the will:** An Athenian court could award an inheritance to a claimant on the basis either of a will or of kinship; cf. on 'won the case against those who claimed on the basis of the will', below, and 'on the basis of kinship, not a will', §25.

**we never thought of contesting his will:** Since Eubulides had already died, 'we' at this stage refers to Theopompus, Stratocles, and Stratius. Theopompus's words show the appropriate respect for the wishes of his dead relative, and give the impression that neither he nor his associates had taken any part in the litigation. But while it was apparently true that they did not contest the will, Theopompus had, according to Sositheus, been actively involved as a witness for Glaucon, and the will produced by the latter was a forgery ([Dem.] 43.4; cf. on 'won the case against those who claimed on the basis of the will', below).

**Eubulides's daughter:** Phylomache II, who successfully challenged Glaucon for the estate of Hagnias but was later defeated by Theopompus. It is implicit in Isaeus's narrative that Eubulides left no sons, so Phylomache inherited his estate as his 'heiress' (Gk. *epiklēros*). This is confirmed by Sositheus ([Dem.] 43.13, 20, 55), who claimed her in marriage as her father's next of kin (first cousin once removed) and represented her at the two trials described in this speech.

Following the convention that respectable citizen women were not normally named in Athenian forensic oratory (on which see Schaps, 1977), Isaeus never refers to Phylomache by name, but identifies her three times as 'Eubulides's daughter' (cf. §§16, 21) and twice as 'the woman who was in possession of the estate' (§§17, 18). It might have been expected that a married woman would be identified by her husband's name rather than her father's, but in this case the designation of Phylomache as Eubulides's daughter is the natural choice because it reflects the capacity in which she claimed the estate of Hagnias after her father's death.

As Schaps (1977, 329) points out, Sositheus in [Dem.] 43 has no qualms about naming the women involved in the case, including his wife Phylomache: 'Whether Sositheus was trying to make everything as clear as possible by mentioning all names, or to swamp the jurors under a profusion of names they could not possibly remember, is far from clear … What is clear for our purpose, however, is that Sositheus felt that the demands of his case took precedence over any delicacy he may have felt about mentioning women's names in court; he shows no trace of reticence about anyone'.

It is worth noting that, for various reasons, some of the males in the case are also not identified by name in Isaeus 11; cf. on 'the boy', §1, 'you, come forward', §4, and 'our fathers were cousins', §8.

**won the case against those who claimed on the basis of the will:** According to the witness's deposition preserved at [Dem.] 43.31 (the authenticity of which is uncertain), Phylomache won the estate 'in the archonship of Nicophemus', i.e. in the year 361/60. See the introduction to this speech, pp. 112–13, for further discussion of dating and chronology.

Thompson (1976, 19) notes 'how lightly Isaeus skips over' the first *diadikasia*, 'neither explaining how the will was broken nor implicating his client in that losing venture'. If Sositheus's version of the trial ([Dem.] 43.3–4) is to be believed, a fuller account would have risked presenting Theopompus in an unfavourable light, but it would probably have added little to his defence in the *eisangelia*, where his main concern was to show that Stratocles's son was not entitled to a share in the estate.

**Although she was outside the order of succession:** See on 'outside the order of succession', §7. As Isaeus explains it, Phylomache's relationship to Hagnias (second cousin once removed) was the same as that of Stratocles's son (Theopompus's ward), neither of whom was within the order of succession to Hagnias. But that is not the full story: Isaeus does not explain that Phylomache, through her paternal grandmother Phylomache I, was (or claimed to be) also Hagnias's first cousin once removed (see on 'Eubulides', §8, and cf. on 'those who were lying … what was not true', §17). It was on the basis of that relationship that she won the estate at the first *diadikasia*, but was defeated by Theopompus at the second.

**10 Stratius, Stratocles, and I:** If they had all survived, each of Hagnias's remaining second cousins would have been entitled to a third of the estate.

**when the estate became available for adjudication to the next of kin:** When an Athenian will was annulled by the decision of a court, it was open to the surviving relatives of the deceased to submit their claims. According to Theopompus, he, Stratius, and Stratocles had refrained from contesting Glaucon's claim to the estate under Hagnias's will (see on 'we never thought of contesting his will', §9), but now that the will has been annulled by the court's decision in favour of Phylomache, they are willing to challenge her.

**all prepared to submit a claim:** On the use of the verb 'to prepare' (Gk. *paraskeuazein*), see on 'preparing to embark', §8, and 'concocted', §14.

**both Stratius and Stratocles died:** Which of the two died first is unimportant, but the timing of Stratocles's death is crucial to the legal narrative; see on 'when Stratocles died before our claims to half the estate could be heard', §22.

**a cousin's son:** Theopompus, here and at §18, explicitly makes clear that his identity as a 'cousin's son' (Gk. *anepsiou pais*) was the basis of his claim to the estate of Hagnias. For discussion, see the introduction to this speech, p. 123.

**in the same relationship to him:** For the Greek word translated as 'relationship' (*syngeneia*) cf. on 'outside the kinship', §3. Here the word carries its more normal meaning, referring to those who were related to Hagnias in the same degree.

*11–14: The order of intestate succession (law and argumentation)*
Theopompus explains the order of intestate succession under Athenian law in order to demonstrate that he is the only one of Hagnias's surviving relatives who is entitled to inherit the estate. Having established that there is no legal basis for his opponent to claim a share on behalf of Stratocles's son, he then repeats the accusation, alluded to at §4, that the prosecution is motivated by personal malice rather than the pursuit of justice.

**11 But how are you to know ...?:** In addition to the questions put to his opponent (§5), Theopompus addresses 12 rhetorical questions to the judges; cf. §§12, 13, 19, 23, 24, 25 (x3), 26, 33, 44, 47.

**the children of the others, including this boy:** 'the others' are Stratius and Stratocles, both of whom have died, leaving their children with no right of succession to Hagnias. Cf. on 'the sons of Stratius … bringing a claim for the estate against me', §19.

**The law itself will make this clear:** 'Athenian litigants sometimes give special emphasis to the laws they cite, implying that their evidential value is superior to that of other documentary evidence' (Griffith-Williams, 2022, 106). Cf. Isae. 2.16, 17; 8.30, 45, and see Rubinstein (2018, 175–76).

**It is agreed by everyone:** This sounds like a variant of the 'common knowledge' topos, frequently used by Athenian courtroom speakers trying to convince the judges of a 'fact' on which they have no witness testimony or other hard evidence (cf. Griffith-Williams, 2022, 57). In the present context, there was certainly no scope for disagreement on the actual words of the written law, but it is possible that there was some uncertainty over the correct interpretation of the words 'children of cousins'. According to MacDowell (1978a, 107): 'The truth is that "as far as children of cousins" is an ambiguous phrase. The fact that Theopompos and Sositheos could propound different interpretations, each with some hope of convincing a jury that his interpretation was right, indicates that its meaning was obscure to the Athenians, as to us, and both interpretations had some plausibility. The original drafters of the law must have known what they meant, but they failed to express their meaning clearly'. Scafuro (2011, 132) agrees that: 'the answer was probably not simple and known to all. The competing claims of [Theopompus and Glaucus/Glaucon at the second *diadikasia*] can best be explained by a third possibility: that no one really knew what "children of cousins" meant: Theopompus banked on convincing the judges that the phrase meant "second cousins" and Glaucus/Glaucon that it did not'. The fact remains, nevertheless, that Theopompus won the second *diadikasia*, and that his status as a 'cousin's son' is not an issue in the *eisangelia* (cf. on 'whether the law also gives that right to our children', below, and, for further discussion, see the introduction to this speech, pp. 120–22).

**children of cousins:** See on 'the children of cousins', §2.

**whether the law gives that right to our children after us:** Theopompus has established his own right to the inheritance as a 'cousin's son', but denied his opponent's claim that his nephew is also entitled to a share of the estate. So, as Theopompus himself (or Isaeus on his behalf) defines it, the legal point at issue between him and his opponent is not the identity of 'children of cousins', but whether the right of inheritance extended to the next generation after the 'children of cousins' had died. In fact, the prosecutor must have accepted that Theopompus's claim to the estate (or part of it) was legitimate: if Theopompus was outside the *anchisteia* then so, *a fortiori*, was Stratocles's son. (Cf. the introduction to this speech, p. 123.)

**Take the law, then, and read it to them:** The clause of the law which was read at this point is, uniquely in the manuscripts of Isaeus, preserved with the text of the speech. Modern editors (Wyse 1904, Roussel 1926, Forster 1927, Edwards 2007, Cobetto Ghiggia 2012) take it to be an interpolation by a later scribe, based on Isaeus's paraphrase. In any event, the purported text of the law adds nothing to what Isaeus says in §12; the wording, though not the sense, differs from that of the law cited at [Dem.] 43.51 (see General Introduction, pp. 3–4).

Whatever its exact wording, the law read at this point is evidently an excerpt from the longer reading at the beginning of the speech, and the explanation in §12 does not differ substantively from that in §2. Here, though, Isaeus focuses specifically on the point at issue between Theopompus and his opponent: the inheritance rights of 'cousins' children' and their own offspring.

**12 As you hear, gentlemen:** Cf. on 'gentlemen', §8. Here, the address to the judges marks the resumption of the speech after the reading of the law.

**the legislator:** Elsewhere in this speech, Isaeus refers to the agency of 'the law' or 'the laws': the laws have explicitly given Theopompus the right of inheritance (§13); they have given him the right to inherit the whole estate (§25); they have entitled Hagnias's mother to claim a share in the estate (§30); they have created private actions (§§32, 35). Here, at this crucial point in his argument, he seeks to give greater weight to the authority of the law by introducing a personal agent. The judges would have taken 'the legislator' as a reference to the great sixth-century lawmaker, Solon, to whom the law on intestate succession is normally attributed.

**up to the children of cousins:** See on 'the children of cousins', §2.

**But he placed our children outside the order of succession:** This is the crux of Theopompus's legal argument: he and Stratocles, as second cousins of Hagnias, had a legitimate claim to Hagnias's estate, but their children do not. (Cf. on 'outside the order of succession', §7.)

**How, then ... legally in possession of the property?:** Isaeus, characteristically, uses a rhetorical question to ridicule the claim of his client's opponent.

**They have no such right:** Answering his own rhetorical questions, as a way of reinforcing an argument, is a distinctive feature of Isaeus's style. According to Denommé (1974, 144–45), short, negative answers are the most frequent (Isae. 2.39; 3.37, 51, 65; 7.32; 8.11, 32; 10.17), while affirmative answers are also found occasionally (3.33; 8.28, 33 x2).

**13 So isn't it outrageous ... the most serious risks?:** A highly tendentious rhetorical question, inviting the judges to agree with Theopompus about the inconsistency of his opponent's actions and accept his biased explanation of the prosecutor's reasons for bringing the case. As Thompson (1976, 24–25) points out, the Attic orators often begin a question with a phrase such as 'Is it not dreadful that' or 'Would it not be dreadful if' to introduce an antithesis between what the opponent has done and what he should have done.

**the laws have explicitly given me the right of inheritance:** Theopompus's right to possession of the estate was based on the law because it derives from a previous court judgment (cf. on 'property that you adjudicated to me', §14). But to claim that it derives directly from the laws, which have a unique authority, is an overstatement, reinforced by 'explicitly' (Gk. *diarrēdēn*; cf. on 'by explicitly requiring each claimant ...', §23).

**placing my opponents outside the order of succession:** See on 'outside the order of succession', §7.

**bring a malicious prosecution:** See on 'pursuing a malicious prosecution', §4.

**pay a deposit:** In at least some circumstances a litigant claiming an inheritance had to pay a deposit of one tenth of the value of the disputed estate, which would be forfeited to the court in the event of failure (cf. Griffith-Williams, 2022, 102). In the present case, the law cited at [Dem.] 43.16, which required a deposit from anyone challenging an occupant to whom the estate had been adjudicated in previous litigation, must have applied to Theopompus and the other claimants who challenged Phylomache at the second *diadikasia*.

The requirement for a deposit was, presumably, intended as a deterrent against frivolous claims, and it is likely to have been all the more effective when the value of the estate in dispute was substantial. (As Scafuro, 2011, 132, points out, the deposit for a claim to Hagnias's estate would have been expensive, perhaps as much as 1,200 drachmas.) Theopompus implies that the other potential claimants, on behalf of the sons of Stratocles and Stratius, did not submit claims because they were unwilling to pay a deposit that they would inevitably lose. (Cf. on 'did not think it appropriate to pay a deposit', §15, and, for the opponent's explanation, see on 'did not pay a deposit', §27.)

**subject me to the most serious risks:** This foreshadows Theopompus's more explicit criticism of the prosecutor's choice of procedure (cf. on 'remove me from the guardianship', §31). An *eisangelia kakōseōs orphanou* was an 'assessed action' or *agōn timētos* (Harrison, 1971, 81–82), meaning that the penalty to be imposed on a convicted defendant was not fixed by law but determined by the judges after submissions by the prosecution and defence. As Osborne (2010, 185) points out, with reference to this case, an *eisangelia* carried no risk at all for the prosecutor, but 'put the accused in considerable danger, since the penalty was assessed and might be set at complete loss of rights'. Cf. Isae. 3.47, where the speaker points out that there is no risk to the prosecutor in an *eisangelia* for mistreatment of an 'heiress' (Gk. *epiklēros*), even if he fails to receive a single vote, while a convicted defendant is liable to the most extreme penalties.

**14 he doesn't even accuse me about money that is agreed to belong to the boy:** Theopompus reasons that, if his opponent had accused him of misappropriating or mismanaging part of the orphan's paternal estate, the prosecution would be appropriate. As it is, the property in question belongs to him, not to the orphan, so the prosecution is inappropriate. The argument is tendentious; withholding property that belonged to an orphan, whether or not it was part of his paternal estate, would have been grounds for an accusation of mistreatment (cf. the introduction to this speech, p. 129).

**if I had administered property as badly as he has done:** This is Theopompus's first hint at a clash between the two guardians over the administration of the orphan's estate; see on 'if I had allowed him to waste the boy's property and not opposed him', §16.

**concocted:** The Greek verb *paraskeuazein* (lit. 'to prepare', as in 'preparing to embark', §8, and 'all prepared to submit a claim', §10) is often used pejoratively by Athenian litigants, implying unfair tactics on the part of an opponent. Cf. on 'since they are prepared to discuss the inheritance from the beginning', 5.5; and for the similarly pejorative use of the cognate noun, *paraskeuai*, see on 'these devices', §31.

**property that you adjudicated to me:** On the convention of addressing the judges as if they had been sitting at a previous trial, see on 'by your vote', 5.37. Here, Theopompus's point is simply to reinforce his entitlement to the whole of Hagnias's estate by emphasizing that it was awarded to him by a court, following the proper procedure. Cf. on 'you adjudicated in my favour', §18; 'by your adjudication', §19; 'Since you adjudicated this inheritance to me', §26; 'if you vote in his favour', §33; and 'an estate which I received by your vote', §35.

*15–19: The second* diadikasia *(narrative and argumentation)*

Isaeus's account of the second *diadikasia*, although more extensive than that of the first (to which he made no more than a passing reference at §9), is still selective, and it differs in some significant respects from Sositheus's version in [Dem.] 43. Comparisons between the two speeches have, unsurprisingly, provided useful ammunition to scholars determined to discredit Isaeus: 'These sections are a remarkable instance of the boldness with which Isaeus will pervert the truth. If the speech of Sositheus had not been preserved, who would have divined from this narrative that Theopompus opposed and defeated Glaucon and Glaucus his late allies?' (Wyse, 1904, 689). Theopompus's narrative is certainly selective and tendentious (though no more so than that of Sositheus) but not necessarily untrue. His aim was not to provide a complete and impartial record of the *diadikasia* but to highlight those aspects that supported Theopompus's case in the *eisangelia*. A less biased commentator than Wyse might see this passage as an example of Isaeus's skill in directing the judges' attention to the important facts, ensuring that they are not distracted by irrelevant or potentially misleading details. (For a fuller discussion of the divergences between Isaeus 11 and [Dem.] 43, see the introduction to this speech, pp. 115–20.)

**15 I am doing no wrong to the boy at all:** Theopompus has already made the point (§14) that his opponent has not accused him of mismanaging the estate inherited by his nephew from Stratocles (an accusation which, as he concedes, would have justified the present prosecution). He now makes the broader denial that he has not done any wrong at all to the boy.

**when I claimed the estate, gentlemen:** Following a sentence in which Theopompus has used verbs and pronouns in the second person plural, the vocative address adds emphasis to the point he is going to make about his opponent's failure to submit a formal claim to the estate on the boy's behalf. For the sparing use of vocative addresses in this speech, see on 'gentlemen', §8.

**the man who is now denouncing me:** The Greek verb *eisangellein* ('to denounce') alludes to the *eisangelia* or 'denunciation' procedure (see on '*eisangelia*', §6), so the underlying point, elaborated at §§31–32, is that the prosecutor's choice of procedure was inappropriate.

**did not think it appropriate to pay a deposit:** If the prosecutor thought that Stratocles's son was legally entitled to a share in the estate, he ought to have been willing to pay the deposit for a claim on the boy's behalf, instead of 'denouncing' Theopompus. Cf. on 'pay a deposit', §13, and 'did not pay a deposit', §27.

**whose relationship is the same as the boy's:** That is, their relationship to Hagnias: Stratius's sons, like Stratocles's son, were second cousins once removed to Hagnias and thus, as Theopompus insists, outside the *anchisteia* (order of succession). Theopompus implies that they (or their guardians) knew this, and that was why they made no claim on the estate.

**16 causing trouble for me:** See on 'pursuing a malicious prosecution', §4.

**if I had allowed him to waste the boy's property and not opposed him:** Theopompus retaliates against his prosecutor by implying that the prosecutor himself is guilty of the offence with which he is charged: mistreatment of an orphan. (See Kucharski, 2020, 179–82, for discussion of the 'criminal double' as a prosecutorial identity constructed by defendants in public cases.) Isaeus provides no details about the dispute between the two guardians; the vague wording does not explain how Theopompus's fellow guardian 'wasted' the orphan's property, or what Theopompus did to oppose him. If their dispute had resulted in litigation, Isaeus would almost certainly have mentioned it.

Like the allegations of sykophancy at §§4, 13, and 31, this accusation (of which a hint was given at §14) helps to undermine the credibility of the prosecutor although it says nothing directly about the defendant's guilt or innocence.

**knew that they were outside the order of succession:** See on 'outside the order of succession', §7.

**Eubulides's daughter:** Phylomache (see on 'Eubulides's daughter', §9).

**whose relationship is the same as that of the boy and Stratius's sons:** As a second cousin once removed, Phylomache's relationship to Hagnias was the same as that of Stratocles's son and Stratius's sons, and all of them – as Theopompus is at pains to impress on the judges – were outside Hagnias's *anchisteia* (see on 'although she was outside the order of succession', §9). Isaeus never mentions that Phylomache was (or claimed to be) also a first cousin once removed of Hagnias, through her paternal grandmother Phylomache I (see on 'Eubulides', §8, and 'those who were lying … what was not true', §17).

**inclined to oppose me:** Theopompus presents both Phylomache and Hagnias's mother as his opponents in the *diadikasia*, but according to Sositheus ([Dem.] 43.7–10), Theopompus was acting in collusion with Hagnias's mother (and her other sons, Glaucon and Glaucus) to deprive Phylomache of the estate.

**the legal representatives of Hagnias's mother:** An Athenian woman could not participate directly in legal proceedings on her own account, but had to be represented by her husband or other male relative as *kyrios* (cf. on 'legal representative', 5.10). In this case, as Thompson (1976, 27) points out, the plural does not necessarily mean that there were more than one, since Isaeus 'regularly treats the principals in the case not as individuals but as members of a group' (referring, e.g., to 'my opponents' when, in fact, there is only one).

Who, then, were the legal representative(s) of Hagnias's mother? If she was still married to Polemon (Hagnias's father) or Glaucetes (the father of Glaucus and Glaucon) at the time of the trial, her husband would have represented her. If she was widowed or divorced, and not remarried, the duty would have fallen in the first instance to Glaucon and Glaucus, so the plural could have been intended to be taken literally. But they were probably claimants on their own account (see the introduction to this speech, pp. 117–18), so their mother is more likely to have been represented, if not by her husband, then by some other male relative. As suggested by various scholars (see Scafuro, 2011, 129 for discussion), a possible candidate is the mysterious Eupolemus, named at [Dem.] 43.7 as a participant in the 'conspiracy' against Phylomache, but not mentioned by Isaeus. (Cf. the introduction to this speech, p. 119.)

**17 what to write in their claim about her right of succession:** Anyone claiming an Athenian estate under a will, or as the dead man's next of kin, had to submit a written claim (*lēxis*) to the court. In the case of a claim based on kinship, the information required on the *lēxis* included the claimant's relationship to the deceased. (Cf. on 'wrote that I was a cousin's son', §18, and, on the content of a *lēxis*, Griffith-Williams, 2022, 143.)

**the woman who was in possession of the estate:** Phylomache, the daughter of Eubulides, who had previously won the estate from Glaucon (cf. on 'Eubulides's daughter', §9).

**those who were lying when they tried to explain her kinship ... what was not true:** Isaeus does not explain the basis of Phylomache's claim to the estate, saying merely that she and her associates lied about her relationship to Hagnias. In fact, as we know from [Dem.] 43, she claimed as a first cousin once removed, saying that her paternal grandmother, Phylomache I, was a sister of Hagnias's father Polemon. It was on that basis that she won the estate from Glaucon at the first *diadikasia*, but Theopompus, at the second *diadikasia*, defeated her by persuading the judges that Phylomache I was not a full legitimate sister of Polemon. He probably said that Phylomache I was only a half-sister of Polemon, with the same mother but a different father; cf. Thompson (1976, 19): 'If Phylomache [I] did not have the same father as Polemon, that would sever the legal connection between her and Polemon's own son, Hagnias'. Alternatively, he may have said that Phylomache I was not related to Polemon at all, or that she was an illegitimate daughter of Hagnias I, but her marriage to her cousin Philagrus makes that less likely.

By omitting to mention Phylomache's relationship to Hagnias through Phylomache I, and identifying her only as Hagnias's second cousin once removed, Isaeus focuses the judges' attention on what was, for Theopompus, the significant point: that Stratocles's son (also a second cousin once removed) was not within the order of succession to Hagnias. (Cf. on 'whose relationship is the same as that of the boy and Stratius's sons', §16).

**those acting on behalf of Hagnias's mother:** Cf. on 'the legal representatives of Hagnias's mother', §16. Here, the vaguer wording might include other friends or family members who were not formally her legal representatives.

**excluded by the law, which prescribes that males have precedence:** Both Hagnias's mother and Theopompus were second cousins of Hagnias, but Theopompus was considered to be more closely related to him because of the principle of male precedence. (See 'sisters by the same father and their children', §2, and, on the role of Hagnias's mother in the proceedings, see the introduction to this speech, pp. 117–20.)

The Greek verb *keleuein*, rendered here as 'prescribe', occurs five times in this speech with 'the law(s)' as its subject (more often than in any of Isaeus's other extant speeches); cf. on 'by explicitly prescribing that each claimant must claim his own share', §23, 'for that is what the laws prescribe', §33, 'and also what the laws prescribe', §35, and 'the law prescribes … must start again from the beginning', §46.

The semantic range of *keleuein* includes 'command', 'order', 'instruct', 'urge', 'request'. When the subject is *ho nomos* ('the law') or *hoi nomoi* ('the laws'), the verb is normally translated as 'ordain' or 'prescribe'; but, as noted by Todd (2007, 121), its 'useful ambiguity' is sometimes exploited by forensic speakers to blur the distinction between mandatory laws and those that are merely permissive (cf. Edwards, 2024, 26, n.50).

**the closest of all ties by nature, but agreed to be outside the order of succession:** See on 'outside the order of succession', §7. Hagnias's mother and her supporters may have hoped to gain the sympathy of the judges by the emotive appeal of the maternal bond (and perhaps cause some embarrassment to Theopompus who was opposing her).

**18 wrote that I was a cousin's son:** See on 'a cousin's son', §10. In the written claim that he submitted to the court (see on 'what to write in their claim about her right of succession', §17), Theopompus described his relationship to Hagnias as 'cousin's son'. Harrison (1968, 143, n.1) comments: 'The usual view is that Theopompus simply hoodwinked the court. But he must have hoodwinked the archon as well, since the relationship on which his claim was based must have been set out at the *anakrisis* [preliminary hearing]'. As Harrison rightly observes, it is highly unlikely that he could have succeeded in such a deception.

**not within the order of succession:** See on 'outside the order of succession', §7.

**you adjudicated in my favour:** See on 'property that you adjudicated to me', §14.

**those who were then acting as judges ... gave their vote to me:** Theopompus now uses the third person to refer to the judges at the trial where he won the estate from Phylomache. It is unlikely that their decision was unanimous, as the literal sense of his words might imply; 'their vote' stands metonymically for 'the majority vote'. According to Sositheus, who represented his wife Phylomache at the earlier trial, Theopompus won by only three or four votes ([Dem.] 43.10), but this is probably an exaggeration; each speaker is making a rhetorical point rather than giving a factually accurate account of the result (cf. Filonik 2024, pp. 8–9).

**valued justice and their oaths so highly:** On the oath sworn by Athenian judges (the dicastic oath), see on 'having sworn to vote in accordance with the laws', §6.

**in accordance with the law:** These words not only emphasize, yet again, the validity of Theopompus's claim to the estate, but also echo the wording of the dicastic oath.

**19 if I defeated the women in this way:** Here, as at §26, Theopompus summarizes his argument with a string of conditional clauses building up to a conclusion expressed in the form of a rhetorical question.

**according to the order of succession:** As with 'outside the order of succession' (see §7), the repetition of this phrase, later in §19 and at §§22 and 33, reinforces the message that Theopompus alone was legally entitled to inherit Hagnias's estate.

**the sons of Stratius ... bringing a claim for the estate against me:** Stratius's sons did not claim a share of Hagnias's estate, knowing (as Theopompus reasons) that they had no hope of success because they were outside the *anchisteia*. Since their relationship to Hagnias was the same as that of Stratocles's son, this implies that Theopompus's opponent also knew that a claim on behalf of the orphan had no hope of success; that was his real reason for not bringing a claim, not the existence of a private agreement.

A similar argument is used by the speaker of Isaeus 7 (the adopted son of Apollodorus), who points out that Apollodorus's relative Thrasybulus has not contested the estate, despite having a better claim than the speaker's opponent; this (as the speaker argues) shows that Thrasybulus accepts the validity of the adoption (Isae. 7.18–24). In both cases the argument is plausible, but not conclusive; someone entitled to claim an inheritance might have various reasons to refrain from doing so.

**by your adjudication:** See on 'property that you adjudicated to me', §14.

**what further information do you need, and what more do you want to hear about these matters?:** Cf. on 'I don't know what more I need to say', §36. A formula along these lines would more typically be used at the conclusion of a speech, as at Isae. 7.45 and 8.46 (cf. Dem. 20.167; 36.62; 38.28; 54.44, all cited by Griffith-Williams, 2013, 88). By using it here, at the transition to a new section of the speech, Isaeus apparently seeks to reinforce the impression that the only issue of significance – whether Stratocles's son had a legal right of succession to Hagnias – has already been dealt with. Making the point in the form of a question and answer gives it added emphasis (cf. on 'They have no such right', §12).

**I think that what I have said is enough for you, as men of good sense:** Denommé (1974, 145–46) points out that Isaeus, instead of actually answering a question he has posed, sometimes prefers to add a 'personal reflection', strongly suggesting his desired answer to the judges.

Flattering the judges as 'men of good sense' was clearly a good tactic for an Athenian litigant. Citing this passage among his examples, Ober (1989, 157) observes: 'Part of the Athenians' faith in the wisdom of collective decisions made by the masses rested upon their conviction that Athenians were by nature more intelligent than other people'. (Cf. Eur. *Medea* 826–27, 844–45, cited by Ober.)

### *20–26: Was there a private agreement between Theopompus and Stratocles? (argumentation)*

After effectively demolishing the prosecutor's claim that Stratocles's son was legally entitled to half of Hagnias's estate, Isaeus now turns to the allegation that Theopompus was in breach of an informal agreement he had made with Stratocles about the division of the estate. Although this is the first time that Isaeus has mentioned the alleged agreement, the judges had, of course, already heard about it from the prosecutor, and they may well have found his account persuasive. Isaeus's argumentation, designed to convince them that such an agreement would have been impossible, is logically irrefutable but deliberately misleading. First, he ridicules the idea that Stratocles and Theopompus could have agreed to share the estate between them (a possibility that the prosecutor had almost certainly not suggested), and then invites the judges to dismiss the much more likely scenario: an agreement that, if either of the brothers died before the case was decided by the court and the survivor won, he would share the estate with his orphaned nephew.

The argument is framed, throughout, in strictly legal terms, implying not only that Theopompus had always acted in accordance with the law, but that it would actually have been illegal for him to do otherwise. (Cf. Johnstone, 1999, 65: 'The idea that behavior was oriented toward and in fact determined by the law ... provided material for an argument from probability. Speakers sometimes asserted that the actions attributed to them by their opponents were inconsistent with the law and that it was improbable, therefore, that they happened as alleged. Theopompos' speech over the estate of Hagnias provides an interesting example of such argumentation'.) This is in marked contrast with the approach of Menexenus, the speaker of Isaeus 5, who seeks to impress the judges with his magnanimity towards his opponents, claiming that he has treated them more generously than the law strictly required.

**20 thinking he can tell any lie he pleases with impunity, has the audacity to slander me frequently:** These insinuations, carefully placed before Theopompus's denial of a private agreement with Stratocles, are designed to prejudice the judges against the prosecutor's account. (On the language of 'lying' and 'slander' in this speech, see on 'pursuing a malicious prosecution', §4.)

**Now he is saying:** This is the first time that the possibility of a private agreement between Theopompus and Stratocles has been mentioned; up to this point, Isaeus has focused exclusively on the question whether the boy was legally entitled to a share in the estate, as if that were the only issue at stake (cf. on 'if he cannot specify the relationship', §4).

**impossible to reach a mutual agreement:** Isaeus envisages a dispute in which two of the rival claimants to an inheritance agree privately, before the court hearing, that whichever of them wins will share the estate with the loser. As he goes on to explain, such an agreement would have been possible between Phylomache and Hagnias's mother, who were claiming independently of each other and on different grounds, but not between Theopompus and Stratocles, because each of them was claiming half of the estate and their claims stood or fell together. But this is a 'straw man' argument, a deliberate distraction from the prosecutor's real point: that Theopompus had agreed to share the estate with Stratocles's son, not with Stratocles himself.

**21 Eubulides's daughter:** Phylomache (see on 'Eubulides's daughter', §9).

**a separate voting urn:** This speech illustrates the voting system in a *diadikasia*, as distinct from an adversarial trial in the Athenian courts (cf. on 'after the ballots had been tipped out', 5.17). There was no prosecutor or defendant in a *diadikasia*, and the judges simply voted in favour of the litigant(s) whose claim they approved. There could be any number of parties to a *diadikasia*, with a voting urn allotted to each (or shared between two or more who were claiming a share of the estate on the same basis). The trial described here, and in [Dem.] 43, is a rare example of a *diadikasia* involving more than two rival claimants. (There were apparently at least four in the case mentioned at [Dem.] 48.30, but the details are obscure.) In many cases, probably the majority, there would be only two claimants and therefore two urns.

In this case, as Theopompus goes on to explain, there were initially four claimants: himself, Stratocles, Phylomache, and Hagnias's mother. Each of the two women, who were claiming independently of each other, had a separate urn; but the two brothers were claiming half the estate each, so if Stratocles had survived he would have shared an urn with Theopompus (cf. on 'providing one voting urn for those who claim on the same grounds', §23).

According to Sositheus's account of the second *diadikasia* ([Dem.] 43.10), in which there were five claimants to the estate, there were four voting urns, one of which was shared between the half-brothers Glaucon and Glaucus (cf. Scafuro, 2011, 144, n.41).

**22 when Stratocles died before our claims to half the estate could be heard:** Stratocles's death before the case came to court extinguished his claim, and consequently that of his son, to a share in Hagnias's estate. If he had survived and been awarded a share of the estate by the court, that share would have become part of his own property and passed to his son when he died, along with the rest of his estate. That is what happened in the case of Theopompus: he inherited the whole estate, and it passed to his son, Macartatus II, on his death (see on 'adopted into the family of Macartatus', §49). But since Stratocles was already dead when the case came to court, his son had no claim to the estate because he was outside the *anchisteia* (cf. on 'if the boy's father didn't leave him the property because it was never adjudicated to him', §26). That point is misunderstood by Edwards (2007, 175): 'Where [Theopompus] may be suspected of trickery is in his argument against the right of Stratocles' son to share the estate'. What is genuinely questionable about Theopompus's case is not his legal argument but his denial that he made a private agreement with Stratocles to share the estate with the latter's son.

**by law ... according to the order of succession:** Once again, Theopompus emphasizes the legal basis of his own possession of the estate (cf. on 'according to the order of succession', §19).

**only then does my opponent start to devise and fabricate these tales:** In the Greek text the verbs *plattei* ('devises') and *mēchanatai* ('fabricates') are in the historic present tense: 'apparently [Theopompus] is becoming animated as he contemplates his opponent's effrontery' (Thompson, 1976, 55).

**with the expectation of easily deceiving you:** Cf. on 'trying to deceive you', §4. Kremmydas (2013, 66) cites this passage as an example of 'by far the most frequently attested sub-category of anti-deception topoi … used to discredit the opponent by portraying him as an agent of deception. The wording used by the orator is cautious lest he alienate his audience; this topos portrays deception as an attempt, an intention, rather than a certainty'.

**Please take the law and read it to them:** Once again, Isaeus bases his client's case firmly on the law. Nothing is known of this particular law, which evidently prescribed the procedure to be followed when an inheritance claim was disputed, apart from Isaeus's brief paraphrase of the relevant provisions.

**23 Do you think … adjudication?:** Again, the reading of a law is followed by a rhetorical question, this time designed to reinforce the point that the opponent's version of events is unlikely to be true because it does not comply with the law. (Cf. on 'Stop. I will question you', §5.)

**by explicitly prescribing that each claimant must claim his own share:** For the meaning of the Greek participle *keleuōn* ('prescribing'), see on 'excluded by the law, which prescribes that males have precedence', §17. In the present context, the adverb *diarrēdēn* ('explicitly') reinforces the interpretation that the law in question was indeed mandatory and not merely permissive. (For the use of *diarrēdēn* in relation to the law, see on 'the laws have explicitly given me the right of inheritance', §13; and cf., e.g., Isae. 3.68: 'the law explicitly says'; 6.63: 'it is explicitly written in the law'; and 10.10: 'the law explicitly forbids').

**providing one voting urn for those who claim on the same grounds:** See on 'a separate voting urn', §21. Isaeus points out that when two people claim an estate on the basis of the same relationship to the deceased, it is impossible for only one of them to win, because they share a single voting urn. While his reasoning is correct, the point is irrelevant to the allegation made by the prosecutor; see on 'impossible to reach a mutual agreement', §20.

**24 to which, gentlemen, please give your attention:** Isaeus boldly urges the judges to pay particular attention to what he ridicules as 'the most contradictory story of all'. For addresses to the judges in this speech, see on 'gentlemen', §8.

**he says that I agreed to give half of the estate to the boy:** Having tried to distract the judges with the 'straw man' argument that Theopompus and Stratocles could not have agreed to share the estate between them, Isaeus now turns to the possibility that Theopompus did agree with Stratocles that, in the event of the latter's death, he would give half of the estate to his nephew if he won the *diadikasia* against Phylomache. Despite the plausibility of this scenario, it is also possible that it was indeed a fabrication by the prosecutor, who had chosen to attack Theopompus on what could be perceived as his weak point.

**on the basis of kinship:** See on 'on the basis of kinship, not a will', §25.

**why would I need to make an agreement with them?:** A cluster of five rhetorical questions culminates in 'how can you believe what they say?', §26.

**25 the laws have given me the right to inherit the whole estate:** Cf. on 'the laws have explicitly given me the right of inheritance', §13. Here, Theopompus's claim is more specific: he is legally entitled to inherit the whole of Hagnias's estate, and not required to share it with his nephew. Isaeus's insistence on the legality of Theopompus's behaviour seems to have been a strategy to conceal the weakest point in his case. Stratocles's son was clearly unlucky in the timing of his father's death (cf. on 'when Stratocles died before our claims to half the estate could be heard', §22), and it might well have been argued on his behalf that Theopompus was acting unfairly (albeit not illegally) in retaining the whole of the estate for himself. Cf. Johnstone (1999, 66): 'It is possible to imagine that Theopompos might have agreed to share the estate … with his nephew … out of fraternal affection, even if the law did not require it'.

**on the basis of kinship, not a will:** The speakers of both Isaeus 1 and Isaeus 4 argue at some length that a claim to an inheritance is more likely to be genuine if it is based on kinship (Gk. *genos*) rather than a will. The argument, which is clearly tendentious, relies strongly on the possibility that a will might be forged, whereas it is 'impossible to lie' about kinship (Isae. 1.41, with Griffith-Williams, 2022). Theopompus is here making a similar point, though he puts it more succinctly.

**no need for witnesses:** Cf. Isae. 4.15 (trans. Griffith-Williams, 2022): 'So you see how difficult it is to understand whether those who claim an estate on the basis of a will are telling the truth, whereas those who claim on the basis of kinship ... have no need to produce witnesses to testify that the estate is theirs (since everyone agrees that the property of a dead man goes to his next of kin)'. This argument is tendentious, because a claimant to an estate might well need witnesses to testify to his relationship to the deceased. And, in the present context, it contradicts Theopompus's earlier suggestion that his opponent ought to produce witnesses to the boy's relationship to Hagnias (§6).

**26** Theopompus summarizes his arguments about the impossibility of a private agreement with a string of three conditional clauses leading to a rhetorical question that invites the judges to discredit his opponent (cf. on 'if I defeated the women in this way', §19).

**if it was impossible ... while he was alive:** Theopompus has explained at §§20–21 why it was 'impossible' for him and Stratocles to make an agreement.

**if the boy's father didn't leave him the property because it was never adjudicated to him:** For the effect of Stratocles's death on his son's claim to the estate, see on 'when Stratocles died before our claims to half the estate could be heard', §22.

**since you adjudicated this inheritance to me:** See on 'property that you adjudicated to me', §14.

**how can you believe what they say?:** The rhetorical question hardly needs an answer, but Isaeus hammers the point home by adding 'Not at all, in my view'. Cf. on 'They have no such right', §12.

*27–31: The prosecutor's choice of procedure (argumentation)*

Theopompus attacks his opponent for choosing to prosecute him in a public action; while acknowledging that this choice was legally permissible, he claims that it was inappropriate in the circumstances of the case, and asserts that his opponent's real motive for bringing the case was personal malice and a desire to punish Theopompus, not to obtain justice for the orphan.

**27 at the time:** This refers to the situation described at §10: after Stratocles died, and Theopompus was (on his own account) left as the only legitimate claimant to the estate, it would have been possible for the other guardian to file a claim on behalf of the orphan.

**did not pay a deposit:** According to Theopompus, his opponent refrained from claiming the estate on behalf of Stratocles's son because he knew he would lose the deposit if he did so (see on 'pay a deposit', §13, and 'did not think it appropriate to pay a deposit', §15). But the opponent has evidently said that there was no need for him to submit a claim and pay the deposit, because Theopompus had agreed to share the estate with Stratocles's son if he won.

**on their own behalf:** As discussed by Thompson (1976, 38–39), the pronouns in this sentence are confusing. While some editors (including Wyse and Forster) have emended the ms. *autois* ('to them', dat.) to *autous* ('them', acc.), Thompson's solution, which I have adopted, is to retain the dative case but make the pronoun reflexive (*hautois*); this gives the meaning 'for themselves' or 'on their own behalf'.

**because orphans are not allowed to claim against their guardians:** As discussed by Hatzilambrou (2018b, 347), there appears to have been no law prohibiting an orphan from prosecuting his guardian, although in practice he would have needed to have another guardian who was prepared to undertake the action on his behalf. So in this case, as Isaeus argues, there was no reason why Theopompus's fellow guardian could not have brought a private action against him on behalf of Stratocles's son, instead of resorting to a public action (*eisangelia*).

Isaeus never refers specifically to his nephew and nieces as 'orphans' (see on 'the boy', §1), but the term is used here in a more general legal context.

**28 just as the law allows a public action against me:** Theopompus does not question the legality of the prosecutor's action against him, even though he asserts that a private action would have been more appropriate. In the Greek text, here and at §§31, 32, and 35, *graphē* is used as a generic term for any public action, including an *eisangelia* as in the present case. (See on '*eisangelia*', §6.)

**29 not within the order of succession:** See on 'outside the order of succession', §7.

**they would easily have been deprived of it by the next of kin:** Again, Isaeus's reasoning is correct but misleading: if the court had awarded a share of Hagnias's estate to Stratocles's son, the adjudication would have been vulnerable to challenge from a relative whose position in the order of succession was higher. But after the whole estate was awarded to Theopompus, there was nothing to prevent him from simply giving part of it to the boy, and it is possible that he and Stratocles had agreed that he would do this before the latter's death.

**as I have already said … on his mother's side:** Theopompus again reiterates the main point of his legal argument, introduced at §2 and elaborated at §12: that after 'children of cousins' (i.e. second cousins) on the father's side, the next in the order of succession are not their children but the relatives of the deceased on his mother's side.

**30 outside the order of succession:** See on 'outside the order of succession', §7.

**also within the order of succession to her son:** This is not to be taken as suggesting that any Athenian mother was a member of her son's *anchisteia*; Hagnias's mother was also his second cousin. (See on 'Hagnias's mother', §8, and cf. Hatzilambrou (2018b, 348) on the argumentation in this section.)

**31 sykophantic proceedings:** See on 'pursuing a malicious prosecution', §4.

**started a public action:** See on 'just as the law allows a public action against me', §28.

**by slandering me:** See on 'so clever at slander and twisting the laws', §4. On the association of slander with sykophancy, cf. Aesch. 2.145: 'slander (*diabolē*) is the sister of sykophancy'.

**remove me from the guardianship:** Cf. on 'subject me to the most serious risks', §13. A guardian who was defeated in an *eisangelia kakōseōs orphanou* was at risk of being deprived of his guardianship. Theopompus implies that his opponent wants to become the orphan's sole guardian in order to continue defrauding him without interference (cf. on 'squander the boy's property … with impunity', below).

**these devices:** The Greek word *paraskeuai* (lit. 'preparations') may have negative overtones ('devices', 'machinations', 'conspiracy'). Wyse (1904, 375) describes this pejorative usage as 'the stock phrase of Athenian pleaders for an opponent's activity' (citing, *inter alia*, Isae. 4.5, 11.31, Ant. 5.79, Andoc. 1.1, Lys. 3.2, 12.75, 19.2, 28.11, [Dem.] 43.10, 32, 81).

**won't lose anything of his own:** Theopompus has already accused his opponent of failing to claim a share of the estate on the orphan's behalf through the proper procedure, in order to avoid paying the deposit that would have been required. (See on 'did not pay a deposit', §27.) Now, for the first time, he points out that the opponent has gained a further advantage from his choice of procedure: the prosecutor in an *eisangelia* was exempt from the penalty that applied in other public actions (*graphai*) if he failed to secure a specified percentage of the judges' votes. On the prosecutor's freedom from financial risk as one of the 'principal distinguishing features' of the *eisangelia*, see Harrison (1968, 118). For the 'prosecution is risk-free' topos in *eisangeliai* and other Athenian trials, cf. Whitehead (2000, 124).

**squander the boy's property ... with impunity:** Another allusion to the prosecutor's alleged attempts at fraudulent mismanagement of the ward's property (cf. on 'if I had administered property as badly as he has done', §14, and 'if I had allowed him to waste the boy's property and not opposed him', §16).

*32–36: Summary of Theopompus's case*

These sections of the speech, which effectively conclude Theopompus's legal defence, have some of the features of the conventional epilogue that one might expect to find at the end of the speech as a whole. But rather than straightforwardly summarizing the main points of the defence, Isaeus frames them within an attack on the prosecutor's choice of procedure, pointing out what course he ought to have followed if there had been any substance in his allegations. As Thompson (1976, 45) observes: 'This unit plays an important part in the overall design of the speech. Theopompos opened his case confidently, expounding the inheritance law. Then in his narrative he had the opportunity to present the facts according to his own lights. But beginning with section 20 he lost the offensive and was forced to answer specific allegations made by his opponent. Now he has reversed their positions: he goes onto the attack, in effect making his opponent the defendant on a charge of bringing an improper suit'.

**32 You must not ... encourage the bringing of public actions about matters for which the laws have created private actions:** Again, as at §28, the generic term *graphai* is used for 'public actions', while 'private actions' are *idiai dikai.*

Other forensic speakers object to a prosecutor's choice of procedure (Ant. 6.9, Hyp. *Eux.* 1–10) or anticipate such an objection from the defendant (Dem. 21.25–26), but Theopompus goes further with the more general point that a litigant should not resort to a public action in a case where a private action is available. Such a bold assertion, while in keeping with his characterization as a confident and experienced speaker, does not necessarily reflect a wider Athenian consensus or an established policy. (On the choice of procedures available to Athenian litigants, cf. the introduction to this speech, pp. 129–30.)

**leave them in your memory:** Reminding the judges of the salient facts of the case was one of the functions of an epilogue; cf. Arist. *Rhet.* 13.4.

**the rest of my defence against the accusations:** Theopompus looks forward to the concluding sections of the speech (from §37) where he deals with the prosecutor's allegations that he has concealed the extent of his wealth.

**33 So … how would I define them?:** Theopompus's meaning could have been expressed as a direct statement: 'These are the rights of the case, and this is how I define them'. Instead, by using a rhetorical question, Isaeus engages the judges in the argument and creates the impression of a dialogue with them.

**If, on the one hand …:** Again (see on 'If he is shown to be related in some way …', §3), Isaeus uses logical conditions, which convey the impression that Theopompus is being fair and reasonable to his opponent. Here, the seven conditional clauses in Theopompus's summary of 'the rights of the case' also add credibility to his complaints about the prosecutor's choice of procedure by enumerating the range of available alternatives. As Thompson (1976, 43) points out: 'The first three alternatives are ones which [Isaeus] has already discussed, and … he adds one other possibility just for the sake of completeness'.

**according to the order of succession:** See on 'according to the order of succession', §19.

**if you vote in his favour:** See on 'property that you adjudicated to me', §14.

**for that is what the laws prescribe:** Theopompus seeks to convey an impression of fairness by signalling that he would be happy to comply with the law in the event (however unlikely he thinks it is) that his opponent won a legal claim to half of the estate on behalf of the boy. The law cited at [Dem.] 43.16 lays down the procedure to be followed by someone claiming an estate that has already been awarded by the court to someone else. It was on the basis of this law that Theopompus and others contested Hagnias's estate against Phylomache at the second *diadikasia*. For the meaning of the Greek verb *keleuein*, translated here as 'prescribe', see on 'excluded by the law, which prescribes that males have precedence', §17.

**although I deny that there is any truth in that:** Theopompus has already strongly denied (§§20–26) that he agreed to give half of the estate to the boy. By repeating the denial here, he reminds the judges that he is now dealing with a purely hypothetical scenario (perhaps in a tacit admission that he knows this is the weak point in his case).

**for that is only right:** Again, this contributes to the impression of reasonableness that Theopompus wants to convey.

**34 let him say what law forbids this:** See on 'because orphans are not allowed to claim against their guardians', §27.

**but that the property already belongs to the boy:** It is unlikely that the prosecutor claimed that there was no need for any further litigation because the property already belonged to Stratocles's son (although, since we do not have the text of his speech, we cannot be sure). Isaeus is apparently suggesting a hypothetical possibility for the sake of completing his argument (cf. on 'If, on the one hand', §33).

**let him register it ... as belonging to the boy:** This is Theopompus's only reference to the fact that the property left by Stratocles to his children was, or could be, leased by their guardians, and he does not say whether Stratocles had left instructions that this should be done. Property to be leased on behalf of orphans, whether on the instructions of their father or at the guardians' discretion, had to be registered with the archon, who would then put it up for auction (cf. Isae. 6.35–37, with Griffith-Williams, 2022). In this case, Wyse (1904, 702) suggests: 'If guardians were quarrelling about the management of an estate, it would be natural to appeal to the Archon to grant a lease'.

**the orphan's estate:** Isaeus usually avoids referring to Stratocles's son as an 'orphan' (see on 'the boy', §1), but here, as at §27, the term is used in a legal context.

**35 and also what the laws prescribe:** Cf. on 'for that is what the laws prescribe', §33: having indicated his own willingness to abide by the law, Theopompus now demands the same of his opponent.

**If I were holding property that was agreed to belong to the boy, and had harmed him by maladministering any of it:** Again, in a show of reasonableness, Theopompus concedes that maladministration of an orphan's estate would be grounds for an *eisangelia kakōseōs orphanou* – but, of course, he denies any such maladministration.

**by Zeus:** The oath, repeated at the end of §35 and varied with 'by the gods' in §36, is ironic, inviting the judges to join Theopompus in ridiculing his opponent's inappropriate choice of procedure. Isaeus's use of formulaic oaths (imprecations) is relatively sparing; they occur in only five of his 12 extant speeches (3, 4, 6, 7, and 11). As noted by Griffith-Williams (2022, 153), they are a feature of colloquial speech used to convey an impression of spontaneity and often associated with an 'intense effort to persuade' (Denommé, 1974, 122).

**in a public action:** See on 'just as the law allows a public action against me', §28.

**a matter on which the laws have created a private action:** See on 'You must not …', §32.

**put me at personal risk:** Literally meaning 'concerning my body/person', the Greek phrase *peri tou sōmatos* could refer to a penalty of death, exile, or disfranchisement (as distinct from merely financial risk in the event of a fine). Cf. Lys. 1.50 and 9.15 (with Todd, 2007); also Phillips (2013, 127).

Although in theory the most extreme penalties were available for a convicted defendant in an *eisangelia kakōseōs* (cf. Isae. 3.62, where *peri tou sōmatos* refers to the penalty in a potential *eisangelia* for mistreatment of an 'heiress'), it is unlikely in the present case that Theopompus was really at risk of capital punishment or exile. If he lost the case, he is more likely to have faced the loss of some of his civic rights or to have been removed from his role as guardian (cf. on 'subject me to the most serious risks', §13, and 'remove me from the guardianship', §31).

**an estate which I received by your vote:** See on 'property that you adjudicated to me', §14.

**36 greed:** Although it might seem an obvious motive for fabricating a claim to an inheritance, 'greed' (Gk. *pleonexia*) is mentioned only twice in Isaeus's speeches (cf. Isae. 8.2, with Griffith-Williams, 2013; also [Dem.] 44.28, 35, 38).

**slandering:** Once again, Theopompus accuses his opponent of slander; see on 'pursuing a malicious prosecution', §4.

**distorting the laws:** Cf. on 'so clever at slander and twisting the laws', §4. Here, the Greek verb is not *diastrephein* but *paragein*, sometimes used with a personal object in the sense of 'mislead' or 'deceive'. Cf. Dem. 20.98, 22.34, 23.215, 45.87, 46.1 (cited by Kremmydas, 2013, 88).

**by the gods:** See on 'by Zeus', §35.

**I don't know what more I need to say:** These words, which effectively conclude Theopompus's legal defence, add to the impression of an epilogue. A similar formula ('I don't know of anything I ought to add' is used at the conclusion of two other speeches by Isaeus (Isae. 7.45, 8.46); cf.

Dem. 20.167; 36.62; 38.28; 54.44, cited by Griffith-Williams, 2013, 88). Cf. on 'what further information do you need …?', §19.

*37–50: Theopompus's wealth compared with that of Stratocles and his son*

Isaeus presents this part of the speech as the rebuttal of an attempt by the prosecutor to blacken Theopompus's character by portraying him as rich but mean: a 'useless citizen' who conceals the true extent of his wealth in order to avoid performing public services (the Athenian equivalent of tax evasion) and who in the private sphere refuses to contribute to the dowries of his orphaned nieces. Far from being 'beside the point' (Wyse, 1904, 675), such allegations were directly relevant to the prosecution case, because a man who could be shown to have avoided other financial responsibilities would have been seen by an Athenian court as all the more likely to withhold property that he ought (legally or morally) to have relinquished to his nephew (cf. Thompson, 1976, 56). So these were not 'invidious side-issues' (Wyse, 1904, 677), and it was important for Theopompus to defend himself. He does so by claiming, first, that he has not avoided liturgies but performed all the duties required of him by the state; and, secondly, that Stratocles's children were not left in poverty but with more than sufficient resources to pay for the girls' dowries without unfairly diminishing the son's inheritance.

But Isaeus also had another, more subtle agenda: to extend and elaborate his argumentation from probability about the alleged private agreement between Theopompus and Stratocles. Perhaps some of the judges saw through the argument that such an agreement would not have been legally possible, and suspected that Theopompus had simply agreed to give half of the estate to Stratocles's son as a gesture of goodwill. If so, this comparison of the brothers' respective wealth was designed to reassure them: not only was it unnecessary for Theopompus to share the estate with his nephew, but also unlikely that Stratocles would have expected him to do so.

It was clearly in Theopompus's interest to downplay the value of his own property while exaggerating that of Stratocles, and for the modern reader there would be little point in trying to assess the accuracy of his account. This commentary focuses, accordingly, on Isaeus's persuasive technique, while also pointing out the insights the passage provides into the effect of marriage and adoption on patterns of land tenure in fourth-century Attica.

We do not know exactly how the speech concluded, because the manuscript text is incomplete. In the extant text, Theopompus mentions two topics to which he probably reverted in the missing section: his plans for the administration of the orphan's estate (§40) and his claim that his opponents have pilfered part of the estate (§44). On that basis, Thompson (1976, 60) conjectures that Isaeus 'relied primarily on the argument based on character, contrasting Theopompos' efforts to augment his ward's holdings with the other guardian's desire to obtain complete control of the property in order to pillage it'.

**37 I see, gentlemen:** The transition to a new section of the speech is marked by a direct address to the judges.

**contribute to the dowries:** For the dowry as a woman's share of her father's estate, see on 'a dowry of 40 minas', 5.26. Once Stratocles's son came of age, he would take over the whole of Stratocles's estate, and with it the responsibility to provide dowries for any of his four sisters who remained unmarried. In the meantime, the estate would be managed by Theopompus and his fellow guardian (the prosecutor) and used for the maintenance of all of Stratocles's children, including the provision of dowries for any of the daughters who reached marriageable age while the estate remained in the control of the guardians. The prosecutor has, apparently, suggested that Theopompus ought to contribute to the dowries from his own resources, because Stratocles's estate was not large enough to make adequate provision for them.

**38 arouse your envy against me:** Sanders (2014, 82) cites this as one of four statements in the Attic oratorical corpus that the speaker's opponent wants to arouse the judges' envy towards the speaker (the others are Isoc. 11.38, Dem. 21.29 and 29.2). Stirring the judges' envy of Theopompus, and pity for the orphans, may well have been an effect of the prosecutor's character assassination, but his primary motive is more likely to have been convincing them that Theopompus had defrauded his nephew out of meanness.

**so that you know he is lying:** Theopompus accuses the prosecutor of lying not only in his interpretation of the law and his 'fabrications' about a private agreement, but also (here and at §47) by exaggerating the extent of Theopompus's wealth in comparison with that of Stratocles. It is, of course, impossible to know which of the opposing litigants was really telling the truth; it was up to the judges to decide which version was more plausible.

**I would admit, gentlemen:** Once again, Theopompus purports to show magnanimity towards his opponent, using a conditional clause to explain in what circumstances he would concede the case (cf. on 'If he is shown to be related in some way …', §3, and 'If, on the one hand …', §33). Here, though, the balance of the logical condition is abandoned in favour of a much more explicit denial of the proposition.

Another direct address draws attention to Theopompus's 'admission' (in reality a denial that he has neglected or mistreated Stratocles's children). The proximity of the two vocative addresses in §37 above, in a speech with only six such addresses in total, underlines the intensity of Isaeus's effort to engage the judges in his argument at this stage. (Cf. on 'gentlemen', §8.)

**if it were shown that … failed to take care of his children:** Theopompus's exact words are worth noting: he does not say that he would be the most wicked of men if he had failed to take care of his brother's children when they were in need, but *if it were shown* that he had failed to do so. As Dover (1974, 226) observes: 'in cases where a modern speaker would probably make some reference to good and bad conscience, the Athenians tended instead to use expressions such as "be seen to …", "be regarded as …", and these expressions were also used where we would refer neither to conscience nor to reputation, so that an Athenian's "I wanted to be regarded as honest" is equivalent to our "I wanted to be honest". In such cases there was no intention, of course, of drawing a distinction between disguise and reality; it was rather that goodness divorced from a reputation for goodness was of limited interest'.

**39 more secure:** The fortune left by Stratocles to his children is 'more secure' than Theopompus's own in the sense that he is not yet securely in possession of Hagnias's estate because of the pending prosecutions for false testimony mentioned at §45.

**rather, I deserve praise for conserving and increasing their estate:** Again, the wording is significant: the emphasis is on a reputation for virtue rather than virtue in itself.

**I will easily prove to you that this is in fact the case:** In this part of the speech, as Thompson (1976, 49) observes: 'Isaeus is not interested in proof, he is interested in persuasion'.

**40 the details of the boy's property:** The minute detail in which Theopompus enumerates the orphan's property at §§40–43 seems calculated to create an impression in the judges' minds of a very large estate.

**how I see fit to administer it:** Presumably Theopompus dealt with this issue in the missing conclusion to the speech.

**indication:** See on 'more evidence', 5.26, for the semantic range of the Greek word *tekmērion* (here translated as 'indication'). In this instance, the size of the dowry an Athenian received with his wife could be taken as an indication of his own relative wealth, but it was not conclusive proof.

**such a small dowry ... a husband of substantial means:** Theopompus and Stratocles might have had various reasons for accepting a wife with a dowry of only 20 minas, which was certainly modest compared with, say, the 40 minas given to Protarchides with one of the sisters of Dicaeogenes I (5.26). The speaker of Isaeus 2 says that he and his brother (who were left with limited resources after their father's death) gave their two sisters in marriage with dowries of 20 minas each. Menecles, who married the younger sister, was wealthy, and his motivation for the marriage was not financial but rather his friendship with the speaker's deceased father and a desire to strengthen the bonds between the two families (Isae. 2.3–5, with Griffith-Williams, 2022).

**41 Theophon:** An unusual name; Stratocles's brother-in-law is one of seven individuals of that name listed in *LGPN*, of whom only two are in Attica (deme or demes unknown).

**adopted one of Stratocles's daughters:** Theophon, like Hagnias, adopted his niece, and this was evidently another testamentary adoption, coming into effect only after Theophon's death. On the disadvantages of adopting a daughter rather than a son, see on 'adopted his niece as his daughter', §8. In this case, Stratocles had four daughters (§37) but only one son, so he would have been left without a male heir if that son had been adopted into a different *oikos*.

**land at Eleusis worth two talents ... a fine horse:** Denommé (1974, 166) suggests that the rhythmical accumulation of nouns in this list could easily have led the judges to overestimate the value of Stratocles's property.

**Eleusis:** One of the demes of Attica; see on 'the battle at Eleusis', 5.42.

**phylarch:** The fact that Theophon served as a phylarch (leader of his tribe or *phylē*) hints at a distinguished military career (cf. on 'commanding the cavalry at Spartolus', 5.42).

**42 After having control of this property for nine whole years:** Despite the lack of detail in this passage, it is clear that after Theophon's adoption of his niece, her natural father, Stratocles, became her guardian. (Theophon probably appointed Stratocles as guardian in his will, although Theopompus does not explicitly say so.) Control of the estate would have passed to her husband when she married, so, since the customary age of marriage for an Athenian girl was around 16, the length of Stratocles's guardianship indicates that she must have been a small child at the time of her adoption. In fact, it is not made clear whether the guardianship was terminated by the girl's marriage or by the death of Stratocles. Thompson (1976, 53) assumes that Theopompus was also one of the girl's guardians, but that is not certain.

**land at Thria:** See on 'Oenoë', §44.

**a house at Melite:** Melite was a city deme in the western part of Athens, close to the Buselids' ancestral deme of Oeum Ceramicum and 'on a good communication route to the Thriasian Plain where [Stratocles's] property was located' (Cox, 1998, 9).

**43 interest-free loans:** The Greek word *eranos* means 'an interest-free loan granted by a group of men to accommodate a friend or client. The contributors sometimes chose a treasurer to manage the arrangement' (Thompson, 1976, 53).

**the other property left, which my opponents won't disclose:** This vague allusion hints that Stratocles's estate could have been significantly larger than Theopompus is able to enumerate.

**Please call the witnesses to what I have said:** It is striking that the only witness testimony adduced by Theopompus, here and at §44, relates to the accuracy of his statements about the extent of his and Stratocles's property. No testimony was used to support his account of the earlier litigation about Hagnias's estate. On the use of written testimony in the Athenian courts, and the formulae used to introduce witness testimony, see the introduction to Isaeus 5 (pp. 28–30).

**44 I'll speak later about what my opponents have pilfered:** Theopompus has already accused his opponent of mismanaging their ward's property (§§14, 16, 31). Presumably he reverted to this subject in the missing sections at the end of the speech. As Thompson (1976, 60, n.100) points out: 'Not only will this magnify the size of the ward's estate, it will give Theopompos a chance to expand on his theme that the other guardian is the real criminal'.

The Greek verb translated here as 'pilfer' is *parakleptein*. Todd (2018, 255) notes that compounds of *kleptein* ('to steal') are more often used metaphorically than literally: 'The only literal usages of compound verb forms in the orators are Dem. 27.12 (*diakleptō*), Isa. 11.44 (*parakleptō*), and Antiph. 6.35 (*synkleptō*)'.

**And how much is my property worth?:** Again, by posing a question instead of making a direct statement, Isaeus creates the impression of a dialogue between the speaker and his audience. In contrast with his detailed enumeration of the estate left by Stratocles (cf. on 'the details of the boy's property', §40), Theopompus gives only a summary account of his own property, expressing the value in round figures. Specifically, he mentions two pieces of land, worth 5,000 and 3,000 drachmas respectively, and a house worth 2,000. So, before he acquired the estate of Hagnias, the total value of his property was 10,000 drachmas (or one talent and 40 minas).

**Oenoë:** There were two demes of this name; Theopompus does not specify whether his property was in Oenoë of the tribe Hippothontis or of Aeantis. According to Cox (1998, 8): 'If Theopompus's land at Oenoë was in Hippothontis, then it was located in northwest Attica en route to his brother Stratocles' holdings which were at Eleusis, in the same trittys as Oenoë, and which were also at Thria nearby'.

**Prospalta:** An inland deme of the tribe Acamantis, southeast of the city, sending five members to the Boule. Theopompus's wife was a daughter of Apolexis of Prospalta ([Dem.] 43.48). As Cox (1998, 8) points out, Theopompus was therefore unusual among the Buselidae in that he married outside the family and its ancestral deme, Oeum Ceramicum. His wife inherited the estate at Prospalta from her brother (see on 'Chaereleus left the estate at Prospalta', §49).

**a house in the city:** Theopompus does not specify the location of his city house, which may have been in Oeum Ceramicum.

**worth about two talents:** Theopompus gives no details of the property left by Hagnias, and only a vague estimate of its value. Cf. Thompson (1976, 54): 'Just how much Hagnias' estate was really worth, we have no idea. Notice that Theopompos does not magnify its importance by enumerating the properties or monies of which it consisted. Nor, of course, does he itemize the animals or buildings of his farms, nor tell the jury the income of his possessions. The object is not to conceal, but simply to oppose as few discrete units as possible against as many as possible in the boy's estate'.

**45 the property of my son who was adopted out of the family:** The estate at Prospalta (§44) had become the property of Theopompus's son Macartatus II after his posthumous adoption as the son of Macartatus I (§49).

**not yet securely mine:** Despite his confident assertions that the estate of Hagnias has been lawfully awarded to him by the court, it now suits Theopompus's argument to admit that his tenure of the estate will not be finally secure until the question of false testimony is settled (see following notes, and cf. on 'more secure', §39).

**prosecutions for false testimony are under way:** Thompson (1976, 56) sees a discrepancy between this section and §25, where Theopompus 'tried to maintain that he had no need of witnesses in his contest with Phylomache'. But the point made by Theopompus at §25 was that he had no need of witnesses to prove his own relationship to Hagnias; the disputed testimony must have concerned the status of Phylomache (see on 'those who were lying … what was not true', §17), and the prosecutions were presumably started by Sositheus on her behalf. It is not clear whether they ever went to trial; if so, they must have been unsuccessful, since the estate remained in the possession of Theopompus until his death (cf. the introduction to this speech, p. 112).

**46 the law prescribes … must start again from the beginning:** Thompson (1976, 55) sees no reason to doubt that Isaeus's statement of the law is accurate: 'Some scholars object to Isaeus' formulation of the law on the *a priori* ground that it would permit a judgement to be overturned by conviction for a minor or irrelevant falsehood. But this founders on the problem of how to decide what is irrelevant or minor. Today a panel of judges would review a transcript of the trial to determine this question, but the Athenians had neither transcripts nor a Supreme Court. The only practical way would be to stay the previous verdict and rehear all the evidence, i.e. to have a new trial, just as Isaeus indicates'. For an alternative view, see on 'the witnesses who had not yet been convicted', 5.13.

On the meaning of 'the law prescribes' (Gk. *ho nomos keleuei*), see on 'by explicitly requiring each claimant to claim his own share', §23.

**Please take and read the witness statements:** See on 'Please call the witnesses to what I have said', §43.

**47 Is there only a small difference … that of Stratocles's children?:** Yet again, Isaeus engages the judges in his argument by turning what could have been expressed as a direct statement into a question, but he is careful to steer them towards the answer he wants.

**he has had the audacity to slander me by lying:** Theopompus has already accused his opponent four times of slandering him and twice of lying (see on 'pursuing a malicious prosecution', §4), at this point by exaggerating the extent of his wealth.

**three inheritances:** Theopompus had inherited half of his father's estate, which he shared with his brother Stratocles, as well as the whole of that of Hagnias, and (as his wife's *kyrios*) that of his brother-in-law Macartatus I. There was no legal restriction on the number of estates an Athenian could inherit, but this passage, among others in Isaeus's speeches, suggests that there may have been some prejudice against those who received more than one; cf. Isae. 7.44 and 10.23, with Griffith-Williams (2013).

**concealing my wealth:** Theopompus's opponent has evidently accused him of concealing the extent of his property in order to avoid performing public services (liturgies), perhaps arguing that such dishonesty was characteristic of a man who was prepared to defraud his nephew (cf. Thompson, 1976, 56).

On the rhetorical use of liturgy avoidance to slander an opponent, see Christ (1990, 159): 'While the boasts and slanders of individual litigants obviously deserve close scrutiny, it is significant that speakers regularly play off the popular belief that the rich conceal their assets to avoid public service … The frequent claim of litigants that their opponents were liturgy dodgers must also reflect the receptiveness of popular audiences to such charges'.

**Those who have nothing just to say … to get the better of their opponents by slandering them:** On allegations of slander as a tactic in Theopompus's counter-attack on the prosecutor, see on 'pursuing a malicious prosecution', §4. Here, rather than accusing the prosecutor explicitly of using slander as a substitute for legally valid arguments, Isaeus seeks to undermine him with the more general statement that this is a tactic commonly used by litigants who do not have a sound case.

**48 you are all my witnesses:** Theopompus now enlists the judges themselves as metaphorical 'witnesses', in addition to the real witnesses whose testimony has just been read. Thompson (1976, 57) points to the similarity between this rhetorical device and the 'everyone knows' topos: 'It is not unusual for a speaker to call upon the jurors as witnesses to a matter of common knowledge (or wide-spread prejudice). Aside from easing the burden of proof, this device establishes a bond between the speaker and the jury, who share this knowledge between them'.

In a more recent study, Chris Carey has drawn a distinction between what he calls the 'dicast-witness motif' and the 'everyone knows' topos: while the latter often alludes to mere rumour or hearsay, in the absence of hard evidence, the explicit identification of judges as witnesses 'carries implications of direct personal acquaintance with the facts and events' (Carey, 2024, 143). Although it does sometimes provide cover for the lack of real evidence, 'for the most part, the [dicast-witness] motif just offers an effective way of adding dramatic vividness, engaging the audience more personally, or offering a persuasive reconstruction of a moment in time or a set of events'. See Carey (2024, 143–44) for further discussion and parallels.

**my wife's brothers, Chaereleus and Macartatus:** Theopompus's wife is identified by Sositheus ([Dem.] 43.48) as a daughter of Apolexis of Prospalta. On the naming of women in the case, see on 'Eubulides's daughter', §9.

Both of Theopompus's brothers-in-law had unusual names. Six men named Chaereleus, all in Attica, are listed in *LGPN*, while there are only five individuals named Macartatus, of whom four are in Attica (and one of these was Theopompus's son, who may have taken the name only after his posthumous adoption as the son of the older Macartatus; see on 'adopted into the family of Macartatus', §49).

**You know:** See on 'you are all my witnesses', above.

**sold his land and bought a trireme:** Neither the value nor the location of Macartatus's land is mentioned, but it may have been part of his family's ancestral property at Prospalta (see below). He presumably bought his trireme secondhand, at a considerably lower cost than that of building and equipping a new one (cf. Thompson, 1976, 57).

**sailed away in it to Crete ... a war instead of peace between us and Sparta:** The older Macartatus appears to have been involved in an expedition to collect booty on behalf of a Cretan city at war with Sparta (cf. Thompson, 1976, 56).

**a debate in the Assembly:** The wording of the sentence implies that the debate was a fairly recent one, which would have been fresh in the memory of the judges.

**49 Chaereleus left the estate at Prospalta:** Chaereleus evidently died childless and without making a will, so that his property went in the first instance to his brother, Macartatus, as his next of kin. After Macartatus's death it passed to their sister, Theopompus's wife, and subsequently to her son Macartatus II as the posthumously adopted son of Macartatus I (see following notes). Theopompus would have administered the property on behalf of his wife, and it would, presumably, have counted as part of his own property for the purpose of taxation (cf. Thompson, 1976, 57).

**persuaded by her:** Theopompus does not explain why his wife wanted one of their sons to become the adopted son of her deceased brother. (On posthumous adoption, see the General Introduction, p. 4.) Typically, in other cases, posthumous adoption is explained in moral or even religious terms, as a way of ensuring the continuity of the deceased relative's *oikos* (line of descent) and ensuring that there will be someone to carry out the commemorative rituals for him (see, e.g., Isae. 7.31–32, [Dem.] 43.11–12). Rubinstein (1993, 111) sees the absence of such reasoning from Isae. 11 as evidence that 'posthumous adoption was not always construed as an act of piety'. It is, nevertheless, quite possible that Theopompus's wife did use such arguments in their private conversations, but that Theopompus (or Isaeus on his behalf) did not think it necessary or appropriate to mention them in a speech which is predominantly concerned with law and property.

Persuasion, especially through the agency of a woman, is often presented negatively in Isaeus's speeches because it is associated with irrationality or deception, particularly when a speaker argues that a will or adoption is invalid under Solon's law because the testator or adopter was acting under the influence of a woman (Gk. *gynaiki peithomenos*, lit. 'persuaded by a woman'). In this instance, unusually, female persuasion seems to have no such negative connotations; Theopompus gives no indication that he regrets his decision or considers it ill-judged. Perhaps this reflects the reality that Athenian women did have considerable influence in family matters, which was not necessarily irrational or detrimental in its effect.

**our second son:** Since Theopompus had two sons, he was not left without a male heir when one of them was adopted out of his family (cf. on 'adopted one of Stratocles's daughters', §41).

**adopted into the family of Macartatus:** This is one of seven examples of posthumous adoption listed by Rubinstein (1993, 121–23) in her catalogue of attested adoptions. There is some evidence, from the title of a lost speech by Lysias, that the estate of Macartatus I was contested (*On the estate of Macartatus*, or *On half of the property of Macartatus*, Lys. frr. 117–18, *OCT*). If so, it is not clear whether the litigation took place before or after the posthumous adoption (Rubinstein, 1993, 123).

When Theopompus died, his estate, including the property he had inherited from Hagnias, went to his son Macartatus, who had returned to his birth family ([Dem.] 43.77). Since Macartatus inherited the whole of Theopompus's estate, Theopompus's other son must have died, and his death was probably the trigger for Macartatus's return.

**not to avoid performing liturgies:** The negation makes it clear that the prosecutor has accused Theopompus of arranging the posthumous adoption because he would have become liable to the performance of liturgies if

Macartatus's property had been added to his own. (On the technique of 'presentation through negation', as used in Athenian forensic oratory, see Griffith-Williams, 2013, 59–60.)

**50 I did not perform fewer liturgies than before … carried out all the public duties you prescribed:** Theopompus gives no details of the liturgies and other public duties he has performed. That, in other circumstances, might be taken as an indication that they were relatively modest, since a litigant with an impressive record of public service would normally be anxious to enumerate it at length (cf. Lewis, 1959, 164). In this context, however, it is in Theopompus's interest to play down the extent of his wealth as far as possible.

Scholars have, in fact, debated whether Theopompus was really qualified to perform liturgies at all, because his property, on his own account, seems to fall short of the minimum requirement (generally accepted to be three talents). Wyse (1904, 712–13) thinks that Isaeus's use of the vocabulary of liturgies in this passage is a mere *lusus verborum*, suggesting that Theopompus had simply performed duties, such as military service, that were required of all citizens. Lewis (1959, 163) takes issue with Wyse, describing Theopompus's words as 'a guileless statement of fact, to be taken at face value'.

**slandering me:** See on 'so clever at slander and twisting the laws', §4.

**a wealthy but useless citizen:** A typical characterization of an Athenian who has (allegedly) not used his wealth for the benefit of the city. Theopompus's character may have been attacked by his opponent in similar terms to those of Menexenus against Dicaeogenes in Isaeus 5.

**I am willing to combine my estate with that of the boy, and let each of us take half the total:** Theopompus's offer to pool his property with his nephew's and divide the total between them, is reminiscent of the Athenian procedure of *antidosis* (lit. 'exchange') which enabled someone who wanted to evade a liturgy to challenge another, allegedly wealthier citizen, to either perform it in his stead or exchange his property with the challenger. (See Harrison, 1971, 236–38.) As discussed by Thompson (1976, 59–60), the problem, both with the *antidosis* and with Theopompus's challenge, was that only real estate, livestock, and slaves would be exchanged or shared, while cash and investments could easily be concealed. So, in this case, Theopompus could be confident that his opponents would refuse his 'offer'.

# BIBLIOGRAPHY


Adamidis, V. 2017. *Character Evidence in the Courts of Classical Athens: Rhetoric, Relevance and the Rule of Law*, London.

Alwine, A. T. 2015. *Enmity and Feuding in Classical Athens*, Austin, Tex.

Arnaoutoglou, I. 2018. 'Twisting the law in ancient Athens', in *Use and Abuse of Law in the Athenian Courts*, eds C. Carey, I. Giannadaki, and B. Griffith-Williams, Leiden, 181–97.

Avramovič, S. 1997. *Iseo e il Diritto Attico*, Naples. [Originally published Belgrade, 1988, as *Isejovo sudsko besednistvo I atinsko pravo*.]

Blass, F. 1874. *Die Attische Beredsamkeit, zweite Abtheilung: Isokrates und Isaios*, Leipzig.

Blok, J. 2017. *Citizenship in Classical Athens*, Cambridge.

Bonner, R. J. 1905. *Evidence in Athenian Courts*, Chicago.

Bonner, R. J. 1926. 'Administration of justice under Athenian oligarchies', *Classical Philology* 21, 209–17.

Bonner, R. J. and Smith, G. 1930–1938. *The Administration of Justice from Homer to Aristotle*, Chicago.

Broadbent, M. 1968. *Studies in Greek Genealogy*, Leiden.

Brock, R. 2020. 'Civic and local identities in Athenian rhetoric', in *The Making of Identities in Athenian Oratory*, eds J. Filonik, B. Griffith-Williams, and J. Kucharski, London, 15–31.

Cairns, D. 1996. 'Hybris, dishonour and thinking big', *Journal of Hellenic Studies* 116, 1–32.

Calhoun, G. M. 1916. 'ΕΠΙΣΚΗΨΙΣ and the ΔΙΚΗ ΨΕΥΔΟΜΑΡΤΥΡΙΩΝ', *Classical Philology* 11, 365–94.

Calhoun, G. M. 1919. 'Oral and written pleading in Athenian courts', *Transactions and Proceedings of the American Philological Association* 50, 177–93.

Carey, C. 2004. 'Offence and procedure in Athenian law', in *The Law and the Courts in Ancient Greece*, eds E. M. Harris and L. Rubinstein, London, 111–36.

Carey, C. 2007. *Lysiae Orationes cum Fragmentis* (Oxford Classical Texts), Oxford.

Carey, C. 2018. 'Bridging the divide between public and private: *dikē exoulēs* and other hybrids', in *Use and Abuse of Law in the Athenian Courts,* eds C. Carey, I. Giannadaki, and B. Griffith-Williams, Leiden, 75–92.

Carey, C. 2024. 'The dicast as witness', in *Evidence and Proof in Ancient Greece*, eds C. Carey, M. Edwards, and B. Griffith-Williams, Newcastle upon Tyne, 133–44.

Christ, M. R. 1990. 'Liturgy avoidance and *antidosis* in classical Athens', *Transactions of the American Philological Association* 120, 147–69.

Christ, M. R. 1998. *The Litigious Athenian*, Baltimore.

Cobetto Ghiggia, P. 2002. *Iseo, Contro Leocare (Sulla Successione di Diceogene)*, Pisa.

Cobetto Ghiggia, P. 2012. *Iseo, Orazioni: Introduzione, Testo Rivisto, Traduzione, Note e Glossario Giuridico Attico*, Alessandria.

Cohen, D. 1995. *Law, Violence and Community in Classical Athens*, Cambridge.

Cooper, C. 2003. 'Worst of all he's an Egyptian', *Syllecta Classica* 14, 59–81.

Cox, C. A. 1998. *Household Interests: Property, Marriage Strategies, and Family Dynamics in Ancient Athens*, Princeton.

Cudjoe, R. V. 2000. *The Social and Legal Position of Widows and Orphans in Classical Athens*, University of Glasgow PhD thesis: http://theses.gla.ac.uk/2101/

Davies, J. K. 1971. *Athenian Propertied Families, 600-300 BC*, Oxford.

Denommé, J. M. 1974. *Recherches sur la Langue et le Style d'Isée*, Hildesheim.

Dickey, E. 1996. *Greek Forms of Address from Herodotos to Lucian*, Oxford.

Dorjahn, A. P. 1935. 'Anticipation of arguments in Athenian courts', *Transactions and Proceedings of the American Philological Association*, 66, 274–95.

Dover, K. J. 1974. *Greek Popular Morality in the Time of Plato and Aristotle*, Oxford. [repr. 1994].

Edwards, M. J. 2002. 'Two awkward women in Isaeus (IS. 5.9, 26)', *Classical Quarterly* 52, 592–97.

Edwards, M. J. (trans.) 2007. *Isaeus*, Austin, Tex.

Edwards, M. J. 2020. 'Deceptive narratives in the speeches of Isaeus', in *Forensic Narratives in Athenian Courts*, eds M. Edwards and D. Spatharas, London, 71–80.

Edwards, M. J. 2024. 'Oral and written evidence in the speeches of Isaeus', in *Evidence and Proof in Ancient Greece*, eds C. Carey, M. Edwards, and B. Griffith-Williams, Newcastle upon Tyne, 16–27.

Filonik, J. 2024. 'Acquitted/convicted by a single vote? Aeschines 3.252 and vote counts in Athenian oratory', *Mnemosyn*e 2024, 1–14.

Fisher, N. R. E. 1990. 'The law of *hybris* in Athens', in Nomos: *Essays in Athenian Law, Politics and Society*, eds P. Cartledge, P. Millett, and S. C. Todd, Cambridge, 123–38.

Forster, E. S. 1927. *Isaeus, with an English Translation* (Loeb Classical Library) Cambridge, Mass.

Foxhall, L. 1989. 'Household, gender and property in classical Athens', *Classical Quarterly* 39, 22–44.

Gabrielsen, V. 1994. *Financing the Athenian Fleet: Public Taxation and Social Relations*, Baltimore and London.

Griffith-Williams, B. 2012. '*Oikos*, family feuds and funerals: argumentation and evidence in Athenian inheritance disputes', *Classical Quarterly* 62, 145–62.

Griffith-Williams, B. 2013. *A commentary on selected speeches of Isaios*, Leiden.

Griffith-Williams, B. 2014. 'Matrilineal kinship in Athenian inheritance disputes: two case studies', in *Inheritance, Law and Religions in the Ancient and Mediaeval Worlds*, eds B. Caseau and S. R. Huebner, Paris, 91–98.

Griffith-Williams, B. 2016. '"She was treated abominably, gentlemen": women in the Athenian inheritance system', in *The Material Sides of Marriage: Women and Domestic Economies in Antiquity*, ed. R. Berg, Rome, 111–16.

Griffith-Williams, B. 2022. *Greek Orators VIII: Isaeus, Orations 1, 2, 4 and 6* (Aris and Phillips Classical Texts), Liverpool.

Griffith-Williams, B. 2023. 'Blood is (usually) thicker than water: kinship and friendship in ancient Greek inheritance disputes', in *Friendship in Ancient Greek Thought and Literature: Essays in Honour of Chris Carey and Michael Edwards*, eds A. Efstathiou, J. Filonik, C. Kremmydas, and E. Volonaki, Leiden, 306–29.

Griffith-Williams, B. 2025. 'Character evidence in Isaeus's speeches from inheritance disputes', in *Keeping to the Point: Law, Character, and Rhetoric in Athenian Forensic Oratory*, eds E. M. Harris and A. Esu, Edinburgh, 209–31.

Hall, E. 2006. *The Theatrical Cast of Athens: Interactions between Ancient Greek Drama and Society*, Oxford.

Hansen, M. H. 1991. *The Athenian Democracy in the Age of Demosthenes.* Oxford.

Harris, E. M. 2013. *The Rule of Law in Action in Democratic Athens*. Oxford.

Harris, E. M. 2018. 'Trials, private arbitration and public arbitration in classical Athens or the background to [Arist.] *AthPol* 53, 1-7', in Athenaion Politeiai *tra Storia, Politica e Sociologia: Aristotele e Pseudo-Senofonte*, eds C. Bearzot, M. Canevaro, T. Gargiulo, and E. Poddighe, Milan, 213–30.

Harrison, A. R. W. 1947. 'A problem in the rules of intestate succession in Athens', *Classical Review* 61, 41–43.

Harrison, A. R. W. 1968. *The Law of Athens, Volume 1: The Family and Property*, Oxford.

Harrison, A. R. W. 1971. *The Law of Athens, Volume 2: Procedure*, Oxford.

Harvey, D. 1990. 'The sykophant and sykophancy: vexatious redefinition?', in Nomos: *Essays in Athenian Law, Politics and Society*, eds P. Cartledge, P. Millett, and S. C. Todd, Cambridge, 103–21.

Hatzilambrou, R. 2011. 'The use of the "ad hominem" argument in the works of Isaeus', *L'Antiquité Classique* 80, 37–51.

Hatzilambrou, R. 2018a. *Isaeus'* On the Estate of Pyrrhus *(Oration 3)*, Newcastle upon Tyne.

Hatzilambrou, R. 2018b. 'Abuse of inheritance law in Isaios?', in *Use and Abuse of Law in the Athenian Courts*, eds C. Carey, I. Giannadaki, and B. Griffith-Williams, Leiden, 336–51.

Humphreys, S. C. 1983. 'The date of Hagnias' death', *Classical Philology* 78, 219–25.

Hunter, V. J. 1994. *Policing Athens: Social Control in the Attic Lawsuits, 420-320 B.C.* Princeton.

Jebb, R. C. 1876. *The Attic Orators, from Antiphon to Isaeos*, vol. 2, London.

Johnstone, S. 1999. *Disputes and Democracy: The Consequences of Litigation in Ancient Athens*, Austin, Tex.

Kremmydas, C. 2007. *Commentary on Demosthenes* Against Leptines, Oxford.

Kremmydas, C. 2013. 'The discourse of deception and characterization in the Attic orators', *Greek, Roman, and Byzantine Studies* 53, 51–89.

Kucharski, J. 2020. 'Prosecutorial identities and the problem of relevance', in *The Making of Identities in Athenian Forensic Oratory*, eds J. Filonik, B. Griffith-Williams, and J. Kucharski, London, 171–90.

Lanni, A. 1997. 'Spectator sport or serious politics? οἱ περιεστηκότες and the Athenian lawcourts', *Journal of Hellenic Studies* 117, 183–89.

Leão, D. R. and Rhodes, P. J. 2016. *The Laws of Solon: A New Edition with Introduction, Translation and Commentary*, London.

Lewis, N. 1959. 'Pro Isaeo, 11.50', *American Journal of Philology* 80, 162–68.

MacDowell, D. M. 1962. *Andokides* On the Mysteries, Oxford.

MacDowell, D. M. 1976. '"Hybris" in Athens', *Greece & Rome* 23, 14–31.

MacDowell, D. M. 1978a. *The Law in Classical Athens*, London.

MacDowell, D. M. 1978b. 'Review: The estate of Hagnias' [review of Thompson 1976], *Classical Review* 28, 300–01.

MacDowell, D. M. 1989. 'The *oikos* in Athenian law', *Classical Quarterly* 39, 10–21.

MacDowell, D. M. (ed.) 1990. *Demosthenes* Against Meidias *(Oration 21)*, Oxford.

MacDowell, D. M. 2009. *Demosthenes the Orator*, Oxford.

Martin, G. 2006. 'Forms of address in Athenian courts', *Museum Helveticum* 63, 75–88.

McKechnie, P. R. and Kern, S. J. (eds) 1988. *Hellenica Oxyrhynchia* (Aris and Phillips Classical Texts), Oxford.

Miles, J. C. 1950. 'The Attic law of intestate succession (Demosthenes' "Contra Macart." 51), *Hermathena* 75, 69–77.

Ober, J. 1989. *Mass and Elite in Democratic Athens: Rhetoric, Ideology, and the Power of the People*, Princeton.

Osborne, R. 1985. Demos: *The Discovery of Classical Attika*, Cambridge.

Osborne, R. 1990. 'Vexatious litigation in classical Athens: sykophancy and the sykophant', in Nomos: *Essays in Athenian Law, Politics and Society*, eds P. Cartledge, P. Millett, and S. C. Todd, Cambridge, 83–102. [Reprinted with an endnote in Osborne 2010, 205–28.]

Osborne, R. 2010. *Athens and Athenian Democracy*, Cambridge.

Phillips, D. D. 2013. *The Law of Ancient Athens*, Ann Arbor.

Pritchett, W. K. 1955. 'The conditional sentence in Attic Greek', *American Journal of Philology* 76, 1–17.

Rhodes, P. J. 1981. *A Commentary on the Aristotelian* Athenaion Politeia, Oxford.

Roussel, P. 1926. *Isée: Discours*, Paris. [repr. 2003].

Rubinstein, L. 1993. *Adoption in IV. Century Athens*, Copenhagen.

Rubinstein, L. 2018. 'Clauses out of context: partial citation of statutes in Attic forensic oratory', in *Use and Abuse of Law in the Athenian Courts*, eds C. Carey, I. Giannadaki, and B. Griffith-Williams, Leiden, 165–80.

Sanders, E. 2014. *Envy and Jealousy in Classical Athens*, Oxford.

Scafuro, A. (trans.) 2011. *Demosthenes, Speeches 39–49*, Austin, Tex.

Schaps, D. 1977. 'The woman least mentioned: etiquette and women's names', *Classical Quarterly* 27, 323–30.

Schaps, D. 1979. *Economic Rights of Women in Ancient Greece*, Edinburgh.

Sommerstein, A. H. 2013. 'The dicastic oath', in *Oath and State in Ancient Greece*, eds A. H. Sommerstein and A. J. Bayliss, Berlin, 69–80.

Thalheim, T. 1903. *Isaei Orationes cum Deperditarum Fragmentis* (Bibliotheca Teubneriana), Leipzig.

Thomas, R. 1989. *Oral Tradition and Written Record in Classical Athens*, Cambridge.

Thomas, R. 1994. 'Law and lawgiver in the Athenian democracy', in *Ritual, Finance, Politics: Athenian Democratic Accounts Presented to David Lewis*, eds R. Osborne and S. Hornblower, Oxford, 119–33.

Thompson, W. E. 1971. 'Attic kinship terminology', *Journal of Hellenic Studies* 91, 110–13.

Thompson, W. E. 1976. *De Hagniae Hereditate: An Athenian Inheritance Case*, Leiden.

Thompson, W. E. 1981. 'Athenian attitudes toward wills', *Prudentia* 13, 13–25.

Thompson, W. E. 1982. 'The text of Isaeus, XI, 2', *American Journal of Philology* 103, 322–25.

Todd, S. C. 1993. *The Shape of Athenian Law*, Oxford.

Todd, S. C. 2007. *A Commentary on Lysias Speeches 1-11*, Oxford.

Todd, S. C. 2018. '"Theft" as a metaphor for the abuse of legal process at Athens', in *Use and Abuse of Law in the Athenian Courts*, eds C. Carey, I. Giannadaki, and B. Griffith-Williams, Leiden, 249–68.

Usher, S. 1999. *Greek Oratory: Tradition and Originality*, Oxford.

Volonaki, E. 2024. '*Dike pseudomartyrion*: a remedy and measure for retrial?', in *Evidence and Proof in Ancient Greece*, eds C. Carey, M. Edwards, and B. Griffith-Williams, Newcastle upon Tyne, 28–39.

Volonaki, E. and Edwards, M. J. 2023. *A Commentary on Apollodorus'* Against Evergus and Mnesibulus: *A Case of False Witness*, Newcastle upon Tyne.

Wevers, R. F. 1969. *Isaeus: Chronology, Prosopography and Social History*, The Hague.

Whitehead, D. 2000. *Hypereides: The Forensic Speeches*, Oxford.

Whitehead, D. 2022. *Isokrates, The Forensic Speeches (Nos. 16-21): Introduction, Text, Translation and Commentary*, 2 vols., Cambridge.

Wolpert, A. 2002. *Remembering Defeat: Civil War and Civic Memory in Ancient Athens*, Baltimore and London.

Wolpert, A. 2003. 'Addresses to the jury in the Attic Orators', *American Journal of Philology* 124, 537–55.

Wyse, W. 1904. *The Speeches of Isaeus, With Critical and Explanatory Notes*, Cambridge.

# INDEX

The index is selective, focusing on significant people, places and topics mentioned or discussed in the introductions and commentaries. The translations of the speeches are not indexed.

Printed and bound by CPI Group (UK) Ltd, Croydon, CR0 4YY

13/09/2026

14961098-0002